Critical Studies on Heidegger

SUNY series in Contemporary Continental Philosophy
———————
Dennis J. Schmidt, editor

Critical Studies on Heidegger
The Emerging Body of Understanding

DAVID MICHAEL KLEINBERG-LEVIN

Published by State University of New York Press, Albany

© 2023 State University of New York

All rights reserved

Printed in the United States of America

No part of this book may be used or reproduced in any manner whatsoever without written permission. No part of this book may be stored in a retrieval system or transmitted in any form or by any means including electronic, electrostatic, magnetic tape, mechanical, photocopying, recording, or otherwise without the prior permission in writing of the publisher.

For information, contact State University of New York Press, Albany, NY
www.sunypress.edu

Library of Congress Cataloging-in-Publication Data

Name: Kleinberg-Levin, David Michael, author.
Title: Critical studies on Heidegger : the emerging body of understanding /
   David M. Kleinberg-Levin
Description: Albany : State University of New York Press, [2022] | Series:
   SUNY series in Contemporary Continental Philosophy | Includes bibliographical
   references and index.
Identifiers: ISBN 9781438491813 (hardcover : alk. paper) | ISBN 9781438491837
   (ebook) | ISBN 9781438491820 (pbk. : alk. paper)
Further information is available at the Library of Congress.

10 9 8 7 6 5 4 3 2 1

Attention is the natural prayer of the soul.
>—Nicholas Malebranche, *Treatise on Nature and Grace*

Attention is the rarest and purest form of generosity.
>—Simone Weill, *Gravity and Grace*

. . . responsibility of mankind for being . . .
>—Heidegger, *The Principle of Identity*

Contents

Introduction: The Emerging Body of Ontological Understanding — 1

1. Thinking from Embodied Experience — 17
2. Gestures Befitting the Measure — 27
3. The Uncanny Vision of Kalchas — 49
4. The Fourfold: Gathering around the Thing — 75
5. The Incarnate Dialectic of Aesthetic Hyper-reflexivity — 113
6. Insight into Being: On Heidegger's "Einkehr in das Ereignis" — 145
7. A Dawning Sense of Being — 201

Notes — 209

Bibliography — 227

Index — 239

Introduction

The Emerging Body of Ontological Understanding

> The hint half guessed, the gift half understood, is Incarnation.
> —T. S. Eliot, "The Dry Salvages"

> The forming of the five senses is a labor of the entire history of the world down to the present.
> —Karl Marx, *Economic and Philosophical Manuscripts of 1844*

Too many philosophers have either neglected the human body or seriously misrepresented it, treating it as a substance. In many fundamental ways, Heidegger too neglects the body. But at least his representation of the being of the human as *Da-sein* breaks away from the imposition of a substance metaphysics, opening our embodiment, our being, to the world.

The potential half-guessed, the nature only half-understood, is the human body. This is not the body of anatomy lessons, neurophysiology, and mechanics, nor the body as physical object moved by a Cartesian mind, but the body of experience, thrown open to be in the world. Retrieving for initial guidance Aristotle's concept of *dunamis*, we must renounce once and for all the metaphysical projection of the human body as an enclosed material substance and commence thinking of it as an organically organized, livingly unified system of capacities, abilities, and dispositions open and exposed to the world in contexts if interaction. This is the only way by which we can understand (1) how the three stages and dimensions of understanding constitutive of human embodiment—the pre-ontological, the ontic, and the ontological—function, and (2) how the event of being can appropriate us for the history-making task that Heidegger envisions. However, (3) we cannot be appropriated for that task unless we *embody* it in developing a body of *ontological* understanding, a body of sense and sensibility, the character of which would realize its potential for engaging the world in a way that might overcome some of the malignancies and malevolence that Heidegger discerns in his ontologically grounded critique of our time, our epoch. Hence the importance, in my attempt to continue Heidegger's project, of recognizing and retrieving the promising ontological potential in the nature of our capacities and capabilities—for instance, in regard to the contemporary disposition and character of our visual and auditory perception and our gestures. This is a question of developing the potential, the promise, in those natural endowments of our embodiment through mindful practices and processes of learning, so that, as much as possible, habits of comportment conducive to the ontological dimension of an ethical life—that is, in regard to the being of beings—would be encouraged to emerge from the proper cultivation of human nature without the imposition of repressive social discipline. As I conceive it, this work is a continuation of the Enlightenment project, but without its teleology of reason and its excessive faith in progress.

∽

I found my way into the thought of Martin Heidegger only after a long intensive study of the phenomenological writings of Edmund Husserl and Maurice Merleau-Ponty. While I discovered much in Husserl that was congenial, I could not be comfortable in the rationalism and subjectivism constituting his extreme withdrawal into transcendental idealism. In Merleau-Ponty's phenomenology of perception, however, I found a work much more congenial to my philosophical and aesthetic disposition. And I happily immersed my thought in the elegant and eloquent prose of his phenomenology before realizing that I needed to engage with the thought of Husserl's extraordinary student. Entering into that thought was for some time overwhelming. I eventually resolved to put aside secondary sources and venture to understand Heidegger's thought on my own.

However, I did get a chance, while a student at Harvard, where its philosophers were committed to an empiricism scornful of *Being and Time*, to delve into Spinoza's *Ethics*. Born into a family of Jewish culture, I was drawn to the thought of this philosopher. One of the topics that caught my attention and intrigued me concerned his handling of the relation that binds mind and body. It seemed to me that he was venturing a very original way of thinking about it, connecting the character of that relation to spiritual exercises and ethical practices of the self that were inspired by Greek and Roman Stoicism.

In "Of the Power of the Intellect; or of Human Freedom," the final part of his *Ethics*, Spinoza says, "The mind can cause all the modifications of the body, or the images of things, to be related to the idea of God [*ideam Dei*]" (Proposition XIV).[1] Moreover, he also argues that, "In God, there exists an idea which expresses the essence of this or that human body under the form of eternity" (Proposition XXII). Arguing that "it is the nature of reason to conceive things under the form of eternity," he explains what this proposition means, saying, "Everything that the mind understands under the form of eternity it understands [. . .] because it also conceives the essence of the body under the form of eternity" (Proposition XXIX). These propositions, together with others, lead him to the proposition that, as he puts it: "He who possesses a body fit for many things possesses a mind of which the greater part is eternal" (Proposition XXXIX).

Elaborating the significance of this proposition, he argues that, "In this life, it is our chief endeavor to change the body of infancy, so far as its nature permits and is conducive thereto, into another body which is fitted for many things, and which is related to a mind conscious as much as possible of itself, of God, and of objects [. . .]." Developing the potential capabilities of the mind, one correspondingly develops the body, hence its perceptivity; likewise, developing the sense and sensibility of the body, hence its perceptivity, one correspondingly develops the mind. In this regard, what is most important for Spinoza is the cultivation of what he calls the "intellectual love of God." That is, as Spinoza formulates it, love of "God or Nature": "Deus sive Natura." Arguing for a certain version of Idealism and Rationalism that later, in Schelling, would give substance to Romanticism, Spinoza also identifies this "intellectual love of God," perhaps best understood as dedication to an ethical life of virtue and care, with the assumption, or rather adoption, of the viewpoint of eternity (Proposition XXIX).

In other words, it is important for us to *imagine* and project what we think would be the ideal world, a morally perfect world—things as they would present themselves if contemplated from the standpoint of redemption [*wie vom Standpunkt der Erlösung*], as Theodor Adorno phrased it in concluding *Minima Moralia*—because that speculative vision, that projection, would both encourage and guide us to work for the moral improvement of ourselves and the actual world.[2] That, he argues, is "the only philosophy that can be responsibly practiced in the face of despair." Heidegger would perhaps call that standpoint the standpoint of the *Geschick*—the destiny that would befit our humanity. It is not easy, however, to determine what world—what ethical life—Heidegger's vision of destiny imagines.

In his "Letter on Humanism," Heidegger repudiates the Western world's inheritance of Humanism, arguing that in neglecting to think our relation to being, Humanism fails to recognize our true "dignity." However, he leaves his conception of Humanism in a condition of abstraction and indeterminacy. Presumably, our "dignity" is a question of giving thought to being itself, and not getting lost in the world of beings. But surely, that is important not only because, having been endowed with the capacity to think, we human beings should thankfully exercise and fulfill that endowment, but because giving thought to being is *necessary* for protecting the *being* of *beings* from the peril in forms of nihilism—reduction and reification—that are increasingly determining our world. Ultimately, it is not only our relation to the being of all the beings in our world that is at stake, but also, the being of our own being, our very humanity. I think that is what Heidegger means when he argues, all too abstractly, that our true dignity lies in giving thought to being. And I would argue that achieving an insightful understanding of the being of beings, an awareness that brings the different beings to light in their deepest individual and differentiating truth, is a moral task: a task that only we human beings, in touch with our *ownmost* sense of humanity, can undertake. Our "dignity" is in living by that understanding.

Heidegger repudiates and avoids burdening his thought with "morality." But he is against mindless conformity to abstract principles and formulae, codifications of social and cultural practices that reduce "morality" to self-interest and custom. What he wants, I think, is a "morality" rooted in thoughtful caring for the being of beings. Such understanding of being, and the caring for being that it motivates, is what I believe he had in mind when he invoked a "fundamental, originary ethics." Ontology and ethics are not only inseparable: they affect and inform one another. I shall have more to say about this in chapter 6.

†

The *Ethics* may be read as Spinoza's answer to the question: What is the *character* of the perceptivity that must correspond to this "intellectual love of God"? "Intellectual" is in our time a correct yet misleading interpretive translation: it suggests that this love is merely a cognitive or conceptual engagement—just the *thought* of such love. I submit, however, that the "intellectual" nature of this love abides in its attentiveness, its mindfulness. Since the world and all the beings within it are thought to be "in" God and "belong" to God, that love should translate into how we *interact* with all beings and with the being of the world itself, namely, as befits their nature. Thus, Spinoza's ethics, deduced, in effect, from his ontology, essentially concerns the character of that interaction. This interpretation is possible only because of the way Spinoza brings mind and body together. In "Of Human Bondage" (Proposition XXVII), Spinoza brazenly overturns the epistemological priority of the mind in the entire history of idealism from Plato to Descartes. With thinking steeped in Aristotle's *Metaphysics* and *De Anima*, he says, "The more capable the body is of being affected in many ways, and affecting external bodies in many ways, the more capable is the mind."[3] This also bears on the nature of the love that Spinoza had in mind.

My reading of Spinoza stirred me to ponder a difficult question: What embodiment, what perceptual capabilities, would correspond to the mind's "intellectual love of God"? That was one of the questions that launched the project that has become my life's work. In the light of Heidegger's critique of our contemporary world, that question led me to wonder: What transformations in the historical character of perception are needed? How might a perception that redeems its potential change our world? There are hints in Heidegger's texts, such as "Building, Dwelling, Thinking," "Poetically Man Dwells," "The Thing," and "The Origin of the Work of Art." In these texts, Heidegger imaginatively projects a world informed by a new ontology, a new experience and understanding of being.

I suggest that the questions Spinoza's *Ethics* provokes point toward a responsibility engaging the potential inherent in our perception. They point toward a claim carried by, and in, the most fundamental disposition of our embodied nature. That claim, as Heidegger will argue, calls us and appropriates us, demanding that we consciously take responsibility for our role in the necessary conditions for the experiencing of an intelligible, meaningful world that our very existence, our simply being bodily present in the world, makes.

For Heidegger, though, much more is at stake than the realization and fulfillment of our bodily nature, our capacities and capabilities, as *Dasein*. In question is how we should dwell on this planet earth and sojourn amid its beings. But this *is* a question concerning the character of our way of *embodying* openness, hence relationality, in our situated presence—*Da-sein*.

Perception is fundamental in this receptive enquiring openness. Thus, understanding the *character* of our perception is crucial to understanding the world in which we are living—and indeed the history and future of this world, which Heidegger's narrative brings to light through his critical reading of the history of metaphysics. Who we are and who we want to become demands that we reflect critically on the ontology implicit in the contemporary character of our perceptivity, our interactions with the world and the beings appearing in it.

Heidegger seems to have felt an abiding affinity with Aristotle, the one philosopher whose reflections in *De Anima* on potentiality and human capacities might have suggested the key to continuing Spinoza's thoughts in the context of his analytic of *Dasein* and the corresponding phenomenology of perception. Yet he never committed time to thinking in connection with Aristotle about the questions that Spinoza's propositions pose concerning the development, or perfecting, of the human body as endowed with the capacity for an "intellectual love of God."

In the context of Spinoza's ethics, I would argue that the "perfection" of the human body in and as the "love of God or Nature" is the never-ending work of embodying and perfecting ways of feeling, enacting, and living that love in everything one does and says. Now, this "love of God or Nature" is called an "intellectual" love—meaning, I suggest, that what is called for is a mindfulness and dedication to the practice of virtue that comes, in large measure, from our self-reflection and self-examination; and it relates to everything we encounter in the world with due respect and care, *as if* God, or a trace of God's touch, were actually invested in its material nature, or *as if* God left some of Himself on or within the nature of every form of being, so that everything we are engaged with would be received, at least initially, with fitting open-mindedness and generosity of spirit—*as if* it were manifesting the hidden material presence of God or God's work. For Spinoza, I think this process of developing a love of God is a love that touches and affects everything we see, hear, taste, sense, and handle; and it would essentially involve an attitude grounded in the felt embodiment of the teachings inherited from the biblical texts, together with prayer and other sacred rituals and practices, giving this embodiment in voice, words, and gesture the discipline that would shape and perfect its understanding and expression of love, sympathy, and care. The hidden presence of God in all beings, or say the sacredness attributed to everything, is thus to be found in our *interactions* with the world. To think of God as the one and only sub-stance, or as the sacredness of being, is, I wish to propose, to think of the presence of God, or the sacredness of Nature, as manifest in the ethical demand for appropriate acknowledgment, constitutive of everything everywhere. And that comes down to treating everything in a way that befits its "nature." This is *a practice of love*: learning care in openness of heart and generosity of spirit in relating to everything in the world. As for what is dangerous and evil, it is still a question of treating the beings in our world as befits their "nature." This, I believe, is Spinoza's conception of an embodied ethical life with a deeply felt sense of the ontological dimension, guided by the religious teachings.

In giving the body such a significant role, corresponding to the perfecting of the mind in both knowledge and mindfulness, Spinoza ventured a conception of ethical life that was, in his day, and still is in ours, a very bold and radical thought. It was, in effect, an attempt to begin thinking *from* embodied experience. But, first of all, it was an awkward attempt to rethink the omnipresence of a hidden God through a radically new conception of substance: sub-stance not as something merely material, nor as something mystical, but rather as positing, or indicating, the sacredness that is felt to *under-lie and in-form* the presence of every being. That felt sacredness *is* the presence of God. In question is, therefore, is a deep sense of love expressed in all the ways that we inhabit perception, gestures, and words.

The perfection of the human body involves us in endeavoring to draw our capacities and capabilities in perception, voice, and gesture into a mindfulness that realizes a love that corresponds to, and befits, the nature of everything in the world, and the world itself, in which we live. This, I suggest, is the essence of Spinoza's "intellectual love of God." Needless to say, this interpretation takes us far from a substance ontology and metaphysics, situating us in a *dynamic relationship* between us and the beings of the world: an *interaction* with the beings in our world in which we are mindful of their (way of) being and attentive to what befits their particular nature.

And precisely this is the historically persisting subject of Spinoza's *Ethics*. How should we embody, and indeed endeavor to perfect, the intellectual love of God? Because of the fact that everything belongs to and takes part in the divine substance, and is thus an "attribute" of the divine substance, such that the presence of God is "in" all things, ethics concerns how we should relate to everything in our world and how we should relate to the world itself. What is the appropriate disposition and attunement in our worldly interactions? And how should we strive to embody it more perfectly? What does the love of "God or Nature" mean? The *Ethics* is Spinoza's answer.

If what we call God is present in—and, in effect, nothing other than—all that in any way *is*, and therefore *is* even in the mode of absence or evil, then everything is sacred and needs to be treated accordingly—and that means as befits its distinctive nature. An ethical life would consequently *embody* the *character* of this felt relation to the substance, the essence, of all things. This relation to the being of beings would be, then, the loving mindfulness constitutive of the intellectual love of God—"God or Nature."

It is questionable whether Spinoza himself could ever have been comfortable thinking about God solely in this way. What he would think today of his ingenious attempt to reconcile the science of his time with theology is impossible to determine. But my interpretation eliminates the problematic notion of substance, channeling its religious attitude—its sense of the world as a sacred gift and unfathomable blessing—into the thoughtful sensibility required of ethical responsibility: insofar as possible, attentive to the being of all beings with an open mind, respectful, caring, generous, loving, as befits the nature of each being. This is the embodiment of the temperament and sensibility, the "spirit" that inhabits and nurtures an ethical life.

†

With problems and questions about the character of perception and sensibility provoking me, I undertook a project of thought that eventuated in the publication of a trilogy that, as the writing unfolded, I called "the emerging body of understanding," bearing in mind Heidegger's evocation of earth and sky in "The Origin of the Work of Art" and in such later writings as "The Thing" and "Building, Dwelling and Thinking." In this trilogy, the question for us as mortals to ponder was how we should *under-stand* what it means for us to be *standing* on the earth and dwelling *under* the immeasurable sky. For me, this question called for a phenomenology of our embodiment in seeing, hearing, motility, and gesture: a phenomenology that must be hermeneutical, because, inasmuch as motility, gesturing, seeing, hearing, and the other three modalities of perception are forms of disclosiveness, it is a question of a prior holistic context of meaning forming the background of our world; and such a context, with its temporal and historical dimensions, and its inevitable boundary limits, is always at work as the condition for all intelligibility. Meaningfulness accordingly emerges from the background in an interplay of concealment and unconcealment.

Merleau-Ponty's first major work, *The Structure of Behavior* (1942), a critique of Empiricism, Rationalism, and Idealism with regard to understanding human nature and human existence, laid the ground for his second major work, *The Phenomenology of Perception* (1945), which draws on research in empirical psychology, the phenomenology of Husserl (especially his 1900 *Logical Investigations*, his 1913 *Ideas I: General Introduction to Pure Phenomenology*, his 1928 *Phenomenology of Internal Time Consciousness*, his 1929 *Formal and Transcendental Logic*, and his 1931 *Cartesian Meditations*), and Heidegger's first major work, *Being and Time* (1927). Even though Merleau-Ponty's *Phenomenology of Perception* boldly developed Husserl's phenomenological studies, challenging their transcendental idealism in order to reconcile them with the existential phenomenology he found in *Being and Time*, his approach remained to some extent like Husserl's, namely, still under the sway of Cartesian subjectivism. However, he continued to elaborate his phenomenological approach, writing on art, nature, language, and the child's stages of social development in the course of its acquisition of language. And he obviously continued to read and reread Heidegger's published work as well as Husserl's very late texts, such *The Crisis of European Sciences and Transcendental Phenomenology* (1936). I conjecture that this reading and rereading, especially in the 1950s, finally enabled him to think his way toward completing the process of breaking away from the remaining vestiges of Cartesianism troubling his thinking. That movement past Cartesianism is singularly manifest in his last lectures and writings concerning the phenomenology of perception, most notably, perhaps, his "Working Notes," published in *The Visible and the Invisible* (1959–1961). In these last lectures and writings, working with such key constructs as "flesh," "ecstatic" intentionality, "chiasm," "intertwining," and "reversibility," "hiddenness," and "unconcealment," Merleau-Ponty exposed the open pre-objective dimension of being, a figure-ground dynamic that precedes the emergence and formation of the subject-object structure.

In the course of an intense and extensive process, slowly reading through much of the available collection of Heidegger's lectures, seminars, and other texts, I arrived at two strongly compelling conclusions, the second one of them truly surprising and exciting. First, that Heidegger was, from the middle of the 1920s into the time of his death, unwaveringly committed to the phenomenological method as he understood it, namely, as *phainesthai*, a method for letting things reflexively show themselves from out of themselves—a method, therefore, for thinking from out of our lived experience (*aus der Erfahrung*), conceived as even more radical, and more hermeneutical, hence more faithfully phenomenological, than Husserl's method, which claimed to return to "the things themselves." And *second*, that in its essentials, there is ultimately no difference between Heidegger's fully developed phenomenology of perception and Merleau-Ponty's final version of his phenomenology of perception. The chiasm, intertwining, and reversibility that figure in the latter appear in the former as "belonging-togetherness" ("*Zugehörigkeit*"), "mutual pull" ("*Bezug*"), "oscillation" ("*Gegenschwung, Schwingung*"), and "vibration" ("*Schweben*"). And Heidegger, like Merleau-Ponty, attempts to return reflection to experience that dimension which precedes the emergence of the subject-object structure, concentrating on what is, in effect, the dynamic tension in the figure-ground *Gestalt* and the reifying reduction of that dynamic *Gestalt*, in our time, to the *Ge-stell* (for Heidegger, see GA 7: 266/EGT 103; for Merleau-Ponty, see *Phénoménologie de la perception*, 254/*Phenomenology of Perception*, 219). The significance of that return to our belonging-togetherness with being, for Heidegger, is that, as I would describe the matter, that experience can lead us into a bodily felt sense of the claim on our responsibility in regard to being. Heidegger argues for that belonging-togetherness, but he fails to recognize how that implicates our responsibility.

Although the phenomenological method calls for describing our experience just as it is lived, I was at first surprised to discover that both Heidegger and Merleau-Ponty use phenomenology in a way that departs from this discipline, as, for instance, when Heidegger retrieves the "oscillation" in the belonging-togetherness of our experience of being and when Merleau-Ponty retrieves the "melodic arc" in the most ordinary of gestures. How can these descriptions claim phenomenological truth? The answer is that neither philosopher was afraid to delve beneath our common, habitual experience to retrieve a deeper dimension, hoping that the description, functioning performatively like metaphor, would make itself true by a revelation that guides us into recognizing and living in the truth constitutive of the deeper experience. Merleau-Ponty describes this deeper, older dimension as the prereflective, preconceptual, and prepersonal. Heidegger calls it the pre-ontological, to be retrieved for development as the ontological by engaging thought in a process somewhat like Platonic recollection.

In the fiction of literature, truth-telling is always paradoxical. In *Languages of Truth*, Salman Rushdie, making an argument for story-telling, wrote that "tales full of beautiful impossibility, which were not true, but by being not true told the truth."[4] Plato, however, thought that fiction is corrupting because it cannot tell the truth. Yet, in *The Republic*, he resorted to myth in order to communicate a truth not recognized by common experience. Other philosophers recognize the truth in literary fiction, even weaving the insights of fiction into their arguments.

In his *Phenomenology of Perception*, Maurice Merleau-Ponty proposes descriptions of our lived experience that are so much deeper than our ordinary, habitually shallow and reflectively inattentive experience that they can at first seem to be false; yet, if we take them to heart and ruminate on them, these descriptions have the power to make themselves true to our experience. And moreover, we are likely to feel, as the descriptions are absorbed, that, in fact, they *were already true* to our experience. By being not true to the shallowness and distraction of our everyday life, the philosopher's stories can likewise tell the truth—a deeper, keenly felt truth, a deeper realism.

Many of the early scholars working with Heidegger's texts were inclined to regard his more extravagant or bewildering phenomenological descriptions as merely poetic metaphor, thereby effectively denying these descriptions their disclosive, transformative power. For Heidegger, though, the essence of metaphor, as its Greek derivation should always remind us, is its revelatory power, a power to carry us into a new experience.

The convergence of the two philosophers should not, actually, be so surprising, since Merleau-Ponty attended some of Heidegger's lectures and was familiar with Heidegger's work. However, the way he elaborated and formulated the phenomenology is nevertheless entirely wrought in a process of reflection drawn from his own resources. Consequently, he is able to give compelling embodiment—flesh—to Heidegger's much more abstract and less experientially elaborated description of human existence. Whereas Heidegger's thought served to guide Merleau-Ponty's thought toward recognizing the *ontological dimension* of the phenomenology he was exploring, suggesting a way for him to think the ontological dimension of our embodiment and perception, Merleau-Ponty's phenomenology could serve to provide Heidegger's ontological thought with the embodiment it very much needs, since Heidegger repeatedly turned away from giving human *embodiment* the thought it requires. Although in "The Principle of Identity" (1957) and "Time and Being" (1962), as well as in certain other texts, for example, in "The Way to Language" (GA 12: 248/OWL 128) and *The Event*, wherein he discusses the "incorporation" (*Einverleibung*) of our "most fundamental disposition," the "gentlest of laws" (GA 71: 216–24/E 185–92), Heidegger does, in effect, engage the phenomenology of the emergent subject-object structure in a way that moves into the proximity of an embodied felt experience; but he fails to recognize it: an experience, namely, of our ontological appropriation, the claim on our responsibility that is constitutive of our intimate relation—our inseparable togetherness with being. His failure in this regard means that he leaves the appropriation (*Ereignung*) of our most fundamental disposition in responding to an experience of the event of being dangling in the thin air of abstraction.

It was after returning to Spinoza and reading him in the light of a new acquaintance with Aristotle that for the first time I began to give thought to the so-called mind-body dualism from a perspective distinctly different from the one that dominated philosophical thinking in the academies. For me, Spinoza's propositions on mind, body, and the intellectual love of God (God or Nature) were a provocation that caused me to wonder about the nature of a body that would embody, or bear, a mind dedicated to, and stirred by, an intellectual love of God. What would such a body be like? Recognizing that that body must be an extraordinary body, not the body that most of us inhabit, I began to give thought to what the difference is and how it would occur in keeping with a mind that had become appropriated by a deep love of God. The question of transformation suggested that Aristotle's thought, especially what he wrote in *De Anima*, could provide guidance. But what occurred to me first of all was that we must not reduce the living human body to a substance. Aristotle's substance metaphysics has been responsible for this reduction; and it is precisely the sway of this reduction that leads thinking into the intractable aporetic problems confronting us in mind-body dualism. However, at the same time that he argued for a substance metaphysics, he introduced one of his most important, most consequential contributions, namely, a conceptual framework for thinking about, and understanding, the operation of potentiality in the disposition of human capacities. The strength of the argument for this conceptual framework should have compelled Aristotle to abandon substance metaphysics in thinking about the embodiment of the living human being. In any case, the argument did succeed in making me discern the problems with substance metaphysics. And it made sense for me, thereafter, to approach a number of difficult problems in epistemology and ethics in terms of the conceptual framework that Aristotle himself introduced. The living human body (*Leib*, not *Körper*) is an organically organized, unified system of dispositions, capabilities, and capacities continuously interacting with an environment that needs to be understood dynamically in terms of potentiality and actuality. It is in these terms that our embodiment—the body that we are—should be thought. Otherwise, as we witness in Heidegger's struggles to understand the human body, philosophical thought will inevitably get tangled up in a substance metaphysics from which there is no escape. Thinking of the human body as an organically organized system of capacities and capabilities engaging with its world avoids the impasse. Working with Heidegger's thought to bring out its bearing on the emerging body of ontological understanding, I regard the task before our project to be the *development* of these capacities and capabilities in the time-space fields of perception and gesture. At stake in this development is their moral disposition, their character, their "dignity," considered in the light of Heidegger's critique of our way of life in this epoch.

As we have noted, Heidegger formulated a compelling critique of contemporary life, including strong criticisms of the character of our typical ways of seeing and hearing. Implicit within those criticisms, I have discerned a vivid but still inchoate sense of what ways would be more desirable, implying that our modes of perception—in particular, seeing and hearing—are capabilities and capacities within which there are promising potentials that could be retrieved and developed. Getting at those promising potentials—what in *Being and Time* Heidegger calls our *Seinkönnen*—is what lies behind my project: the emerging of an ontological body of understanding. These potentials bear on the character of perception in the comportment of our ethical life. We have, therefore, a responsibility to retrieve and develop them.

In scholarly studies after Heidegger, it is not only the human body as such that has been neglected; our capacities and capabilities in perception and gesture have also been woefully neglected. My lifetime project has sought to give this subject the attention it requires, especially considering the fact that Heidegger's compelling critique of the *character* of perception and gesture in contemporary life figures only occasionally and mostly in marginality. Although he makes a strong critique of metaphysics and challenges the metaphysical representation of the human body, rejecting a history that assumes it to be an enclosed substance, he nevertheless fails to find a way to represent it in a fitting way, somehow unable to complete his escape from the metaphysical picture. I suggest that thinking of the body in terms of capacities and capabilities the *character* of which can be developed makes that escape easier.

Pursuing this trajectory, I have attempted to subject the *character* of our perception and gestures to a critique that indicates, beyond the faults of character that Heidegger's critique of contemporary life accuses, ways for these capacities and capabilities to be developed for the sake of ethical life. Learning such development, transforming the character of our seeing, hearing, and gesturing, calls for Socratic self-examination and work on ourselves. In experiencing the event of being itself—what Heidegger calls "*Ereignis*," we deepen and strengthen this Socratic work, and we dedicate the questioning and the caring to the being of all beings, past, present, and future.

†

In a poem concerning death, T. S. Eliot says, "I see the eyes but not the tears / This is my affliction."[5] Our eyes, we think, are for seeing. But our eyes are also capable of tears. What is the significance of that second capability? Why and how are those two functions organically connected?

Perhaps the root of our seeing is the capacity for seeing with sympathy, manifest in tears. If, in a phenomenology concerned with the nature of human vision, methodically disciplined attention could guide us into a felt sense of that rootedness, a prereflective, pre-ontological understanding of our intimate connection to the very being of beings, then the sympathetic character of our seeing might be encouraged to develop, greatly benefiting our ethical life and overcoming some of the contemporary tendencies that Heidegger subjected to criticism. Such could be the performative force of phenomenological description.

A similar approach to our capacity for listening and hearing, taking us into a bodily felt sense of our prelinguistic, pre-ontological sense of our connectedness to being, hence to the being of audible beings, could likewise benefit ethical life, improving the quality of communication (*Gespräch*) and consequently improving mutual understanding and sympathy. We may hear the other in an objective, scientifically confirmable sense; but such mere hearing is not enough. We need to listen wholeheartedly to the other in order to hear *properly*. That kind of listening is encouraged when we retrieve our pre-ontological sense of being and learn to live in an ontological understanding of being.

It is unfortunate that, while Heidegger formulated compelling critical observations and arguments regarding the character of our seeing and hearing, which in today's world tends to be either atrophied or malevolent, he does not undertake any corresponding endeavor to explore how we might redeem the potential promise in these modalities by retrieving their underlying ontological dimension, their inseparable connection with being, and accordingly ameliorating, at least to some extent, how seeing and hearing experience the being of the beings with which they are engaged. If he had undertaken this work of recollection in regard, say, to perception, then it would have been apparent how the ontological dimension serves to ground the "original ethics" that he invokes in *Being and Time*. He projects in the realm of thought the way from ontology to ethics, but does not draw on phenomenology to illuminate what that really means for the achieving of a life in which our seeing and hearing would approach, in the character of their self-development, an appropriation that could make possible the redeeming of their promise. Derrida nicely illuminates how phenomenology is related to ontology and ethics.[6]

Philosophical thought is still only now beginning, as it frees itself from Idealism, Rationalism, and Empiricism, to approach an appropriately phenomenological understanding of this gift, this endowment, the human form of embodiment thrown open to be and dwell in the world, exposed, vulnerable, mortal. The lived body: *die erlebter Leib*. The chapters in this book gather together some of my contributions to this project, the emerging body of ontological understanding.

Chapter 1

Thinking from Embodied Experience

> To be a body is to be woven into a certain world.
> —Maurice Merleau-Ponty, *Phenomenology of Perception*[1]

In these studies, Heidegger's thought is carried critically and constructively beyond its original limitations, re-presenting his project in terms of an emerging body of ontological understanding, making sense of this project not only in its historical, cultural significance but also in its bearing on the emergence of future possibilities. Continuing Heidegger's commitment to a way of thinking that is formed from reflectively lived experience, I explore what can be learned regarding the character of our typical and habitual ways of looking and seeing, hearing and listening, and touching, holding, handling, and gesturing. The body of ontological understanding consequently emerges as we learn how to take responsibility for the meaning of being in forming and developing the character of our relationship to all the beings in our world. In this reading of Heidegger's thought, I attempt to show what his project could mean for an ethical way of life.

Heidegger never ceased to stress the importance, for his project, of working "from out of the experience of thinking" ("*aus der Erfahrung des Denkens*"). But does this not mean that, in commitment to phenomenology, he wants our thinking to *come out of* our lived experience (*Erfahrung*)—all of our experience, not only the experience we undergo when "genuinely thinking"? For much too long, there has been an unfortunate tendency among some scholars to treat the expression of some of Heidegger's most important thinking—especially thinking that challenges fundamental concepts and beliefs—as nothing but poetic metaphor, in effect reducing his thought to harmless expressions that will not threaten to disrupt or unsettle our experience. Some have even argued, contrary to Heidegger's own testimony, that he abandoned phenomenology in order to commence what he calls "thinking." This defensive resistance to the truth in experience, effectively removing his philosophical thought from the realm of experience, makes it a meaningless game of words.

However, if there were to be a deeper understanding of metaphor, drawing on the word's Greek etymology, such that the word would signify an experiential movement, a shift or transition from something familiar to something new and revealing, then that attribution would respect the way the philosopher's thinking works with experience, and would show what difference ontological thinking could make in our lives. The German word "*Erfahrung*" suggests an adventure, a journey, experience as inherently meta-phorical, taking us into a different topology.

Heidegger's commitment to phenomenology is a commitment to experience—a commitment, however, to which he is unfortunately not consistently faithful. The same should be said regarding his commitment to hermeneutics, which compels recognizing the hidden, the unknown, the absent, the uncertain, the unpredictable, and steadfastly warns against the doctrine-driven imposition of interpretations. Because of these commitments, he challenges, as did Merleau-Ponty after him, both rationalism and empiricism, both idealism and realism, both subjectivity and objectivity, hence too the primacy of the subject-object structure. All these philosophical systems and methods betray experience by prematurely imposing conceptual frames on its open-endedness and its preconceptual richness. The "sensations," "sense data," "impressions," and "sensory stimuli" that empiricism and rationalism love to work with are nothing but attempts at conceptual approximation—attempts at the clarity and precision of science that inevitably fail to guide us into actually experiencing what is at stake in Heidegger's thought.

However, Heidegger's project does not fully live up to the promise in these two commitments, because it does not sufficiently recognize, and work with, the felt embodiment of experience. The fundamental fact that all our experience is embodied should be the starting point for understanding the human experience of life. Heidegger is at least clear that this embodiment cannot be reduced to the condition of a physical object, as in physics, mechanics, biology, chemistry, and medicine. The body is neither a physical nor a metaphysical substance. It is a living nature. Aristotle got closer to understanding the human body than did generations of philosophers after him, because he thought of the body in terms of potentiality and actuality, hence in terms of capacities and capabilities. Despite Heidegger's intensive studies of Aristotle's extant works and his manifest admiration for Aristotle's achievements in the realm of thought, he missed the importance of Aristotle's terms for working with the phenomenological body and its embodiment of experience. However, in *The Event*, he does observe that

> To the unique claim of being, namely, that it *is*, there pertains, as deriving from that arrogation [*Zu-eignung*], the gathering of all capacities into the effort to preserve the truth of beyng [i.e., the *aletheic* interplay of concealment and unconcealment that is the necessary condition for the presencing of beings]. (GA 71: 161–63/E 139)

It is unfortunate, though, that Heidegger does not further explore the phenomenology of this engagement of our capacities and capabilities.

In "What Is Enlightenment?" Michel Foucault recognized in Aristotle's *De Anima* some of the philosophical importance of capacities and capabilities, asking us to consider: "How can the growth of capabilities be disconnected from the intensification of power relations?"[2] He understood that, for a flourishing democracy, much is at stake in this growth.

In my appropriation of Heidegger's project, I approach the phenomenological task in terms inspired, in part, by Aristotle: the human body is an organically organized system of capacities and capabilities, a system of dispositions: potentialities than can be actualized and, in many ways, further developed, further unfolded. This approach to embodiment, working with the potential in the nature of our capacities and capabilities, has decisive advantages: (1) it avoids entanglements in the problematic of the body theorized as substance; and (2) working from Heidegger's critique of the modern world and the character of our habitual ways of handling things, gesturing, looking and seeing, and listening and hearing, it enables us to consider transformative possibilities, overcoming the ways that, according to his critique, are complicit in the nihilism of *Gestell* that dominates our time. My project, committed to the hermeneutical phenomenology of embodied experience, is an attempt to carry forward Heidegger's critique of our world, exploring the way to a new understanding of being and to corresponding changes in the character of our relation to beings.

The emerging body of understanding involves the achieving of an *ontological* understanding, that is, an understanding of the nature of our relation to being, hence our responsibility for being. This ontological understanding emerges when we hermeneutically circle back, as it were, to retrieve the *pre-ontological* understanding of being that—I would argue—is always already carried from the very beginning of our life by the very nature of our embodiment. In his Introduction to *Being and Time*, Heidegger introduces the notion of a pre-ontological understanding; but he makes no further use of it in the elaboration of his project; moreover, he never explains how, if it is prereflective, prelinguistic, and preconceptual, operating without our awareness as it presumably must be, we could have such a pre-ontological understanding without its being carried by the body.

The human body, endowed by nature with a promising potential of capacities, capabilities, and dispositions, must not be ignored and neglected by philosophical reflection on morality and ethical life. Since the human body, the body we are and live (*erleben*), engaged in the world, is capable of feeling pain and can suffer in sympathy with those who are suffering, we are called on to *embody* our endeavor to achieve a morally desirable world. This means that our bodies must take part in any transformation of our world, to make it a world in which genocides, and other forms of inhumanity, some more common but less conspicuous, could not continue to happen.

In *Negative Dialectics*, Theodor Adorno argues for "a new categorical imperative" that, he says, "has been imposed by Hitler upon unfree mankind: to arrange our thoughts and actions so that Auschwitz will not repeat itself."[3] And, although, as Jay Bernstein points out, "Adorno has offered no concrete policy proposals or action-oriented political recommendations, [. . .] he has been providing immanently good reasons for us to transform our usual habits of thought and action."[4] And, as Bernstein rightly observes, "Since the argument for a transformation of reason had been, until the moment when Auschwitz entered into the account, fully reflective, reason immanently criticizing itself, the introduction of the *fact* of Auschwitz into the argument demands a shift in rational register. The rational demand for transformation becomes both bodily and ethical, which is exactly what Adorno goes on to state."[5] He then proceeds to quote Adorno.

> Dealing discursively with it would be an outrage, for the new imperative gives us a bodily sensation of the moral addendum— bodily, because it is now the practical abhorrence of the unbearable physical agony to which individuals are exposed even with individuality about to vanish as a form of mental reflection.[6]

Kantian morality cannot be grounded in pure reason; the horrors and terrors of inhumanity touch us and affect us bodily, and the imperative emerges from this experience.

Without explicitly referring to the potential in our capacities, capabilities, and dispositions, Heidegger's critique of our way of life in the contemporary ontological epoch nevertheless requires the development and transformation of our embodiment, as in the character of our seeing, hearing, and gesturing. His critique of perception and gesture is compelling; but it implies, and calls for, a phenomenology of their transformation—a fleshing out—that, for the most part, is missing. So, in this volume, I am attempting to use that extensive critique as a significant indication of what is needed for this development and transformation.

What is needed is not only a phenomenology of human embodiment, but also a phenomenological narrative regarding infancy and childhood, and the transition into an adult world. Heidegger has very little to say in this regard (see GA 27: 123), limiting his inquiry to the mortality of an adult *Dasein* without natality, infancy, and childhood, but always already living toward death. What is missing from Heidegger's treatment of Dasein is a phenomenological narrative regarding the *development* of our nature-given potential: in particular, the retrieving and developing of our pre-ontological understanding of being as it functions in our percipience and gestures.

The emerging ontological understanding, never totally achieved, situates our lives as beings who are *standing* on the earth and *under* the sky. This embodiment, deeply attuned in its connectedness to being, unsettling the subject-object structure into which we have habitually cast the experience of being, emerges in a gradual Socratic process of *propriation* that we of course must initiate. This process is never complete, never final. But Heidegger emphasizes the belonging-together of *Mensch* and *Sein*, for instance, in his lecture on "The Principle of Identity," in order to argue that it is our responsibility to safeguard the meaning of being *for the sake of all beings*. Experiencing the event of being (*Ereignis*) is what calls; and it appropriates (*aneignet*) our response-ability for the assumption of that responsibility (*Verantwortlichkeit:* GA 11: 40 n53/ID 31, 33).

Now, it should be noted here that the "call of being" is a very misleading locution. I deny any agency to being itself; but that in no way makes it impossible to think of being as making a claim on us—"calling" in this perfectly ordinary sense. If there is any call, that is, if any call is heard, the call is, and comes from within, our *experience* of being. *We expe-*

rience ourselves to be called, claimed, summoned. And what we are called and summoned to, and claimed or appropriated for, is work on ourselves, fulfilling our potential as much as we can, in relation to an understanding of being. That is why, and how, we are *pre-disposed* to answer the call. It comes from our own sense of the meaning of our life! Are we not "called" to do something if we see someone about to be struck by a car, if that person is not stopped from going across the street? Does a pot of soup boiling over not *call* for some action? So *where* is that calling? In the soup or in me? Unacknowledged metaphysical assumptions here are provoking mischievous questions!

Heidegger's account of the relation between human being and being is good; but it neglects the phenomenology of embodiment that this relation engages. Merleau-Ponty expands this belonging-together, arguing that the *Zusammengehörigkeit* Heidegger wants us to recognize is not, first and foremost, a reflectively generated understanding, but rather a bodily felt sensory connection. He also argues that there is an ontological dimension of chiasmic continuity between *all* beings: in their distinctness, each and every being is the center of a singular web of relations. No being exists without differentiation; identity always emerges and forms in difference—a web of relations. Our bodies silently sense and understand this relationality, despite a culture of individualism that defies that sense and sensibility. Putting Heidegger's phenomenology together with Merleau-Ponty's "ontological rehabilitation of the sensible,"[7] I suggest that the belonging-together of *Mensch-Sein* and *Sein*, which Heidegger describes as an oscillation, a *Schwingen* and *Schweben*, is a pre-ontological bodily experience of chiasmic reversibility and reciprocity (Merleau-Ponty's terms) that constitutes the phenomenological basis for our ontological responsibility for being: the highest and foremost of our responsibilities. Moreover, it would be the source of the ontologically grounded ethics and body politic that Heidegger envisioned but left undone.

Thinking *from* embodied experience, experiences that are brought into a process of conceptualization that is in touch with the very depths of our sense and sensibility, is ultimately what Heidegger's project of critique and transformation requires. In the studies presented in this volume, I have attempted to explore some features of this experience in seeing, hearing, and gesturing, concluding with a chapter on how, in the beholder's perception of paintings and other forms of art for vision, perspective, and positionality, the figure-ground *Gestalt* and the subject-object structure are unsettled in ways that could open us to the emergence of a new understanding of being—and a new bodily felt sense of our belonging-together with the beings of our world. From this experience, philosophical thinking can emerge to assume the task of *Wächterschaft*, caring for the meaning of being—the events in which the meaning of being, and being itself, are disclosed. Because we need to keep in mind that we cannot take fitting care of the beings in our world without caring for being itself.

Heidegger's compelling critique of the character of our habitual ways of seeing, hearing, handling things, and gesturing offers invaluable guidance for the project of transformation that he envisioned. In Heidegger's vision of a new world epoch in the experience and understanding of being, a promising possibility of existential and ontological importance is, no doubt, the Fourfold gathering; but his critique also suggests the need for a genuine transformation in our relation to the natural environment, our use of technology, our political economy, our sense of community and the common good, and, last but not least, our current form of individualism, in which the egocentric will to power flourishes without any moral and humane restraint.

If we are stirred by the insight that comes from our embodied experience as we enter into the event of being and accordingly let ourselves be appropriated by its summons, I believe that we have an opportunity to learn ways to move beyond the present ontological epoch, beginning with our habits of perception and gesture. As Foucault urged us to appreciate,

> There are times in life when the question of knowing if one could think differently than one has been thinking, and perceive differently than one has been seeing, is absolutely necessary if one is to go on looking and reflecting at all.[8]

A key preconceptual, prepersonal experience and under-standing of being that our bodies undergo, even without any initial awareness, is our essential belonging to an intricate network of interrelations and interactions—interdependencies—sharing a world with all human beings and a natural environment with all animal species. In an essay on Jean-Luc Nancy, Walter Brogan notes that "our body is home to an infinite multiplicity of organic life and host to an infinite variety of healthy bacteria without which we could not flourish. The 'matter' we are is uniquely our own and yet teeming with life forms that co-habitate with us."[9] We are, in fact, both singular and plural, individuated and yet bound inseparably, by need and comfort, to all other beings—and bound, also, to earth and sky. It is a convenient assumption that our embodiment is confined, as if it were an organic, thinglike substance, contained within our skin. In truth, our flesh is inherently, as Merleau-Ponty argued, our exposure to the world, our body's natural intentionalities weaving us into the world that our presence, our existence, has opened us to, connecting us in identity and difference, in life and in death, in history and destiny, to the being of all beings.

Although Heidegger begins *Being and Time* affirming that we have a "pre-ontological understanding of being," an understanding of our belongingness in relation to being that he later argued for compellingly in "The Principle of Identity," he nevertheless does not acknowledge that, as Merleau-Ponty would surely have immediately recognized, it could only be our bodies that bear this "pre-ontological understanding." But at least he steadfastly maintained the thought that existence is exposure, openness, interconnectedness, and vulnerability. And I suggest that it is in this recognition that Heidegger will project the sublime ground for the endlessly precarious emergence of ethical life, leaving it to other philosophers to think this emergence from embodied experience.

†

The world epidemic that we have been living through should demonstrate the importance of our interconnectedness, hence our individual and collective responsibility, fundamental for the flourishing not only of ethical life on this earth, but of all life and all of nature. Heidegger understood our interconnectedness, our *Mit-sein*, and our belonging to being occurring in a deep ontological dimension of our experience; but he did not give thought to how that affects our ethical life—our life with others.

Da-sein, human existence, is, in essence, *Mit-sein*, being-with-others. From this fundamental fact of essence (*Wesen*), Heidegger challenged the form of individualism that is prevailing in our world today and attempted to break the appeal of the metaphysics that has reflected and validated it. The hope I want to impart is that, in thinking *from* our embodied experience, from our bodily felt sense of our being-with-others, the unsettling conflict between that sense and our form of individualism might motivate efforts to encourage the emergence of a different form of individualism—a form much more hospitable to the common good and a democratic body politic. In this regard, the clearing we open in the world must provide for a flourishing public space where people with different points of view can gather to discuss and debate matters of common concern, exercising their freedom in goodwill for the benefit of all.

Heidegger's bold insight, rendering the essence of human existence as *Da-sein*, requires abandoning the metaphysical representation of the body as substance; and so he begins to lay out what *Da-sein* actually means for our everyday experience of embodiment; but he can do little more than indicate a direction, a formal sense, for thought to pursue, because what is needed involves not merely thinking *of*, or *about*, the thrown-open, *ek-static* body, but, more radically, actually thinking *from* that very different experience of embodiment. To experience ourselves as *Da-sein* is to experience ourselves as an opening of our presence in the midst of the world.

We are still learning today—and others coming after us will also be learning in the futures to come: What difference does it make in our experience, our way of living, when we understand our embodiment as *Da-sein*, beings cast in uncanny openness, each one of us situated in a web of relations? And what difference could it make in our experience, our way of living, if we were to learn to embody an ontologically informed understanding of the world? These questions constitute a project for all of humanity to work on together: a project that is endlessly rewarding precisely because it is never to be completed.

Chapter 2

Gestures Befitting the Measure

§1

I would like to begin by invoking the painting by Michelangelo that adorns the ceiling of the Sistine Chapel, showing a mighty God reaching out and touching the Adam he has created, who correspondingly stretches out his arm so that he may receive the divine blessing of life. The painting concentrates our attention on the two gestures, one of them giving, the other receiving. By analogical extension, it might remind us at once not only of the creative potential in our gestures, but also of their role in the expression of sympathy and caring.

On Greek funerary monuments sculptured in stone, one often sees the gesture of a friend or loved one gently placed on the shoulder of the deceased as he or she departs from this world. The gesture imparts so much good feeling.

There is a very moving narrative about the hand that figures in a poem,[1] perhaps one never completed, written by Rainer Maria Rilke in 1921.

> Look at the little titmouse,
> astray in this room:
> twenty heartbeats long
> It lay within my hand.
> Human hand. One resolved to protect.
> Without possessing protect.
> But
> now on the window-sill

> free
> in its fear it remains
> estranged
> from itself and what surrounds it,
> the cosmos, unrecognizing.
> Ah, so confusing a hand is
> even when extended to save.
> In the most helpful of hands
> there is death enough still
> and there has been money.

What is a hand? What is the hand for? In this poem, Rilke evokes its fateful duplicity. Heidegger will invoke the fitting measure: "gestures befitting the measure." (GA 7: 202/PLT 223). But what is that measure and how do we learn to know it? Measure, as such, is also ethically ambiguous: there is measure in restraint, but also measure in unrestrained quantification; and there is disregard of measure in greed but also disregard of measure in generosity. In care, our hands can rescue and save beings, mindful of their being. But, as Rilke reminds us, our hands can also use and abuse, careless. And they can be aggressive and violent. Heidegger recognizes this violence, conceptualizing it as an expression of the will to power; and he accordingly interprets its prevalence in terms of the ontological nihilism that reigns in our modern world. But he nevertheless believes that we are still sufficiently free of this epochal ontology to redeem the potential in our gestures, breaking through their nihilism, their propensity for violence, and developing a different character. His critique of the gestures defining our time projects, in desperate hope, the possibility that the critique might somehow induce a transformation in the character of our gestures that would begin another epoch in the history of being. Our ontology cannot be separated from our gestures. The fate of ontology is in our hands.

†

In this essay, I shall argue that, for Heidegger, the gesture is a world-disclosing, hence hermeneutical form of expressive bodily movement, a movement that bears the intentionality of an action. Gesture projects, lays out, and articulates a world of meaning and intelligibility. Every gesture is the clearing, or opening, of a time-space field for the interplay of concealment and unconcealment; and it takes place within this projected phenomenal field of being.

In "Le monde sensible et le monde de l'expression," Maurice Merleau-Ponty argues that "the configuration of a field is part of the genesis of the movement."[2] Hence, he says, "motility is a revelation of being."[3] In other words, as David Morris nicely puts it, "the phenomenal field participates in the creative operation through which we are in it."[4] Gesture, and our bodily movement in general, occasion and generate the context, the field of being, through which they move. The clearing of being is not laid out once and for all time. This phenomenological explication of gesture and bodily motility in relation to the field of being further illuminates Heidegger's discussion of the intimate, inseparable and dynamic connection between being and human being—*Sein* and *Mensch-sein*. Merleau-Ponty refers to the reciprocity and reversibility occurring in this connection as "chiasmic." In "The Principle of Identity," Heidegger describes it as an "oscillation."

The two ontological modalities of being that Heidegger recognizes in world-history, namely, being-ready-to hand (*Zuhanden-sein*) and being-present to hand (*Vorhanden-sein*), originate in our ways of using our hands and our relations to the things with which our hands are engaged. Are other ontological modalities of being possible? The answer to that question lies, perhaps, in the ontological attitude that Heidegger calls *Gelassenheit*, letting-be, letting-go: releasement. Might *Gelassenheit* shepherd in a new ontological epoch in the unfolding history of our experience, understanding and interpretation of being? Heidegger gave much thought to some of the common gestures of our hands, exploring their historical and ontological significance. Among all the animals who have lived on this earth, we humans are not only unique in being endowed with a linguistic ability of singular articulatory and expressive power; we are also unique in being endowed with hands that are capable of an extraordinary range of disclosive and expressive movements and actions. We are capable of using our hands in amazing ways, for instance, in writing, painting, carving, and sculpturing. But also in sewing and surgery. These gestures are unique to human beings. The things in our world tend to conform to the ways the gesturing of our hands relate to them; but things also require, or invite, our gestures, our hands, to conform to their most natural way of being.

Gestures have an important role in our moral, political, and ethical life—a role that Heidegger's phenomenology brings to our attention: greeting, praying, embracing, and giving support. Although the philosopher refrained from developing a phenomenologically grounded ethics and morality, he did urge, influenced by the poetic thought of Friedrich Hölderlin, that the conduct of our lives—hence our gestures—fit the proper measure most appropriate to each situation: "Gebärde die dem Maß entsprechen" (GA 7: 202/PLT 223). But what *is* the fitting measure and what *gestures* correspond to it? I want to argue that, while all our gestures as mortals are finite in measure, the measure of their true character can only be the immeasurable, unconditional demands of an ethical life. If the earth binds us to mortality, the sky teaches us a measure beyond our power: through the spatiality of the sky we experience the possibility of dimensions of meaning for life that exceed the bounds of conceptual understanding.

§2

It seems that, among the ancient Greeks, no gesture carried greater significance than the hand gently placed on a shoulder: a gesture of greeting, a gesture of friendship, a gesture of consolation, a gesture of farewell to a friend or loved one departing from life in the world, or a gesture of shared mourning. Rilke commemorates this gesture in the second of his "Duino Elegies" (1912).

> On Attic steles, did not the circumspection [*Vorsicht*] of human gesture amaze you? Were not love and farewell so lightly laid upon shoulders, they seemed to be made of other stuff than with us? Remember the hands, how they rest without pressure, though power is there in the torsos. The wisdom of those self-masters was this: we have got so far; ours is to touch one another like this; the gods may press more strongly upon us. But that is the gods' affair.[5]

There was, belonging to ancient Greek culture, a gesture that, in its way of embodying expressive meaning, could be disclosive of the symbolic and metaphorical dimensions in which it takes place. It is of that sublime gesture, bearing the truth of mortality, that, in this stanza, Rilke writes, painfully aware of how different the gestures of our time, our world, have become.

Reading one of the early pre-Socratic philosophers in the Western world, Heraclitus by name, Heidegger connected the Greek noun *Logos*, meaning word, speech, discourse, dialogue and logic, with its grammatical verb form *Legein*, suggesting or implying that the *Logos* is, in its different modalities, an in-gathering and laying-out, laying down the structural field of meaningfulness, whether that field be perceptual, a projection of the imagination, a field of recollection, or a field of faith and hope invoking the future (GA 7: 212–34/EGT 59–78; GA 55: 186–387/H 137–288). Given this interpretation of the Greek *Logos*, I want to argue that our gestures, understood as embodiments of *logos*, are manifest in *legein*, organizing and laying out their field of action.

Unfortunately, Heidegger repeatedly evaded giving sufficient thought to our embodiment, cognisant of the fact that understanding the subject requires the overcoming of Western metaphysics, with its persistent conviction that the human body is essentially a material substance.

In any case, once Heidegger has interpreted the Greek notion of *Legein* as a gathering and laying-out that takes place in language as a form of disclosive articulation, the way is open for us to consider gesturing—also a form of *Logos*—as a gathering lay-out (*legein*) that opens, or clears, and in-gathers a field of comportment or action for the intentional trajectory of the gesture. *Logos* is not limited to language (speech and writing); it is also in our gestures—in their *legein*. Then what is important is (1) that our gestures always keep open for questioning the gestural meaning that figures in the fields that they open; and (2) that our gestures should take as their measure what in each situation is most fitting. Thus, in "Poetically Man Dwells," Heidegger, influenced by Hölderlin's retrieval of ancient Greek culture, reminds us to keep in mind "the gestures befitting the measure": "*die Gebärde die dem Maß entsprechen*" (GA 7: 202/PLT 223). We must wonder, though, whether what is most fitting could ever be, or could ever have been, what *exceeds* the measure. Heidegger refrains from asserting any determinate measure; but he is vehement in his critique of our modern epoch, arguing against a way of life that exceeds proper measure.

In this critique, he repudiates the common interpretation of the words attributed to Protagoras of Abdêra, who is supposed to have said that, "Of all things, the measure is Man, of the things that are, that they are, and of the things that are not, that they are not."[6] According to Heidegger, in this, the Anthropocene age, the pre-Socratic philosopher's words have been appropriated in a distortion that manifests precisely the arrogance, the *hubris*, the excess of our time: We reduce everything, including the immeasurable, to something we can measure and thereby dominate and control.

For Heraclitus, there is wisdom in achieving a correspondence (*homologein*) between (1) our words (*logoi*), the words we use, and (2) the potential for meaningfulness granted by the *Logos*, language as such (GA 7: 211–34 /EGT 59–78). That is, wisdom lies in using words that work with the potential that language grants. For Heidegger's "Heraclitus," what that means for ethical life is that we should keep our *logoi*, and the gestures we use, and the fields they open and lay out, open to being in its interplay of concealments and unconcealments, hence open to questions of interpretation and challenges to their achievement. That would be how, like our words, our *logoi*, our gestures would "correspond" in *homologein* to their articulatory potential, as formally indicated by the *Logos*, for disclosing and imparting meaning.

§3

According to Heidegger's account in *Being and Time*, the human being (*Dasein*) is fundamentally, that is to say, in essence, *Da-sein*, a being who is *da*, situated in the world and thrown open. This thrown-openness (*Geworfenheit*) is how we find ourselves: our condition, our *Befindlichkeit*, is to have been born and cast open into the world. We did not choose to be born; we did not choose to be cast, thrown-open, into the world. But what we make of this condition, whether, and if so, how, we appropriate it, is very much a matter of our choosing. Therefore, Heidegger argues that our being, our existence, and indeed our way of life, will always be in question. Who we are, and who we want to become, both as individuals and as taking part in various social communities, is always in question. But, distinguishing between essence and actuality, Heidegger thinks of human beings as not yet realizing and actualizing their essence: to the extent that we do not recognize our being as *Da-sein*, and do not live our lives according to the situated world-openness it involves, that essence remains as merely our potential, a potential never ceasing to call us into question as it awaits its authentic appropriation. But it is not easy to appreciate just how radical this understanding of human existence really is. To take it seriously is at least at first bound to be very unsettling, very disquieting. We tend to experience ourselves as self-contained, encapsulated bodies, our skin serving as substantial boundary between ourselves and the world. To experience ourselves as *Da-sein*, as situated and open, as laying out and in-gathering fields of experience, a world with its limiting horizon, is not only unsettling; it can be disturbing and even frightening, because it compels us to experience ourselves in a radically new way and to recognize our finitude and vulnerability in the knot of relations into which we are woven.[7]

In *The Visible and the Invisible*, a collection of late texts, Maurice Merleau-Ponty formulated a definition of "essence" that is very useful for interpreting Heidegger's conception of essence (*Wesen*), which does not mean, as in the history of metaphysics, an immutable and permanent, or eternal complex of qualities or characteristics totally detached from interactions with the world, but rather "a certain style, a certain manner of managing the domain of space and time over which it has competency, of articulating that domain."[8] After metaphysics, this is the way to think of *Da-sein* and its gestures.

Although reluctant to devote much thought to the philosophical representations of the human body he inherited, Heidegger's representation of the essence of the human being as *Da-sein* already ventures far in deconstructing the metaphysics of substance into which the human body was brutally cast. In "Building Dwelling Thinking," Heidegger elucidates in easily understandable phenomenological terms just what our being *Da-sein* means. The example he uses to illustrate it directs us to consider our visual and spatial experience. In fact, it is not only the openness of our existence that determines the nature of our embodiment; it is also that our embodiment is such that it is the medium through which we are opened to the world we enter. It is the *Da-sein* nature—the *Da-sein* structure—of our bodies that makes possible, and indeed *is*, the laying out and in-gathering of the clearing that forms the world as we experience and live it (GA 66: 328/M291). Insofar as we *Dasein* become *Da-sein*, we *are* that clearing; our very presence *is* the opening of a clearing. Consequently, the clearing is dependent on us, dependent on our existence; but also, it is dependent on our keeping it open, hence dependent on our recognition and understanding of that dependency. That awareness and understanding are crucial, because the clearing we open in the world is always situated, not reducible to the confines of our experience, knowledge, and understanding.

Heidegger makes our dis-positioning thrown-openness as embodied *Da-sein* phenomenologically concrete in a description that figures in "Building Dwelling Thinking."

> When I go toward the door of the lecture hall, I am already there, and I could not go to it at all if I were not such that I *am* there. I am never *here* only, as this encapsulated body

> [*abgekapselte Leib*]; rather, I am *here and also over there*, already pervading the room, and only thus could I go through it. (GA 7: 159/PLT 157)

My eyes take me "over there" to the door; but also, through the orientation of my movement and the pacing and spacing of my steps, my body has already projected me from here to the door.[9] *Where*, then, *is Da-sein? Where am I?* The same phenomenology also illuminates our gestures. In the simple act of drinking a cup of tea, lifting the cup and bringing it to our lips, our gesture must from the instant it begins already anticipate and calibrate the gestural trajectory. The gesture must be appropriately measured—typically done without any conscious, reflective measuring. Heidegger's phenomenology denies us the solid, self-contained embodiment we settled into, opening us into a world of interactions, trajectories of gesture and movement.

Moreover, understanding ourselves as thrown-open, as situated beings, beings whose sheer being, or presence, as such, is the opening and constituting of fields, or "worlds," of experience, is to repudiate the philosophical representation of the human being that, beginning with Descartes, thought of the human being as an inherently solitary subject standing opposite its objects in a kind of otherwise empty space, a timeless encapsulated world. For Heidegger, though, we are through and through relational, woven into the very textures of the spatial-temporal world we live in and experience. His existential phenomenology challenges the persistence of the Cartesian dualisms—the subject and its object, the mind hidden in the body. Hence solipsism, or radical skepticism about the very existence of the world is not a "problem" needing to be resolved.

§4

In 1951–1952 lectures gathered under the title *What Is Called Thinking?* (GA 8), Heidegger turned his thought toward articulating the meaning-disclosive character of the hand, implicitly inviting us to experience in some other way the gestures of the hands and, in particular, the character of their disclosiveness in regard to meaning, and their relation, therefore, to the very being of the beings with which, as with some intent or purposiveness, they pragmatically engage. The intention behind this turning to the hand is to supplement the philosopher's critique of the contemporary world for the sake of illuminating the question of being and the nihilism—the negation, denial, or reduction of being—that prevails. However, it is not possible for him to question and critique the character of our common gestures from an ontological perspective without engaging how, from an ethical-moral standpoint, this character figures in our everyday life. For Heidegger, influenced as he was by Nietzsche, this essentially means addressing the nihilism operative in the power of the will: the will as manifested in all aspects of contemporary life—including our gestures, the gestures of our hands.

Because, for Heidegger, our epoch—in the unfolding of the Anthropocene—is ruled by the nihilism in our will to power, nothing could be more important, more urgent, than protecting being, its dimension of self-concealment, from the will to power (GA 8: 10–11/WCT 9).

> What withdraws [i.e., from our control, knowledge, and use] may even concern and claim man more essentially than anything present that strikes [*betrifft*] and touches [*trifft*] us. Being struck by actuality is what we like to regard as constitutive of the actuality of the actual. However, in being struck by what is actual, man may be prevented from precisely what most concerns and affects him [*angeht*]—affects him in the surely mysterious way of escaping him [*entgeht*] by its withdrawal [*entzieht*]. The event of withdrawal could be what is most present [*gegenwärtigste*] in all that is present [*gegenwärtigen*], and consequently infinitely exceed the actuality of everything actual.

Heidegger's attention to gesture and hand is an effort to begin putting into practice this understanding of the fate of being in the nihilism of our time. We need, he argues, to learn what it means to neglect our connection to being. Everything we do needs to be an opportunity for genuine ontological thought to guide us. And he represents this argument in terms of an exemplary analogy.

> A cabinetmaker's apprentice, someone learning to build cabinets, must make himself answer and respond above all to the different kinds of wood and to the natural shapes slumbering within the wood—the wood as it enters into man's dwelling with all the hidden riches of its nature. (GA 8: 17/WCT 14–15)

The art of the craft depends entirely on this relatedness to the wood: a relatedness that brings out the natural grain of the wood, or rather lets it come forth into presence.

"We are," he says, "trying to learn thinking. Perhaps thinking, too, is just something like building a cabinet. In any case, it is a craft, a handcraft." And it is inherently related to being.

> The word "craft" literally means strength and skill. The hand is a peculiar thing. In the common view, the hand is part of our bodily organism. But the hand's essence can never be determined, or explained, by its being merely, or only, an organ that can grasp [*leibliches Greiforgan*]. (GA 8: 18–19/WCT 6)

The argument continues, drawing the all-too-familiar distinction, which Heidegger persists in maintaining in an absolute form, between the being of the human and the being of the animal.

> Apes, too, have organs that can grasp, but they do not have hands. The hand is infinitely different from all [merely] grasping organs—paws, claws, or fangs—different by an abyss of essence. Only a being who can speak, that is, think, can have hands and be handy in achieving works of hand-craft.

And so, our destiny (*Geschick*) as human beings accordingly lies, to some extent, in the character of our gestures and the forms of skilfulness (*Schicklichkeit*) distinctive of—and proper to—our hands. Thus, says Heidegger,

> The craft of the hand is richer than we commonly imagine. The hand does not only grasp and catch, or push and pull. The hand reaches and extends, receives and welcomes—and not just things: the hand extends itself and receives its own welcome in the hands of others. The hand holds. The hand carries. The hand designs and signs, presumably because the human *is* a sign. Two hands fold into one, a gesture [*Gebärde*] meant to carry the human into the great oneness. [. . .] Every motion [*Bewegung*] of the hand in every one of its works carries itself [*gebärdet sich*] through the element of thinking [*im Element des Denkens*]: every bearing of the hand bears itself in that element. All the work of the hand is rooted in thinking.

According to the philosopher, our gestures are, in virtue of their essential nature, always already, and yet not yet, rooted in thinking. They are *to be* so rooted. Hence, *properly* rooted only by virtue of bearing in mind, and accordingly relating to, being as such. But does our thinking not need to be embodied in our gestures, our hands? That, however, is a task, a process, that Heidegger's thinking neglects. In this regard, he remains bound by the very metaphysical thinking from which he is attempting to escape.

He does, however, use the rootedness of the hand in thinking as a way to formulate his critique of our contemporary world—in particular, for example, demands determining the manual labor of the industrial blue-collar worker (GA 8: 26–28/WCT 23–25).

Drawing on the etymological root-connection between thinking and thanking, but also on his interpretation of the *Legein* (layout and gathering) constitutive of the *Logos* in Heraclitus, Heidegger elaborates what the rootedness of the hand in thinking means.

> The *thanc*, the heart's core, is the gathering of all that concerns us [*uns angeht*], all that we care about and care for [*uns anlangt*], all that touches us [*woran uns liegt*], insofar as we fulfill our being as human beings. What touches us [*anliegt*] in the sense that it defines and determines our nature, what we care about and for, might be called the contiguous [*das Anliegende*] or that which lies in contact with us [*das Anliegen*]. (GA 8: 149–50/WCT 144)

And Heidegger argues that, "whenever we speak of subject and object, there is in our thoughts an oppositeness [*ein Gegenüber-liegen*]—but even so, there is always contact [*das Anliegen*] in the widest sense." As he says in "The Principle of Identity" (GA 11: 37–48/ID 29–39): between us human beings and the event (*Ereignis*) of being itself, there is always a dynamically oscillating belonging-together (*Zusammengehörigkeit*). "It is possible," he explains, "that the thing that touches us [*was uns anliegt*] and is in touch with us [*woran uns liegt*], insofar as we achieve our being-human [*Menschsein*], need not be represented by us constantly and specifically. But even so, it is concentrated, gathered toward us beforehand." Consequently, "In a certain manner, though not exclusively, we ourselves are that gathering" (GA 8: 150/WCT 144). In other words, we are clearings (*Lichtungen*) that gather beings into the experiential field that our bodily presence opens up and lays out: we are, then, in our essential nature, thrown-open, situated and situating *Da-sein*. And this presence, this thrown-open existence, is, in and as a clearing, a *legein*, a gathering layout, a topology, within which various beings can be, and are, encountered in their presence and absence. For instance, in the field laid out by the trajectory of our gestures.

§5

In the later lectures that he gave in 1952, Heidegger turned his thought to the Greek word χρη that appears in an apothegm attributed to Parmenides, which, translated loosely, says that one should both think and say that being is (GA 8: 182, 186, 195/WCT 178, 182, 191). This word, he notes, derives from, or is in any case related to, the Greek word for the hand: Χειρ (GA 8: 190/WCT 186); it is accordingly also related to the Greek verb referring to handling and using. This provokes the philosopher to begin a meditation, asking: What does it mean to use something? "Using [*Das Brauchen*]," he says, "does not mean merely utilizing, using up, exploiting. Utilization is only the degenerate and debauched form of use." Use as manipulation can take many forms, indicating its actual *character*.

> When we handle something, for instance, our hand must fit itself to the thing. Use implies fitting, accommodating response. Proper use does not debase what is being used. On the contrary, use is defined and determined by leaving the used thing in its essential nature. But this leaving it [*Lassen*] that way does not mean carelessness, much less neglect. On the contrary: Only proper use brings the thing to its essential nature and maintains it there [*Wahrung im Wesen*].

Thus, as he states,

> To use something is to let it enter its essential nature [*in seinem Wesen lassen*], keeping it safe in its essence. [. . .] Utilizing and needing always fall short of proper use. Proper use is rarely manifest, and in general is not the concern of mortals. Mortals are at best illuminated by the radiance of use [*vom Schein des Brauches beschienen*].

In translating χρη as "It is useful" in the context of the assertion attributed to Parmenides, Heidegger says that, "We are responding to a meaning of χρη that echoes in the root word."

Χράομαι means turning something to use by handling it—[a gesture] that has always been a turning to the thing in hand according to its nature, thus letting that nature become manifest in the handling.

Heidegger argues, however, that the sense of "useful" that "must here be given thought, and that Parmenides nowhere elucidates, conceals a still deeper and wider sense" than the word does even in Hölderlin's great poem, "The Titans."

It is toward that deeper concealed sense that Heidegger wants to draw our attention and thought. Succinctly stated, that deeper sense is an *ontological* sense, hence a sense from the standpoint of which it becomes possible to conceive and formulate not only a searing critique of the *character* of our habitual and typical gestures in making use of things, but also, more generally, a critique of the nihilism, the violence and abuse at work in the ways in which we handle and manipulate: ultimately an assault on being itself, even challenging the very possibility of meaningfulness in a philosophical critique grounded in the thought of being.

The ontological sense thus pertains to the *logos* and its *legein* that are constitutive of the gesture as the bodily articulation of an ontical meaning that emerges from the conditions of intelligibility operative in the situation of the clearing that the gesture projects and lays out. (See GA 8: 211–15/ WCT 196–204.) And if cognition, the forming of concepts (*noein*), is not compelled to be grasping and clinging, the same could be said of our gestures; both could rather be, practising the phenomenological method, a hermeneutical "letting come what lies before us" (GA 8: 214/WCT 211).

The Greek word for disclosiveness, unconcealment, is *aletheuein*. The *ground* of propositional truth (truth as correctness) is the underlying dimension of concealment and unconcealment: *aletheuein*, the dimension that makes possible the correctness and failure of correctness in regard to all our ontic truth-claims. We are consequently responsible, according to Heidegger, for safe-guarding and sustaining being, the openness of this fundamental dimension. That responsibility for disclosedness and the safeguarding of concealment can alone secure the practice of truth-as-correctness. However, our responsibility is even more compelling, and even more urgent, with regard to safe-guarding and sustaining the dimension of concealment, which withdraws from, and resists, efforts by the will to power to abolish this dimension for the sake of total domination. René Magritte understood the character of the prevailing disposition of the will to power when he is said to have remarked that "we always want to see what is hidden by what we see."[10] In regard to the disclosiveness of our gestures, it is not only a matter of exploring and unfolding their still unknown potential for disclosing and imparting meaning; it is also a matter of recognizing and questioning the disclosive *character* of our gestures. Heidegger's meditation on the hands and their gestures avoids getting explicitly entangled in a critique of the ethical and political life that the character of our gestures institutes. However, his ontological exposition of hand and gesture shines an unequivocally critical light on the abusiveness and violence of the gestures that are favored and predominate in our time. We cannot read his phenomenological exposition of *Zuhanden-sein* (being ready-to-hand, pragmatically available) and *Vorhanden-sein* (being-present as an object for theoretical or abstract contemplation, questioning and deliberation) without at least wondering whether there might possibly be other ways of relating to being, as yet undeveloped ways of relating to what is and what is not: ways that might perhaps inaugurate another ontological epoch, another epoch in the human experience and understanding of being—the being of beings.

§6

Drawing on his ruminations pertaining to Nietzsche's critique of Western metaphysics and the corresponding worldview that Heidegger identifies as nihilism, namely, the negation of being in denial, neglect or reduction (GA 6.1 and GA 6.2), Heidegger ventures, in his "Αγχιβασιη: Triadic Conversation on a Country Path between a Scientist, a Scholar, and a Guide" (GA 13), to think beyond *Zuhandensein* and *Vorhandensein*, the only two modalities in which we have been experiencing being, toward another way of approaching and encountering being, hence the being of all the beings in our world. This other way he calls "*Gelassenheit*," letting-be, letting-go—releasement. *Gelassenheit* requires that the will release its "objects" from its domination, its reifications, reductions, and violence. It requires that the will give up its *willfulness* and embrace an open *willingness* to accommodate in proper measure "things as they are." Thus, as an *ontological* attitude in approaching the being of beings, *Gelassenheit* is in essence not other than the phenomenological method, which, as Heidegger deploys it, is, as it must be, rigorously hermeneutical, acknowledging and protecting the dimension of concealment underlying the interplay of concealment and unconcealment.

As an *ontic* attitude, however, *Gelassenheit* is not necessarily desirable. Desirability depends entirely on the circumstances. Thus, for instance, letting-be would not be right as an attitude if one were the sole witness to someone about to drown; nor would it be right as an attitude if one saw a child being forcefully abducted. As an *ontological* attitude, though, *Gelassenheit* is of great importance for the conduct of our ethical and political life: it is, in effect, an essential feature of what Aristotle called *phronesis*—practical wisdom. Practical wisdom begins when one restrains the will's immediate urge to impose its unquestioned interpretation on things and events. Heidegger is right to challenge the will to power at work in our gestures and hands in the name of an ontological *Gelassenheit* that might keep us open to promising possibilities for the future transformation of our world. Who knows of what skillfulness and artfulness—what *Geschicklichkeit*—our gestures and hands are ultimately capable? Who can say what ontological sense and destiny (*Geschick*) our hands and gestures might bring forth? How can we create a world in which our gestures and hands are not drawn toward abuse and violence?

§7

In his 1942–1943 lectures on Parmenides, Heidegger for the first time engaged in a lengthy discussion of the hand, using reflections stirred by the Greek philosopher's thought to question the human capacity for hermeneutical disclosiveness in relation to the historical change from handwriting to the mechanical writing of the typewriter.

> The human being acts [*handelt*] through the hand [*Hand*]; for the hand is, together with the word, the essential distinction of man. Only a being which, like the human, "has" the word (*logos*), can and must "have" "the hand." Through the hand occur both prayer and murder, greeting and thanks, oath and signal, and also the "work" of the hand, the "hand-work," and the tool. The handshake seals the covenant. The hand brings about the "work" of destruction [*Verwüstung*]. The hand exists [*west*] as hand only where there is disclosure and concealment. No animal has a hand, and a hand never originates from a paw or a claw or talon. [. . .] The hand sprang forth only out of the

word and together with the word. The human does not "have" hands, but the hand holds the essence of the human, because the word as the essential realm of the hand is the ground of the essence of the human being. The word as what is inscribed and what appears to the regard is the written word, i.e., script. And the word as script is handwriting. (GA 54: 118/P 80–81)

"It is not accidental," he says, "that modern man writes 'with' the typewriter and 'dictates' [*diktiert*] (the same word as 'poetize' [*Dichten*]) 'into' a machine."

This "history" of the kinds of writing is one of the main reasons for the increasing destruction of the word. The latter no longer comes and goes by means of the writing hand, the properly acting hand, but by means of the mechanical forces it releases. The typewriter tears [*entreißt*] writing from the essential realm of the hand, i.e., the realm of the word. The word itself turns into something "typed." Where typewriting, on the contrary, is only a transcription and serves to preserve the writing, or turns into print something already written, there it has a proper, though limited, significance. In the time of the first dominance of the typewriter, a letter written on this machine still stood for a breach of good manners. Today, a hand-written letter is an antiquated and undesired thing; it disturbs speed reading. Mechanical writing deprives the hand of its rank in the realm of the written word and degrades the word to a means of communication. In addition, mechanical writing provides this "advantage," that it conceals the handwriting and thereby its character. The typewriter makes everyone look the same. (GA 54: 119/P 80–81)

Heidegger's argument against the typewriter—and indeed against everything printed, or reproduced in print—continues, making it clear that he is not arguing against all technological innovation, but rather against what he believes we lose in understanding ourselves, what we lose in contact with who we are as human beings, and what we lose in the mediation that separates the hand from the word.

When writing was withdrawn from the origin of its essence, i.e., from the hand, and was transferred to the machine, a transformation occurred in the relation of being to man. It is of little importance for this transformation how many people actually use the typewriter and whether there are some who shun it. It is no accident that the invention of the printing press coincides with the inception of the modern period. The word-signs become type, and the writing stroke disappears. The type is "set," the set becomes "pressed." This mechanism of setting and pressing and "printing" is the preliminary form of the typewriter. In the typewriter we find the irruption of the mechanism in the realm of the word. The typewriter leads again to the typesetting machine. The press becomes the rotary press. In rotation, the triumph of the machine comes to the fore. Indeed, at first, book printing and then machine type offer advantages and conveniences, and these then unwittingly steer preferences and needs to this kind of written communication. The typewriter veils the essence of writing and of the script. It withdraws from man the essential rank of the hand, without man's experiencing this withdrawal appropriately and recognizing that it has transformed the relation of his essence to being. The typewriter is a withdrawing concealment in the midst of its very obtrusiveness, and through it the relation of being to man is transformed. (GA 54: 125/P 85)

That the typewriter and the word processor introduce mediations between the hand and the written word that are transformative cannot be denied. And to some extent, the machine unquestionably eliminates, or hides, the character and mood of the writer. But Heidegger needs to explain how and why these machines withdraw us from an experience of the essence of the hand and from the essence of the word. After all, the hand is still involved in typing the letters and words. And the word still comes forth to communicate and share. Is the meaning of the word somehow lost or distorted when it is typed or printed? What is there in the *essence* (*Wesen*) of the word that typing or printing distorts or loses?

Heidegger's critique, then, is not only about a loss in our capacity for disclosiveness, the communication of meaning—a loss that could also be attributed in certain respects to all writing as such in contrast to speaking, which conveys much meaning by the expressive qualities of the voice—but also about our loss of self-knowledge, above all our distinctively human relation to being as such—that is, our relation to the conditions of disclosiveness: the interplay of concealment and unconcealment that is always involved in meaning and truth.

The gesture in typing the word is of course reduced to digital repetition; and, in the printed word, the gesturing of the hand is indeed completely removed and lost.

> I have not been presenting a disquisition on the typewriter itself, regarding which it could justifiably be asked what in the world that has to do with Parmenides. My theme was the modern relation (transformed by the typewriter) of the hand to writing, i.e., to the word, i.e., to the unconcealedness of being. A meditation on unconcealedness and on being does not merely have something to do with the didactic poem of Parmenides; it has everything to do with it. In the typewriter the machine appears, i.e., technology appears, in an almost quotidian and hence unnoticed and hence signless relation to writing, to the word, and to the distinguishing essence of man. A more penetrating consideration would have to recognize here that the typewriter is not really a machine in the strict sense of machine technology, but is an "intermediate" thing, between a tool and a machine, a mechanism. Its production, however, is conditioned by machine technology. (GA 54: 126–27/P 85–86)

There is much truth in Heidegger's critique; but he neglects the role of printing and typing, not only in the dissemination of knowledge and the education and enlightenment of mankind, but also in the emancipation and freedom of many populations. While I recognize that the typewriter, the printing press, and our more advanced technologies have been enormously transformative of social relations and cultural life, I must continue to press the crucial ontological questions, namely: How are these machines disturbing our relation to the concealment and unconcealment of being? How are they concealing from us the *essence* of the word, the essence of gesture, and the *essence* of the human being? What is it that they necessarily make us forget?

Heidegger states, "There is a 'hand' only where beings as such appear in unconcealedness and man comports himself in a disclosing way toward beings. The hand entrusts to the word [and to the gesture] the relation of the human being to being as such and, thereby, the relation of human being to beings" (GA 54:124–25 /P 84). But the mediating machine also makes beings appear in unconcealedness; and it, no less than the hand itself, connects us to the being of beings. Moreover, the hand still remains engaged, even when the relation to the word and to that which the word signifies is mediated. The hand, after all, still needs some kind of tool in order to write. Perhaps an answer to the questions I am raising is that the less mediated, less remote relation can strengthen our *felt sense* of a *responsibility* for the words and gestures we are using and for the being of the beings our words and gestures bring into unconcealment. This suggestion is strengthened, I suggest, when we consider that, even today, a handwritten signature is still required to determine the legitimacy of many documents. So, what ultimately concerned Heidegger was the weakening of a sense of ontological responsibility for being, and consequently for the being of beings.

§8

In the time when writing by hand was both necessary and prevalent, and when a black ink, color of mourning, was used by the feather, pen, or brush, the ink, both in substance and in qualities, was a subtle and sublime reminder of impermanence and mortality. The one who writes lays out a gathering of words on an empty white surface, paper or parchment, entrusting meaning to an alphabet of letters that are like shadows retracing the gestures that embody in writing what has been thought, leaving the letters, the words, to their natural fate: a slow process of disintegration, turning the ink into nothing but a scattering of dust withdrawing meaning from easy mastery by the gaze. That experience of the written text, and of the gestures that brought it forth, is, as Heidegger claims, nearly lost in the mediations of our technology-dependent world. Impermanence no longer appears in the dust of words shrouded in black: our distractions conceal its evidence. And the compelling intimacy of writing by hand, an intimacy that once gave rise to an intensely felt care and responsibility for the carefully written word, has now virtually vanished. There is not only much to criticize; there is also much to lament. Heidegger's lectures join lamentation to critique. The insights they suggest might bring us a little closer, though, to recognizing and achieving something essential to our imperiled humanity.

In the beauty of the traditional Japanese and Chinese art of calligraphy, as in the encrypted and effaced, sometimes almost obliterated writing that appears in Cy Twombly's drawings, we are reminded of the intimate hermeneutical connection between the gesturing hand's writing and the phenomenology of being. The meditative calligraphy and the artist's aesthetically disciplined writing and drawing are examples of art's ways of *Wächterschaft*, caring for *aletheia*—the discreetly sublime truth of being: not truth-as-correctness, but truth as the clearing of a world that is the necessary condition making it possible for beings to appear in some mode of presence within a field of experience where concealment and unconcealment are forever in immeasurable time-space interplay. Everything depends on our assumption of responsibility in taking part, through the gestures involved in writing, in the event of being. For the monks in the Middle Ages, the calligraphy they engaged in the creating of illustrated and decorated manuscripts constituted a discipline and practice requiring the most intense concentration of attention. It was felt to be a form of devotional prayer and meditation. Calligraphy was the enactment of a sacred responsibility. The gestures themselves were acts of prayer, bringing mind and body into sacred communion. And in this painstaking endeavor, their identity, their individualism, was submerged. And so, as I read Heidegger, he is telling us that, in belonging to being, taking part as *Da-sein* in its clearing, we incur a responsibility that challenges our habits of perception and sensibility—and even our very sense of identity. But writing, even though always mediated by some kind of tool, can still be a gesture of kindness, a practice of mindfulness, and a medium disclosive of truth. And, regardless of the tool, a sense of responsibility to the being of that which has been entrusted to the work of writing remains essential. Writing in that spirit, that *Stimmung*, can remind us of the redeeming power in words and gestures.

†

In *Being Singular Plural*, Jean-Luc Nancy nicely recapitulates some of the thinking that has motivated my sense of a need for this chapter on measure and responsibility in regard to our gestures.

> Either the time to come will know to take the measure [of things], or else there will be a loss of all measure, and existence along with it. In both a disturbing and exhilarating way, this is what is immensely grand in what is happening to us today, to the extent [*à mesure*] that we are exposed to it.[11]

For Heidegger, gestures befitting the measure are of the utmost importance. Living in a fitting way, we would acknowledge our finitude, our limitations, our ignorance and powerlessness. We would practice caring with humility. But what *is* the fitting measure? From where could it come, if not, ultimately, from our body's felt sense of what the being of each situation calls for? Ethical life emerges, precariously, painfully, and without any ultimate transcendent grounding, from a sensibility attuned to being. But if we lose all sense of appropriate measure, no longer attuned by a sense of being, how could our gestures avoid the corruption of their meaning? And how could they avoid violence and injustice? If, in our gestures, we become more mindful of the being of the beings with which we are engaged, I think there is reason to hope for a better world.

Chapter 3

The Uncanny Vision of Kalchas

§1

In the course of his 1946 reflections on the only extant fragment attributable to Anaximander, Heidegger ponders "the riddle of being" in the Greek understanding of what we call "being," taking note of the fact that, "in the duality of the participial significance of the *ón*, the distinction between 'being' and 'a being' remains concealed" (GA 5: 321–73/EGT 13–58). Pursuing the fateful historical formation of the Greek word, which in Parmenides and Heraclitus was written in the singular as *eón* and, in the plural, as *eónta*, Heidegger turns to a consideration of that word in Homer's *Iliad*, concentrating on the bard's words, evoking the assembly of warriors at which Achilles commands Kalchas the seer and soothsayer to interpret the wrath of the god, who has sent down on the Achaeans nine days of plague. In an English translation by Richard Lattimore, the passage Heidegger wants to discuss reads thus.

> And among them stood up Kalchas, Thestor's son, by far the best of the bird interpreters, who knew all that is, is to be, or once was, who guided into the land of Ilion the ships of the Achaeans through that seercraft of his own that Phoibos Apollo gave him. (GA 5: 345/EGT 33)

The Greek word for "knew" here is the same word that also was used, Homer's time, to say "saw," or "has seen." Both in ordinary language usage and, later, as reflected in Greek philosophical thought, the Greek philosophers' word for knowing maintained its derivation from seeing. This is evident in the words that Plato depends on for thinking about metaphysics and epistemology. So Kalchas the "seer," the one who knows, can see what no others can see. In fact, says Heidegger, sharpening the claim to the point of paradox and enigma, he has "always already seen"—seen, in fact, everything (GA 5: 345–46/EGT 33–34). Consequently: "having seen in advance, he sees into the future." If we take this seriously, what might it mean? Can we give it any phenomenological truth? *How is it possible* for him to see, so exceptionally, into the future? *How is it possible* for him to have *always already* seen everything that was and even everything that will ever be? What characterizes the distinction of his sight or knowledge? How does he possess this uncanny, seemingly impossible recollection and foresight?

Everything seems to hinge, for Heidegger, on the grammar of the words *tá t'eónta* (all that is, namely, beings), *t'essómena* (what was, or has been), and *pró t'eónta* (what is to be). But if, as I suggest, it is reasonable to understand the grammar of these words to spell out the *ek-static* temporal gathering layout (*legein*) of the seer's vision, then it makes corresponding sense to suppose that the "gathering layout" that figures in Heidegger's commentaries on the pre-Socratic texts is to be identified with the functioning of the clearing, the *Lichtung*, that "primordial self-illumination of being" (GA 5: 336/EGT 26), which, in our appropriation as *Da-sein*, engaged in the world, is assigned an essential role in Heidegger's hermeneutical phenomenology of perception. The clearing, the event of being itself, is the dimension of the world of our experience in and through which everything must pass that in any way was, is, and will be. The clearing is an openness that lets be, lets happen, what was, what is, and what will be; but that openness is always bounded by the given situations, the material and historical conditions, and it extends far beyond the known—into the realm of the invisible, the realm of the unfathomable, in all of which we have to learn to live. Kalchas does *not* gather all the events of time and history, including all future events that have not yet occurred, into the totality of a living present. That advance knowledge of distant events is humanly impossible; not even a seer can escape the conditions of finite experience and knowledge. What distinguishes Kalchas's vision is that he *understands* events in terms of, or from the standpoint of, the transcendental conditions that make events in time possible. His vision is situated in that transcendental dimension. But we must not misunderstand what this means. Thus, we must not confuse the transcendental with something transcendent, exceeding the realm of experience, the realm of appearances. The transcendental is not autonomous, independent of experience; in fact, it is not entirely separate from what empirically appears: it is a structure of conditions for appearing occurring *together with* that which appears: a structure visible in its recessive invisibility. Now, expressed in terms of being, Kalchas's vision is a transcendental vision *of being*; but being is not to be understood as an abstraction behind or apart from what appears. Being is neither totally visible nor totally invisible. Rather, it is visible, or manifest, *as the invisible ground of the visible*, hence to be discerned in its withdrawing from attention within the field of that which is appearing. Kalchas's vision is therefore nothing mystical; but it is possible simply and only because he *understands* the phenomenology of appearing and the functioning of being itself, within the field of appearing.

Kalchas's extraordinary ability is not possible, however, merely because of his being a *Da-sein*, that is, a situated and situating thrown-open-aheadness. After all, that is a description true of every *Dasein*, even, to a certain more limited extent, of the other animal species. What makes the seer different is that what he sees he sees with a singularly keen *awareness* of being thrown-ahead into the *ek-static* openness of temporality (GA 5: 338/EGT 27). That temporality takes place as the openness of the clearing. Ultimately, it is the seer's exceptional *awareness* of his bodily *Da-sein* in, and as, the open *ek-static* clearing, the projected time-space in the receptive but bounded openness of which he lives, that makes possible the exceptional dimensionality of his always already seen. The truth dwells in that awareness. "Awareness": the etymology of the very word, in fact, bespeaks its relation to truth—truth not as correctness, correspondence between thought and world, assertion and fact, but truth as *aletheia*, the dimension of openness for the interplay of concealment and unconcealment that is the necessary condition for the very possibility of truth as correctness.

†

Before proceeding to consider further the seer's vision in its uncanny temporality and historicality, we should understand at the outset that this vision, as Heidegger understands it, has nothing to do with an ability to *predict* specific *events* taking place at a set date and time in the future. Nor does his vision have predictively in view the fate of any particular *objects*. That "common" interpretation is, undoubtedly, how the warriors, peasants, and perhaps even Homer himself, must have understood Kalchas's peculiar ability. It is not at all, however, how Heidegger proposes to understand it. The seer's words are not empirical predictions; nor are they prophecies in the common sense of that word, although the vision, the foresight that they claim does *precede* the events to which they refer. Of course, in the literal sense of *prediction*, namely, speech that precedes, that comes before the event, the seer's words *are* pre-dictive—and, correspondingly, bearing in mind the Greek derivation, his words are also pro-phetic. His seeing, and the words that, pro-phetically, come from that seeing, come from the temporality of a thrown-aheadness that makes possible an "always already."

The uncanny ability that Kalchas enjoys is accordingly possible, I argue, because of two conditions, two connected factors: (1) an exceptional awareness and understanding of the ontological functioning of the open spatiotemporal clearing in the phenomenology of his perception and cognition, and accordingly, (2) a shift from living within the conventional time-series of our calendars and clocks (*Zeitlichkeit*) to dwelling in its phenomenologically underlying ontological dimension, namely *ek-static* temporality (*Temporalität*). These two factors are inseparable, because in the phenomenology of the clearing, there is not only a spatial openness; there is also a temporal dimension in which the three time-orders—past, present, future—that we experience are intricately intertwined: (1) a past experienced as past, a past made present again, and a future past, that is, a past projected to be experienced as having been past but retrieved for a renewing presence sometime in the future; (2) a present experienced in its immediate presence, a present experienced as if already past, a present experienced as belonging to some future present; and (3) a future experienced as if already past, a future experienced as if it were already present, and a future projected to be experienced in the future. Other intricate weavings of temporalities on the loom of time are recognized in the conditional and subjunctive inflections of our grammar, together with the simpler grammatical forms and their various temporal permutations. In this weave of events that mark our time, there are wrinkles and folds, knots and tears—and sequences of events in which we mortals experience fate and fatality. But the seer is one who sees events without imposing on them the metaphysical determinism of a linear series.

†

The shift from everyday *Zeitlichkeit* to transcendental *Temporalität* is crucial for Kalchas's vision. *Zeitlichkeit* tends to be experienced as an irreversible succession of now-present points in a linear series, according to which the past is completely past, finished, irretrievably buried, and the future is absolutely future, as if without any sense of expectation or anticipation preceding its event. In the ontological dimension of *Temporalität*, however, the past is never completely past, as it can resonate and reverberate long past its moment in time; and some of its originally missed opportunities and possibilities might even be retrieved later on for the sake of the present and the future. And the future, which may involve recalling a past, is already present to some extent in the mode of anticipation or expectation, while the present is not a discrete, monadic, self-contained moment in time, but instead a rich, complex weave involving retained pasts and anticipated futures.

Now, if, as Heidegger argues, *thinking* is, in its truest sense, a phenomenological letting-appear, then of course, *a fortiori*, modes of *perception and knowing* must also be ways of bringing forth and letting-appear. And in one of its meanings, "being" is a name for the appearing, the presencing, as such, of *all* that appears, *all* that presences—in any way and in any of the temporal dimensions—in correspondence with the *letting*-appear, the *letting*-presence, of the clearing, which is always operative in the course of human perception and cognition as the necessary condition for the very possibility of such appearing, such presencing. This letting-appear or letting-presence (*Anwesen-lassen*), which Heidegger will describe as a "sending" or "giving," and which is the function of the clearing, being itself, provides an openness-to-beings that makes all presencing, all appearing, possible: an openness, however, that, in the seer's vision, is exceptionally expansive in the interplay of concealment and unconcealment that takes place within the extent of the time-space field. What Kalchas sees he sees with a keen *sense* of the whole, including, therefore, that which he lets remain in concealment. There is in his vision a deeply felt sense that gathers all temporal forms of presencing into its open protective embrace (GA 5: 347–50/EGT 35–38).

We need to give thought to this clearing, the underlying ground of the visionary experience, because it is only by way of that open clearing, to which his vision has been appropriated in exceptional mindfulness, that the seer's vision can become proleptic. With words that engage the Greek *legein* of the *logos*, Heidegger explains that the seer grounds the possibility of his vision in a gathering layout (*legein*), a hermeneutically disclosive spatiotemporal clearing, comprehending the course, the passage, of "all that is, is to be, or once was" (GA 5: 348/EGT 36).

§2

In a world-time belonging to a very distant past, Periander, the sage Tyrant of Corinth (668–584 BCE) is supposed to have urged us to take into our care the whole of beings. If the essence of perception (*Wahr-nehmung*), as

Heidegger has argued, is to take truth (*Wahrheit*), the truth of being—*aletheia*—into our care (*Wahren*), then that means perception bears a summons to care for all beings in the wholeness, or integrity, of their being, hence even—and indeed especially—in their dimensions of concealment. And that wholeness, that integrity, concerns their intrinsic being-in-time. There are no beings not in time—and no beings not subject to time's irrevocable law. The seer (who could very well be a woman, though in the present context, namely, our reflections on Heidegger's brief discussion of Kalchas, visionary soothsayer, the seer happens to be a man), is one who sees this great law at work in the presencing of all beings, letting them come into being and linger for a while before seeing them inevitably withdraw, called away.

As I have argued, the secret of this visionary man essentially lies in his exceptionally thoroughgoing temporal awareness. So it is worth noting, here, that this English word, *awareness*, is etymologically related to the German word for truth: late Old English gewær, from Proto-Germanic **ga-waraz* (source also of Old Saxon *giwar*, Middle Dutch *gheware*, Old High German *giwar*, German *gewahr*), from the joining of **ga-*, an intensive prefix, and *waraz*, which can mean "wary," or "cautious," but also "mindful," and "very attentive." Considered in this light, awareness is care for the event of truth. Kalchas's seemingly impossible foresight, his supposed skillfulness (*Schicklichkeit*) in prognostication, in foreseeing destiny (*Geschick*), is not madness, nor is it a magical power; rather, it is essentially nothing more than the wisdom that comes from authentically living his phenomenological being-in-time—and, before all else, his appropriation to the clearing—with much more thoughtful awareness, much more attentiveness, hence much more understanding, than the rest of us. This makes all the difference in the world. The seer's way of seeing is a way that protects and sustains the clearing—the *aletheic* truth of being, into the temporal openness of which he is, with singular awareness, always already thrown-ahead (GA 5: 348/ EGT 36). But it is a way of seeing that sees everything in its ultimate finitude, its impermanence, its subjection to the law, the justice, of time: the justice of time as Anaximander understood it in his days of life on earth (GA 5: 321/EGT 13).

†

For the moment, however, let us concentrate on the temporality of the seer's perception. The seer is one who understands, and dwells in, a temporal and historical order fundamentally different from the ordinary, because, unlike most of us, his experience of the temporality and historicity in which he lives is thoroughly saturated by his awareness. Hence it is, in actuality, just as Husserl describes that experience in his phenomenology of inner time-consciousness. This phenomenology brings out the true nature—the deep structure—of our experience of temporality: our being-thrown into the *ekstasis* of time. However, the experience that Husserl's phenomenology describes is not something most of us are sufficiently aware of or attentive to in thought. We live *within* the intricacies of that *ek-static* structure, but without sufficient awareness of its temporal dimensionality, even when we correctly and judiciously use the grammar of temporality in all its tenses.

According to Husserl's phenomenology, which I shall recapitulate only in the briefest of summaries, in every moment of experience there is a present that gathers into itself "retentions" and "protensions," intentionalities that carry the immediacies of what has just passed and anticipate the immediacies of what might be about to come. What might seem to be an *Erlebnis*, a discrete, encapsulated monadic experience of the moment, is always in truth an *Erfahrung*, an experience drawn out into temporal relationality. Kalchas does not fall into our common, habitual temporal myopia. Aware of the deeper structure of time, he does not experience time as *Erlebnis*, a narrowed-down, linear succession of discrete, self-contained now-points, such that the present is the presentness of an isolated, self-contained, totally present now, a discrete point in time, while the past is irretrievably gone, absolutely absent from the now-time, and the future is totally futural, likewise absolutely absent from the dimensions of the immediately experienced now. The seer's vision is thus a capacity to experience the world in a way that is markedly different from how we are ordinarily aware of experiencing it, hence it involves a capacity to see what others do not see. As such, it is uncanny, but not in fact divine madness.

The seer's vision is grounded with exceptional awareness in the deeper phenomenological structure of his being-in-time: an *ek-static* temporality involving *Gewesenheit*, remaining in touch with a past that in some way still *is* (hence *da-gewesen*), and *Zukunftigkeit*, living not merely in existential thrownness (*Geworfenheit*), cast into the context (*Befindlichkeit*) of a world, but, because of the retention of what has passed, carrying it into a present (*Gegenwart*) that is always protentional, and because of the protention that carries past and present forward, living also in the aheadness (*Vorlaufen*) of an always already. Hence, as Heidegger says, "Only when a person has seen does he truly see. To see is to have seen. What is seen has arrived and remains for him in sight. A seer has always already seen" (GA 5: 345–46/

EGT 34). Moreover, what has not yet been, what has not yet come to pass, is foreseen—seen, as it were, in advance, not in the sense that it is predicted or prophesied, but rather in the sense that the seer does not dwell in a momentary, sealed present, but instead in a dimension of time in which the present is open to the future and will, at some future time, receive all that is still to come: the seer knows only that what will come to pass will be coming into the openness of a present. In other words, the seer understands the transcendental conditions that make the experience of events possible. But, knowing that, he accommodates the future in its coming; he lets it be; and thereby, in a certain nontrivial sense, may be said to have *already seen* it. He has *not* seen the particular object or event—that will be possible only in the future, when it happens, or comes. But what he *has* seen is the *fact* that all future objects and all future events will belong to the fundamental structure of *Temporalität*. The seer is one who "truly sees," because he knows how time is the very condition of the phenomenology of being.

The seer is someone for whom the present moment is always already *gewesen*, passing on its way into the past—which is not to say it is passing into *Vergangenheit*, as absolutely gone, but rather, it is passing into a past that remains operative in the present, livingly, vividly engagingly present as past, background to what is to come; and that passing away within the present is simultaneously the leaving behind of the present as the present stretches out into future time, opening by the inherently projective structure of time to what is waiting to come. Thus, the seer gathers into his seeing what is present as passing and, simultaneously, interdependently, what is present as to-come. For what is past and what is to come are also ways of presencing in the embrace of the present.

†

The seer is one who, exceptionally, lets himself be mindfully appropriated by his *essence* as *Da-sein*. This feature is crucial, indeed decisive. What it means is that, unlike most of us, he is keenly aware of his being in, and belonging to, the openness of a world-clearing: "an open expanse [*Gegend*] of unconcealment, into which and within which whatever comes along lingers."

This different experience of the temporality operative in the clearing is the secret of the seer's seemingly paradoxical capability in visionary perception. In the final analysis, the vision of the seer is actually nothing mystical—nothing more than what Heidegger would have described as the appropriated (*ereignete*) capability, exceedingly difficult to achieve, of someone living authentically in the care of truth—the truth in its time. And this purports that the seer's way of seeing—the seeing itself—is as difficult and as exceptional as his experience with time. Among other things, it means that the character of this seeing is inherently immersed in time, so that the seer is seeing everything as touched and affected by the passage of time. Even the future of things is seen as *already* touched and affected by that passage. Impermanence touches everything, leaving its traces, its cinders and ashes—for those who, like Kalchas, have eyes to see it.

§3

Anaximander's only extant fragment of thought concerns the being of beings in the cosmological relation of law connecting time and cosmological justice: that is, the destiny of beings according to the justice distinctive of time and the time that is distinctive of nature's justice. Although the principal reason Heidegger discusses how Homer speaks of Kalchas's vision is to reflect on the way that, because being is inseparable from time, the grammar of the Greek word for being undergoes temporal inflection, I would suggest, especially in light of the later pages in the text on Anaximander, that an attempt to *envision* the possibilities confronting our historical freedom in the *Geschick* of being (i.e., in the context of the meaning that *being* has in our present historical epoch) was also a reason why Heidegger's thought was drawn to reflect on the secret of Kalchas's seeing. That there is a philosophy of time and history powerfully influencing Heidegger's interpretive reading of the history of philosophy is something we should not underestimate.

†

This vision will seem stranger than it is, so long as we think of this seeing in terms of a correlation between the seer and a particular object. Rather, what the seer has seen and carries forward into all her future seeing, such that we should say that she has always already seen what comes, always already seen what is, is not other than this: that the essence (*Wesen*) of being is time. In other words, the seer sees being—sees the presencing of all that in any way is—through the optics and grammar of time. She sees being in the *wholeness* of its time—and thus she has always already seen everything in its coming, lingering, and departing. Kalchas sees the world *in the light of* the temporal-spatial clearing, sees the future illuminated by carrying through the clearing what has already been. The temporal-spatial clearing is the theater in which everything appears insofar as it in any way *is*, whether present or absent in its pastness or futurity. To understand the time-structured functioning of this clearing and be in touch with it is, from that perspective, to have seen everything already.

§4

In addition to questions about the temporality of the vision, there is a question regarding the phenomenological correlate—the intentional object, so to speak—of that seeing. So, Heidegger asks, "*What* is it that the seer has seen in advance?" To engage our thinking, he answers his question by suggesting, at first, what seems obvious: "Obviously, only what becomes present in the lighting that penetrates her sight. What is seen in such a seeing can only be what comes to presence in unconcealment. But what is it that becomes present?" That is indeed the question. And the answer is not at all the most obvious one, because it is not any object or event. What the seer sees "in advance," what "becomes present" to his vision, is *the belonging-together of being and time in the openness of the clearing*. The clearing, as Heidegger has argued, is structurally *prior* to all perceptual, imaginative, and conceptualizing engagements: it is a dimension of being laid out in advance of all subject-object encounters in the realm of vision. *Consequently, it is ultimately the a priori clearing that the seer sees* as *making possible* her uncanny vision. She sees it *as* prior, *as* the structure of openness that lets beings show themselves in the interplay of concealment and unconcealment. And because of that, she can see things in advance, always ahead of their coming into presence, still in touch with what has been, and always ahead of things in their trajectory.

†

In order to make sense of the seer's vision, we need to free our thinking from the "historiological" conception of historical time. In the first of the five 1957 Freiburg lectures, "Basic Principles of Thinking,"[1] Heidegger argues against this conception and indicates the phenomenology constitutive of a very different, truly authentic (*eigentlich*), appropriated (*ereignet*) relation to the temporality of history.

> As long as we represent history historiologically, history appears as occurrences, these however in the sequence of a before and an after. We find ourselves in a present through which what occurs flows away. Starting from here, on the basis of this present, the past is calculated. For it, the future is planned. The historiological representation of history as a sequence of occurrences prevents us from experiencing to what extent authentic history is constantly an impending present [*Gegenwart*] in an essential sense. By "present" ["*Gegenwart*"] here we do not mean what is directly present-at-hand in a momentary [self-contained] now. The impending [*Gegen-wart*] is what waits toward us [*uns entgegenwartet*], waits for whether and how we expose ourselves to it or, contrarily, close ourselves off from it. That which waits toward us also comes to us; it is the future [*Zu-kunft*], rightly thought. It pervades what is impending as a summons or directive [*Zumutung*] that approaches the *Da-sein* of the human, seeming [*anmutet*] to him, in one way or another, such that he would surmise [*vermute*] the future in its claim. (GA 79: 84/BF 79)

This impending present that waits must not, of course, be misunderstood to imply that the future is present as *vorhanden*, already set and simply waiting to appear in its due time, as if the future were waiting in concealment like actors waiting behind the stage sets for the moment of their entry onto the stage. Heidegger's exposition of the phenomenology continues.

> Authentic history is an impending [*Eigentliche Geschichte ist Gegen-wart*]. What impends is the future as the summoning directive, or assignment [*Zumutung*], of the inceptual—i.e., of what is already enduring, essencing—as well as its concealed gathering. Impending is also the concernfully approaching claim of what-has-been [*des Gewesenen*]. (GA 79: 84/BF 79)

And he concludes this description with a lament regarding how we of today are living our time.

> For historiological calculation, history is what is past and the present is what is current. Yet [because it is separated from the

rich potential in what has been] the current time remains eternally futureless. (GA 79: 84/BF 80)

"We are," he says, "flooded by historiology and only seldom find an insight into history" (GA 79: 84/BF 80). This means that the seer is not, and could not be, a Cartesian subject, "closed off against the arriving of the dispensation avowed to us [*gegen die Ankunft des uns zugesprochenen Geschickes*]" (GA 79: 100/BF 95). To see with the seer's eyes, we must, according to Heidegger, abandon this false experience of ourselves in relation to the world "in favor of an experience in which [whether we know it or not] we are already residing [*daß wir sie zugunsten einer Erfahrung preisgeben, in der wir uns schon aufhalten*]" (GA 79: 100/BF 95). "In all brevity," he says, expressing his point in a paradoxical metaphor, "this can be stated so: We can catch sight [*erblicken*] only of that which has already sighted us" (GA 79: 100/BF 95). In other words, we can see visible things only because we ourselves belong to the realm of the visible. And this belonging-together in the field of visibility is possible only because that field takes shape within the situation of the open clearing we have been granted. Likewise, we can experience the timeliness of beings only because, in our way of being, we ourselves are immersed in temporality.

By situating us in a linear serial order of time, historiology can actually deny us the retrieving and redeeming of our historical past, just as it can deny us the promise and hope in a future. How we understand historical time really matters.

However, if the oscillating relationship between sighting and being sighted is ever to hold sway, we must, he adds, "abandon the position of the human as a subject, and thereby the subject-object relation, and find our way back into the more originary dimension of the human essence" (GA 79: 100/BF 95; in his *Phenomenology of Perception*, Merleau-Ponty argues for this dimension).[2]

†

Parsing the metaphysical question of being in terms of its tense, or say voice, in grammar, in language, the "shelter of being," Heidegger shows that being is essentially, inherently temporal, given only in and as belonging to time. This argument plays a crucial role in his endeavor to make sense of the soothsayer's experience (GA 5: 345ff/EGT 33ff). Correlatively, Heidegger argues that time is given only in the grammatical forms of being (GA 5:

346/EGT 34). The now-time, presently present [*Gegenwart*], is actually, he argues, "an open expanse [*Gegend*] of unconcealment," a clearing in relation to which what is past and what is to come are present, but present as adumbrations indicative of what *is* outside that expanse of unconcealment—in other words, present as absent: "Even what is absent is something present, for as absent from the expanse, it presents itself in unconcealment" (GA 5: 347/EGT 35).

Thus, as Heidegger points out, the seer "stands in sight [*im Angesicht*] of what is present, in its unconcealment, which has at the same time cast light on the concealment of what is absent as being absent. The seer sees inasmuch as he has seen everything as present" (GA 5: 347/EGT 35). "Present"—but not in a sense that excludes hiddenness, absence, incompleteness, echoes, shadows and adumbrations, invisibility. For the many, this *ek-static*, open vision, the experience of a man "outside himself," is an incomprehensible madness. But, as Heidegger demonstrates, it is merely, in fact, a phenomenologically truthful description of the essential, inherent nature of *all* vision: an experience with vision mindful of itself, which, unfortunately, is only exceptionally experienced as such: "All things present and absent are gathered and preserved [*versammelt und darin gewahrt*] in *one* presencing for the seer" (GA 5: 348/EGT 36). This "presencing," however, is not gathering everything into the closure of a totality; nor is it gathering and reducing everything into the immediacy of presentness—a now-time in which everything past and everything to come are all at once paraded in perfect totality before the sovereign gaze. It is crucial, first of all, that we distinguish a whole from a totality, a closed whole, and that we do not construe the gathering-into-one of the seer's vision as an expression of the will to power, attempting to master and control time and being. In fact, this vision is possible only by *renouncing* such authority and power, relinquishing Platonic metaphysics in favor of the truth in time—being as a function of time. In fact, part of what makes the seer's vision exceptional is precisely its protection of the dimensions of concealment, misrepresented by our ordinary experience as nonexistent. The seer sees the invisible—but in its presence *as* the invisible, the self-concealing.

§5

These reflections lead Heidegger into a discussion of the constellation of words surrounding *Wahrnehmung*, the German word for "to perceive" (GA

5: 348/EGT 36). He mentions *wahren*, *gewahren*, and *verwahren*, signifying preserving and protecting; *wahren*, signifying a securing and safekeeping that clears and gathers; *Wahrheit*, signifying truth; and finally, *Wahr* and *Wahrnis*, nouns signifying truth as protection and preservation. Hence, he says, "Presencing [*Das Anwesen*] preserves [*wahrt*] in unconcealment what is present [*das Anwesende*] both at the present time [*das gegenwärtige*] and not at the present time [*das ungegenwärtige*]" (GA 5: 348/EGT 36). One may therefore say that the seer is also a soothsayer, a *Wahr-sager*, "one who speaks from the *preserve* [*Wahr*] of what is present": one who, moreover, contrary to Platonism, experiences the truth even in perception, realizing that the essence of perception, unrecognized both by Platonism and by the many, is—and must be—the preservation [*Wahrnis*] of the being of beings in the interplay of concealment and unconcealment, presentness and absence.

> If what is present stands in the forefront of vision, everything presences together; one brings the other with it, one lets the other go. What is presently present in unconcealment lingers [*weilt*] in unconcealment as in an open expanse [*Gegend*]. Whatever lingers or whiles in the expanse [*Das gegenwärtig in die Gegend Weilend (Weilige)*] proceeds to it from concealment and arrives in unconcealment. But what is present is arriving or lingering only insofar as it is also already departing from unconcealment toward concealment. [. . .] This must be said precisely of whatever is truly present, although our usual way of representing things would like to exclude from what is present all absences—all sense of absence. (GA 5: 350/EGT 37)

Heidegger's argument continues, drawing out the phenomenology of the seer's vision: "The seer is the one who has already seen the whole [*das All*] of what is present in its presencing. [. . .] To have seen is the essence of knowing" (GA 5: 354/EGT 40).

> In 'to have seen' there is always something more at play than the completion of an optical process. In it the connection with what is present subsists behind every kind of sensuous and nonsensuous grasping. On that account, 'to have seen' is related to self-illuminating presencing. [We forget that] seeing is determined, not by the eye, but by the lighting [i.e., clearing] of being. Presence within the lighting articulates all the human

senses. The essence of seeing, as 'to have seen,' is to know. Knowledge embraces vision and remains indebted to presencing. (GA 5: 349/EGT 36)

And he concludes this paragraph of thought declaring that knowledge is "remembrance of being"—that is, "thoughtful maintenance of being's preserve." This "preserve" is the open clearing, in which, as appropriated to it, the seer as *Da-sein* stands.

†

Heidegger's investment in this understanding of the past ultimately goes far beyond Husserl, far beyond acknowledging the threads of retentional intentionality that keep the present open to the past as what has been; what ultimately concerns him is rather a remembrance that keeps alive the creative, transformative originality of the inception of metaphysics, enabling it to continue being that creative source of originality. For there is a past that has *never* actually been present, a past never made now-present. What is past in the sense of having-been bears possibilities that have remained unrecognized, unappreciated, and unrealized, possibilities still available for retrieval, appropriation and actualization in the time that is now coming present. This nonlinear temporality, in which the past is never entirely lost and beyond retrieval for transformative effectiveness in the present, is one of the momentous truths that the seer's vision of the present maintains and holds open. It is, in a sense, a vision grounded in the *reversibility* of the temporal sequence, the temporal order, since even what was never present in the past, never actualized, can sometimes be retrieved in, and for, the futurity of its worldly meaning. This has decisive implications for our reception of heritage and our commitment to a free destiny.

†

Now, according to Heidegger, being, "as the presencing of what is present, is already in itself truth, provided we think the essence of truth as the gathering that clears and shelters [*als die lichtend-bergende Versammlung*]; and provided that we dissociate ourselves from the modern prejudice of metaphysics [. . .] that truth is a property of beings or of being" (GA 5: 349/EGT 37). This *aletheic* understanding of the truth of being as the gathering-and-laying-out of a clearing for the interplay of concealment and unconcealment, is, however, incomplete without a corresponding understanding of the role of the human being in relation to that clearing for presencing. Heidegger consequently reminds us of what he takes to be the essentially hermeneutical nature of the human being in relation to the clearing.

> The human too belongs to *eónta*; he is that present being which, illuminating, apprehending, and thus gathering, *lets* what is present as such become present in unconcealment. (GA 5: 350/ EGT 38; italics added)

So, what is exceptional about the seer's vision is its mindfulness as a bodily thrown-open *Da-sein*, appropriated to be a site for gathering-into-a-whole, gathering and laying-out a temporal clearing, organizing in responsive attunement to the truth of being the conditions of possibility for a world of meaning into which the appearing or presencing of all beings, the bygone, the present, and the coming, could be welcomed and received. The seer's vision is an exceptionally mindful, exceptionally open letting-presence. It is in virtue of that self-abandonment, that dis-position of openness and receptivity, sustaining and preserving in its time-space clearing the originary potential in what-has-been that the seer has already seen the future in a past that, never before present, now comes as a future possibility. And it is in virtue of that same appropriated openness, that same receptivity, clearing the conditions that make meaningful presencing possible, that the seer has already seen all that is still to come.

†

Again: "Only when a man *has seen* does he truly see. To see is to have seen" (GA 5: 345/EGT 34). To see is to know, to understand how, in the presencing of the hawk, the clouds, and the sky, such beauty in nature, the priority of the clearing, that *Zeit-Spiel-Raum* within the welcoming openness of which these things can appear, is—so to speak—"announced." The seer sees *through* the beings that show themselves, penetrating into what makes the presencing of beings possible in the first place. Thus, in the time-space openness of the clearing, the structurally prior dimension of the ever-possible, Heidegger can say—poetically but also, considering the historical context, perilously—that *beyng* has always already "announced" itself. But only insofar as the one who sees understands and corresponds in the self-abandonment of *Da-sein* to the essential role of the clearing, the letting-presence of beyng, in the taking place of perception.

†

Here is a textual passage that I have taken from Heidegger's 1954 meditation on Parmenides' ruminations on "Moira," goddess of the crossroad, symbolic expression of history-making decision, destiny.

> The play of the calling, brightening, expanding light is not actually [*nicht eigens*] visible. It shines imperceptibly [i.e., the clearing is not only unnoticed, but is a fact without further explanation or grounding], like morning light upon the quiet splendor of lilies in a field or roses in a garden. (GA 7: 256/EGT 96)

Because Heidegger's Parmenides has already understood the function of the open clearing in making possible the presencing of what he sees, he has not only been able to see the glorious blooming of flowers emergent from the earth; he has also been able to see their perishing, their disappearing, *long before* they actually withered, faded, and died. So, because he has already seen all beings as appearing in the clearing, he has always already seen their essential unfolding. Indeed, even long *before* they emerged and appeared for the very first time, he had *already seen* the possibility of their appearing—and their whiling, and, sooner or later, too, their withering, fading, and dying. All of this, the *aletheic* truth of being: already seen. For the seer, we are mortal; and that means the seer has already seen our departure, our death.

The lighting that Heidegger invokes is not visible—or rather, as I would argue, not visible in the same way that the sunlight or moonlight is. It shines, he says, "imperceptively." He says this, paradoxical though it is, in order to differentiate the open clearing from the light that fills it—or from, at night, a light that gently withdraws. I cite this passage because, as I read it, it invokes the clearing, and it does so in a way that brings out how the clearing, as that dispensation, that "Es gibt" which, in its openness to transformative possibilities, symbolized by the flowers, encourages seeing intimations of promise. The way that this promise is seen is a poignant and exemplary instance of *seeing already, seeing as having seen*. And it depends entirely on *seeing the promise* as made possible by the gift of the clearing, that field of vision in which things are granted their time to presence.

Although the clearing is not explicitly named in this textual passage, there is textual support for the reading I am suggesting. Even in this passage, though, there is a clue, in that the light invoked is said to be invisible, imperceptible. I am taking this to mean that what Heidegger is referring to here is the clearing. If so, then we should rather say that the clearing *is* visible, belonging to the perceptible, but *not* in the same way that things are, since it is rather the necessary condition of possibility for all presencing—or, more concretely, it is the *ground*, or time-space *field*, within which things like lilies and roses and meadows and clouds, birds and bridges can show themselves, entering for a while the interplay of concealment and unconcealment. So when, in *The History of Beyng*, Heidegger asserts that "it is beyng itself which, in clearing, veils and cloaks itself as clearing, precisely through those [beings] that come to presence," what he means is that the clearing—the background that occurs (*ereignet*) as beyng itself—is commonly ignored and neglected, and its function unacknowledged in favor of the various things that show up in the clearing (GA 69: 141–42/HB 131). This is a point he makes many times over the years; and it is irrefutably demonstrated by every perceptual experience. The textual passage continues: "Everything depends on the clearing, that it come to be appropriated, and that in the appropriative event a 'that' (that beyng is) first ground itself in its own and thereby differentiate itself from everything that is capable of coming to presence in the clearing." In further support of my argument that what makes possible the seer's having always already seen is his *bodily felt sense* of the clearing, consider what Heidegger wrote in *The History of Beyng* (1938–1940).

> Truth, in its veiled and ungrounded essence, is the revealing "of" that which is self-concealing. As revealing, it is on each occasion a clearing of beings. With this clearing, [. . .] beings are opened up as such and as a whole through it; and this opening happens, in each case, in accordance with the brightness of the clearing [. . .].[3]

However, as Heidegger observes in discussing the Anaximander fragment, in the unconcealment of beings, the brightness or visibility granted them by this "primordial self-illumination of being," that is, by the clearing, distracts from and obscures that very same clearing—"obscures," as he words it, "the light of being [*verdunkelt das Licht des Seins*]" (GA 5: 337/EGT 26). The seer, however, always remembers the appropriated place in this clearing, gathering accordingly the three temporal dimensions of presencing into his proleptic vision. The 1954 Parmenides text on "Moira" echoes this brightness, here once again associated unequivocally with the clearing. Likewise, in *The History of Beyng*, in a textual passage just a few pages earlier than one we just read, Heidegger identifies the clearing with beyng itself—*physis*: that in which "the arising of self-revealing emergence" (*das aufgehende Erscheinung in das Offene der beständigen Anwesung*) takes place (GA 69: 159/HB 136). Beyng provides the conditions of meaning, conditions of intelligibility, for everything that appears: what was, what is, and what will be.

§6

Unlike "ordinary perception" ("gewöhnliche Vernehmung," "alltägliche Vernehmung"), the seer-philosopher's perception speaks out of a singular experience of the history of being: "[This] history is the destining of the duality [*das Geschick der Zwiefalt*, thought and being]. It is the revealing, unfolding bestowal of luminous presencing in which what is present can appear [*Sie ist das entbergend entfaltende Gewähren des gelichteten Anwesens worin Anwesendes erscheint*]" (GA 7: 257/EGT 98). Although not totally determined by its historical context, our perception *is* subject to its conditions, our given situations. This is also true for the way in which the beings belonging to our world can present themselves in perception: the being of such beings is subject to historical conditions, conditions that have differed considerably in different historical periods and epochs. How in the course of Western history we have viewed what presences in the clearings of the perceptual field is consequently of significance, for Heidegger, in his interpretation of the history of being, understood in terms of the "Seinsgeschick," the historically conditioned configurations of meaningfulness in terms of which the being of beings is given and received in the clearing that *Da-sein*'s existential openness prepares.

In reflecting on how Parmenides understands this, Heidegger points to *Moira*, personification in Greek mythology of the *Geschick*, the allotment and dispensation of the historical conditions determining the possibilities for presencing, the metaphorical power "into whose grasp *eón* [being] has been released as the duality [of being and beings], [and who] reveals to the thinker the breadth of vision fatefully reserved [i.e., as the possibility of meeting the calling of destiny] for the path he treads" (GA 7: 257–58/ EGT 98). This nicely characterizes the seer's ability to speak of the destiny that history can grant. And it addresses us, too, as mortals gifted with the ability to see and envision possibilities for the transformation of our shared world—always bearing in mind, of course, the prevailing facts of givenness (*das Geschick, was uns geschickt ist*) in regard to the prevailing ontological conditions, that is, the conditions determining the projection of the meaning of being, hence the conditions determining the very presencing of beings, in our troubled historical situation. The given conditions need to be received as given to us in our freedom.

There is, in the passage I have quoted from Heidegger's reflections on Parmenides, an invisible calling or summoning operative within or behind the visible beauty of nature—a claim on the philosopher, a claim silently appropriating him, that Heidegger can "see" with his mind's ontologically appropriated eyes. The field of lilies and the roses in the garden show the beauty of nature. But while Heidegger calls attention to the sensuous, sensible qualities of the light, what concerns him is what lies *concealed* by the visible: the background of the *Gestalt*, forgotten, commonly, habitually hidden, and for all intents and purposes, invisible and inaudible. It is from this clearing that we say there comes a calling, a summoning, an appropriating claim, which I would identify as the self-withdrawing, self-concealing dimension—beyng, the lighting, not to be identified with the sensible light, but rather with that which, commonly, habitually unnoticed, unrecognized, *lets* things come into meaningful presence within our field of perception.

†

In the 1836 Proceedings of the American Lyceum, there is a lecture on "American Scenery" by the great American painter Thomas Cole, Romantic and Transcendentalist, in which we find a statement that finds resonance not only in Heidegger's sentiments, but even in his very words.

> It was not that the jagged precipices were lofty, that the encircling woods were the dimmest shade, or that the waters were profoundly deep; but that over all, rocks, wood, and water, brooded the spirit of repose, and the silent energy of nature stirred the soul to its inmost depths.[4]

The painter sees what is beyond the present: beyond in time, beyond in space. And in this beyond he finds even more consolation than what actually appears in all its beauty and sublimity. In a letter to his friend Durand, another painter of American landscapes, Cole confides, "I never succeed in painting scenes, however beautiful, immediately upon returning from them. I must wait for time to draw a veil over the common details."⁵ Cole is a painter of the unconcealing: what he wants to paint is the unconcealed *as* the unconcealed—but an unconcealed that lets us see its belonging to the forever self-concealing. He is a careful observer of the visible; but he feels within it what he calls the "spirit" through which we belong to the invisible. And so, despite his "sorrow that the beauty of such landscapes is quickly passing away," he continues to have *faith* in the redeeming power of what is still to come—faith, we might say, in what is "announced"—or what is "conveyed," as I would prefer to say—in the beauty of nature.

In one of the volumes of Heidegger's recently published *Black Notebooks*, a collection of dated ruminations and ponderings belonging to the wartime years 1931–1941, we find a thought of the clearing I want to consider in juxtaposition to the passage I have taken from Heidegger's text on "Moira" and the passage I have drawn from Thomas Cole's writings.

> No matter how much the unrestrained distortion of everything rages on, there remains to the wise the mature calm of the mountain, the gathered illumination of the alpine meadows, the silent flight of the falcon, the bright cloud in the expansive sky—that wherein the great stillness of the farthest nearness of beyng [*des Seyns*] has already announced itself.⁶

What is *added* to this wonderful landscape of nature by the invocation of "beyng"? Why leap from the poetic evocation of nature into what seems like an abstract and prophetic-sounding "announcement" of beyng? How different is it, really, from the sentiment expressed by Cole—or by the poet Wordsworth, who speaks of "a motion and a spirit [that] rolls through all things"? And in what way has beyng "*already* announced itself"? Although we might be tempted to suppose that Heidegger is imagining something mysterious—perhaps another "Annunciation," announcing the coming of another god, I suggest that with his invocation of beyng, he is instead simply calling to mind the ground of the *clearing* to which the human being, in its essence as *Da-sein*, is appropriated, and calling to mind the open time-space expanse (*Zeit-Spiel-Raum*). This time-space clearing is at once always as *near* as it could be, namely, as the projection of *Da-sein*'s very essence, its ownmost, always already appropriated dis-position as projective openness, yet also *farthest*, and that in two ways: first, because we are commonly exceedingly far from recognizing ourselves in our role as *Da-sein*, site of a projected world-clearing, and, second, because the clearing reaches, in its expansive extent, far beyond the horizon that surrounds the visible, deep into the farthest—not only beyond the visible, the presently present, and beyond the invisible past and future that are present in their absence, deep into the unimaginable and the inconceivable, that sublime stillness from out of which promising if unforeseen possibilities might always come forth. The locution "des Seyns" should best be understood as adjectival, rather than invoking a metaphysical *being*: it is merely a formal indication that there is an ontological dimension to the phenomenon that calls for our recognition. If we turn our thinking and enter into that ontological dimension—a clearing in the world—then we can understand that, and how, everything has, in effect, "already announced" itself.

So what Heidegger introduces into the scene of beauty by invoking the stillness of beyng is an affirmation of the clearing in its sublimity: that within which and by grace of which it has become possible for the things he describes—the mountain, the meadows, the clouds, the hawk—to be meaningfully present in the realm of the visible. But why does Heidegger say that beyng has "*already* announced itself"? That is because, I suggest, he wants to say, first, that beyng—the open clearing—is structurally prior, preceding the appearing of all those things as the necessary condition of the possibility of their presencing; and he wants to say, second, that, in light of the openness of the clearing, the appearing of those things in all their natural beauty is an intimation that encourages the genial conviction, and indeed the faith, that the future is promising: the openness of the clearing encourages the philosopher to believe that there is *more* that is beautiful beyond the time and space horizon of visibility—even beyond all we know. Heidegger's conviction that the beauty of nature will endure, since "beyng has already announced itself," is very much like Kalchas's "foresight" regarding the future: it is grounded in an awareness and understanding of the temporal-spatial openness of the clearing. In Heidegger's expression of faith, we should also recognize indications of his philosophy of history.

Is the philosopher yielding, in his closing affirmation, to a metaphysical longing for some new *theologoumenon*? Not necessarily. However, I suspect that, particularly during the war years, Heidegger let himself be overcome by the *Sehnsucht*, the longing for the Absolute that figured so significantly in the German Romanticism of Hölderlin, Schelling, Novalis, and the youthful Hegel. I imagine Heidegger disgusted with the political situation in Germany at that time and contemptuous of its "distortion of everything," including the grandiose political vision he himself once had of Germany's historically new possibilities. Thus, I think, he turned away from all that and realized that, despite the insanity of the human world, there still nevertheless remains, "to the wise," the beauty and sublimity of nature—and "announced" within that, intimations of a new *Geschick*, an ordering of the world according to a higher law of spirit: hope in the coming of a future beyond the raging war, the conflagration consuming the present. Something of a consolation. He felt heartened, consoled, and encouraged by that realization—and by the thought, the sense, that what he was seeing pointed into the openness of the clearing, here called "beyng," as that ontologically prior condition that makes possible the manifestation of nature's emerging and unfolding, the wonder of it all—so much beauty and splendor. So, what "beyng" "announces" is simply that what there is (*das, was es gibt*) gives some hope in what is to come. The present beings in their belonging to nature will perish; but the open clearing, the world into which they briefly appeared, will still remain—as long as there is human life. That he believes.

Some of Heidegger's letters to his brother Fritz, written during World War II, support this interpretation. In one letter, he says, "Each new day we need to let our gaze once more rest in the indestructible."[7] And in another, he writes, "In all the desolate darkness of beings [*Verdüsterung des Seienden*], the bright light of beyng [*das helle Licht des Seyns*] is around me."[8] By this reading, the note in the *Notebooks* would express the philosopher's finding shelter from the depressing political realities of the moment in a deeply Romantic, but also essentially Platonic, philosophical vision—a sublime cosmological vision, not just of nature, but of time, history, and world. And in keeping with the spirit of that vision, the note would implicitly, obliquely, distinguish the beauty of nature from the sublimity of the ontologically prior dimension of beyng, the dimension of the clearing, as that "open expanse" which allows all beings to presence and be, and in relation to which we, we mortals, are the guardians and grounders.

†

For Heidegger, then, it is in the saving truth of this dimension—the open dimension of the clearing—that the promise in a future historical *Geschick* is to be found. But despite his pretensions, Heidegger was not a prophetic seer, and his great vision of "nationalism" was not at all the revolutionary vision that stirred in Hölderlin's heart. However, neither the disgust and despair and mourning Heidegger felt at seeing his traditional "world" collapse, nor the hope he expressed in his poetic evocations of the beauty and the sublimity of nature, dangerously envisioning the political in an aesthetics born of nostalgia, will ever absolve him of his moral blindness in giving his public support and allegiance to National Socialism.

§7

The seer is one who knows the clearing, dimension of truth. At stake is a certain perspective informing the seer's perception, the seer's *Wahr-nehmung*. Although parting ways from metaphysics, this is a sublime vision one might nevertheless feel like calling, or be tempted to call, a dis-position that is *sub specie aeternitatis*—were it not for the fact that in its very essence it belongs to the world of time, is appropriated by time, and speaks of being only in the grammar of earth-bound time—time, the invisible and mysterious host of being that, in the seer's vision, brings forth and takes away.

The seer is commanded to interpret the wrath of the gods; but the unfolding of being in accordance with time is really all he knows, all he can see in advance in the appropriation of the clearing. For the wisdom of Kalchas, the temporality of presencing in the openness of the clearing is sufficient. Even that clearing, however, though withdrawing right before their eyes, is already far beyond what his contemporaries, immersed in their everyday pursuits, can see. Seeing everything as present and absent in relation to the clearing—beyng—that is what gives Kalchas his supposed pro-phetic powers. Seeing everything that happens as happening from the perspective of, or in the light of, the clearing, being itself, Kalchas has already seen everything that has happened and everything that will ever come to pass. It is *as if* he could see every event, every entity, in its passage through time into a dimension of the world that is to be thought *sub specie aeternitatis*. I insist here on the "as if," however, because I do not want to reify time, as in Platonism, or represent everything as eternal, meaning beyond change. Kalchas's vision is rooted in a knowledge altogether *beyond* the conceptual grasp of metaphysics. Heidegger attempts to make sense of this knowledge and vision by presenting it in a radically new way—but still with concern for the meaning of being on which everything ultimately depends. And belonging to the event of being as we do, this concern must become our foremost concern, our foremost responsibility.

What is truly "visionary" or "prophetic" in the character of the vision Kalchas bears is simply its sheer structural openness, its laying out (*legein*) of a *Zeit-Spiel-Raum*, a clearing the logic (*logos*) of which draws its strength, its ontological truth, from a deep understanding of the temporal nature of all beings. He understands that it is not only the beings in our world that change over time; he understands that being itself, that is, the meaning of being—what it is to be—also changes in the course of historical time. And he has, in a sense, seen all events already before: births, deaths, joys, sorrows, pain, grief, pleasure, greed, sacrifice, generosity, selfishness, kindness, cruelty, cowardice and heroism, war and peace. For Kalchas the visionary seer, all temporal dimensions—even the past and the future—are *as if* present, extending their lifetime into the gathering of the now-present. But only in the mode of *as if.* For he knows that the greatest of all illusions would be to believe that there are no illusions—that there is nothing new under the sun. That, too, the unknown, the unknowable realm of concealment encompassing all events in time and even beyond the time of events, he already acknowledges and knows. For, in effect, he entered long ago into the sublime event of being. This is what Heidegger would call *Einkehr in das Ereignis*: entering into the event of being. So, in sum, Kalchas simply understands how being (*Sein, Seyn*) works—how it *wirkt*, how it gives (*gibt, schickt*) space-time to beings, and why it *geht vor*, taking precedence as the clearing, the conditions making events of appearance possible.

Chapter 4

The Fourfold

Gathering around the Thing

We seek the unconditioned Absolute [*das Unbedingte*] and only ever find things [*Dinge*].

—Novalis, *Miscellaneous Observations*[1]

What something [*etwas*] is in its very being [*in seinem Sein ist*] cannot be reduced [*erschöpft sich nicht*] to its being an object [*Gegenständigkeit*].

—Heidegger, "Letter on Humanism"[2]

Each beloved object [*geliebte Gegenstand*] is the center of a paradise.

—Novalis, *Miscellaneous Observations*[3]

Attention without feeling is only a report. An openness—an empathy—is necessary.

—Mary Oliver, *Our World*[4]

Nothing characterizes us as much as our field of attention.

—José Ortega y Gasset, *On Love: Aspects of a Single Theme*[5]

> [May] you be vigilant, watchful [*wach*] for the saving power [*das Rettende*], able to savor everywhere the secret sense of things [*den geheimen Sinn der Dinge zu kosten*].
>
> —Heidegger, *Reden und andere Zeugnisse eines Lebensweges*[6]

> The world is Eden enough, all the Eden there can be, and what is more, all the world there is. [. . .] Romanticism's work [is] the task of bringing the world back, as to life.
>
> —Stanley Cavell, *In Quest of the Ordinary*[7]

§1

In his treatise *On the Origin of Language*, Herder argued, "The first vocabulary was collected from the sounds of the whole world. From each resounding being its name rang forth."[8] What happened to those names when cultures ceased listening to the *singing* of things—the rustle of dry autumn leaves, the creaking of the wooden floorboards, the swinging of the window shutters, the sound of a spoon tapping the edge of a tea cup—in favor of what presents itself in sight, writing and reading? What happened to *things* after their singing was no longer heard and they lost those "original" names?

The argument that the historical origin of language began in the singing of things can be, today, only a lovely fable. Science properly assigns it to the realms of metaphysical fantasy and mythology. However, if the babbling of infants could be called a beginning in song—the beginning of a child's acquisition of language, then the full acquisition in mature speech and writing would be the necessary regimentation of sound and voice and the vanishing of that singing. And, if there is a third phase in the maturing of language, as in the retrieving through memory of a long-forgotten felt sense of that singing, the singing of things and words, it would surely appear, transformed, in the sensuous language of poetry, surrounding the things it names with evocations of their sense, their context of relations in the Fourfold—the singing of earth and sky, of us as mortals and the gods giving voice to our ideals. Poetry, the purest recollection of the singing of things—and the singing of the words themselves.

There is a poem by Rainer Maria Rilke called "I love to hear the singing of things" (*Die Dinge singen hör ich so gern*), the first stanza of which reads thus:

> I am frightened of human words.
> They speak so clearly of things:
> This is a dog and that is a house,
> And here is the beginning and there is the ending.

The poet is lamenting the fact that our words seldom sing. Instead of embracing words and surrounding them with lively sounds and names that would bestir the imagination to contemplate in their uncanny presence an abundance of appearances, a ring of suggestive meanings, the names we attach to things reduce them to predictable objects we can always count on: things bereft of mystery, song and vibrant color, their names worn out by use. It is, perhaps, with this same sentiment in mind that, having given philosophical thought to the thing and argued against an economy of abuse that reduces things to mere "standing reserve" (*Bestand*), Heidegger lets his imagination envision the thing as surrounded by four contexts of meaningfulness.

†

In this chapter, we shall give thought to the thing, envisioning it, following Heidegger, as a *Geviert*, possible site for the gathering of the Fourfold: earth and sky, mortals and what Heidegger unfortunately still thinks of as their "gods."[9] The *Geviert* is an allegorical figure of redemption modeled, I suggest, after the perceptual *Gestalt*. It is, I believe, Heidegger's visionary projection of a transformed humanity (*Menschentum*) and a correspondingly transformed world, in which all things would be rescued from objecthood (*Gegenständlichkeit*) and from further reduction to a mere standing reserve (*Bestand*), to be finally returned to their redeemed being as *things*. It is his projection of the fitting destiny—*Geschick*—that he hopes it might be possible for us, inheriting our history, to appropriate and approach. Leaving aside difficult, perhaps unresolvable questions about Heidegger's own interpretation of the "gods" he invokes, I shall take his invocation of "gods" to *embody*, metaphorically, the highest values, ideals, and principles constitutive of the ethical and political life we conceive for our humanity; as such, they accordingly represent a projection of the life that would redeem the promise of happiness I take to have been granted us—but only in the achievement of a morally grounded historical existence.

Although deliberately abstaining from moral theory and the phenomenology of ethical life, Heidegger does not actually refrain from judgment, and even implicit ethical prescription, in arguing for his critique of the contemporary world. Why he abstains from the phenomenology of ethical life is not made clear. But he never denies, as a matter of principle, that an ethical and moral life grounded in an understanding of the meaning of being, is a desirable possibility. Moreover, in his "Letter on Humanism," he ventures some significant reflections that indicate his conception of a Humanism that, in contrast to all the conceptions that have held sway from the Renaissance into our own time, would fully represent what he believes to be the true dignity—the potential humanity—of the human being: our capacity for reflecting on the character of our life, questioning ourselves in steadfast commitment to achieving our sense of what it means to be a human being: a being responsible for the meaning of being.

Although Heidegger never attempts to formulate an ontologically grounded, hermeneutically aware phenomenology of perception, one can find, scattered throughout many of his texts, compelling critiques of the contemporary character of our perception: critiques that accordingly serve implicitly and formally to indicate ways in which we could, and presumably should, transform that prevailing character. Heidegger avoids exhortation; but he does give us, in the *Geviert*, an allegorical image that is engaging, as if he were simply suggesting that we might try to see and hear and live with things in this way, determining for ourselves whether it is worth attempting to sustain. Can the perceptual *Gestalt* that has been forced to submit to the imposition of the *Gestell* be released from that violence to take place in the gatherings of the *Geviert*? In the present chapter, I will suggest the possibility of an affirmative answer to this question—although the way to this objective is fraught with enormous obstacles and dangers. And I cannot even say, like Kafka, that there is hope, only not for us.

The essence of the *Geviert* must be a gathering into interconnectedness. It not only calls for a very different relationship to things; it also summons us to experience a very different relationship to earth and sky, the whole realm of nature, and a very different relationship to our fellow mortals. In this way, phenomenological description can become performative, turning the formal indications of metaphorical imagination—*aus der Erfahrung des Denkens*—into living actuality.[10]

§2

As is widely recognized, our perceptual experience is inherently organized, conforming to a fundamental structure (*Gestalt*) that consists of a prominent figure—whatever is the principal object of our attention—standing out from, or against, a background, a context or field, that withdraws from attention, remaining present but receding in keeping with the degree of prominence accorded to the figure.

What Heidegger argues in his critique of the contemporary world manifestly applies, I suggest, to the perceptual *Gestalt*. According to this critique, the things we perceive have become reified, violently reduced to mere objecthood, totally available for our use; moreover, the entire world has become reified. We ourselves, together with our way of life, have undergone a devastating reduction—standardized, technologized, commodified, dehumanized, and increasingly subjected to forces imposed by our technological and geopolitical economy. When nothing matters except what can be quantified, objectified, and made readily available for use, our lives are emptied of meaning. Heidegger characterizes times such as this, our time, in ontological terms as falling under the order of the *Gestell*. "Gestell" names the universal imposition of a regime that, in its destructive rage, attacks the very being of beings. It is, he argues, the pervasive imposition of nihilism, the utmost in devastation—a *Verwüstung* that even corrupts and lays waste to what we think of as our "inner life."

Calling attention to what happens to the perceptual *Gestalt*, I suggest that the situation Heidegger describes in his critique has increasingly been turning this *Gestalt* into a *Gestell*. That is to say, the *Gestalt* structure of perceptual experience is increasingly reified: the ground, which inherently refuses to be totally grasped, is constantly subjected to attempts to grasp it in its totality and reduce it to the position of a stable figure, ignoring the new, ever more elusive ground, ultimately abyssal, that inevitably emerges in response to this effort. Thus, as the *Gestell* takes over the *Gestalt*, imposing its order, its positionality, the naturally free dynamic flow between figure and ground is arrested.

Although Theodor Adorno adamantly repudiated Heidegger, accusing him of using deceptive jargon, and Heidegger publicly ignored Adorno, nevertheless the fact remains that they both derived some very important thinking from Goethe. In "The Essay as Form," Adorno uses one of Goethe's maxims: "Destined to see what is illuminated, not the light."[11] Heidegger makes similar critical remarks in texts concerning the pre-Socratics. Casting the ontological difference between being and beings in terms of the "duality" differentiating the ontological dimension of lighting from the ontic light, Heidegger is, in effect, articulating the figure/ground structure of the perceptual *Gestalt*, arguing that we do not experience the ground as ground, that is, as receding, withdrawing, and yielding to the figure of our attention, but instead we either ignore the ground or, if recognizing it, then we attempt to reify it, making it itself into a stable figure, a *Ge-stell*, subject to our total control. In "Aletheia (Heraclitus, Fragment B 16)," Heidegger says, "Mortals are irrevocably bound to the revealing-concealing gathering which lights everything present in its presencing. But they turn from the lighting, and turn only toward what is present, which is what immediately concerns them in their everyday commerce with each other. [. . .] The *Logos* [i.e., one of the names for being], in the lighting of which they come and go, remains concealed from them and forgotten. [. . .] Everyday opinion seeks truth in variety, the endless variety of novelties that are displayed before it. It does not see the quiet gleam (the gold) of the mystery that everlastingly shines in the simplicity of the lighting. [. . .] But the golden gleam of the lighting's invisible shining cannot be grasped. [. . .] The invisible shining of the lighting streams from wholesome self-keeping in the self-restraining preservation of destiny" (GA 7: 287–88/EGT 122–23). And in "Moira (Parmenides VIII, 34–41)," Heidegger remarks, "Ordinary perception [*alltäglichen Vernehmen*] certainly moves within the lightness of what is present and sees what is shining out in color, but is dazzled by changes in color, and pays no attention to the still light of the lighting that emanates from the duality. [. . .] The destining of the disclosure of the duality [i.e., between the *ontic light* and the *ontological lighting*, which is the open clearing that welcomes the light that illuminates what is present] yields what is present to the everyday perception of mortals. [. . .] How does this fateful yielding occur? Already only insofar as the twofold as such, and therefore its unfolding, remain hidden" (GA 7: 258–59/EGT 100).

For instance, in *Being and Time*, he calls attention to how our way of looking objectifies what we see, grasping everything in a kind of dominating stare, imposing the affront of a frontal positionality that in effect reduces the seen to a commodity and endeavors, insofar as possible, to make what we see totally visible, hence, insofar as possible, totally under control and manipulation. Nothing, I think, can represent the character in perception of what Heidegger calls the *Gestell* (the total imposition of reification) better than the Gorgon's stare. In this major publication, there are three brief references to the stare: "ein starres Begaffen eines puren Vorhandenen" (GA 2: 82, 93, 99/BT 88, 98, 104). Heidegger seems to realize intuitively that visual perception, and the stare in particular, is a compelling instantiation of the way that the impositional character of the *Gestell* functions: not merely objectifying, but also fixating, holding in place, imposing a position, permitting no movement. The stare is a form of violence: it is, in fact, deadening, mortifying.

The stare is not the same as the gaze that tarries; nor is it the same as passively watching or observing. It is an aggressive fixation. Heidegger reflects on it in discussing the phenomenology of our different ways of relating to the being of things, the being of beings. To stare at something, in contrast to using it, or in some other way interacting with it, is to relate to it as being in the mode of presence-at-hand: *Vorhandensein*. Heidegger defines it as preeminently "representational," because "representation" in German is *vor-stellen*, meaning "to set before" or "to position before." What is stared at is held constant in its positionality of presence before one. Thus, it is inherently aggressive, *confrontational*, compelling what it sees to stay directly in *front* of its narrowly focused visual beam. And it is imposing, forcing what it sees into reification within the subject-object structure. In the time of the *Gestell*, perception tries to achieve absolute control over the presencing of what presences, imposing a *frontal* view, a *frontal* ontology. It is not accidental that contemporary art does everything it can to challenge and defeat our perceptual habits, turning their reification, their aggression, their violence, and their impatient need for totality back onto themselves. (See the next chapter on hyper-reflexivity in the experience of art.)

In lectures assembled under the title *What Is Called Thinking*, Heidegger likewise gives voice to a critique of our hearing, which increasingly favors univocity and tries to suppress the dimensions of tone, resonance, and echo. In those lectures, Heidegger argues that we "need first of all to hear [*hören*] the appeal of what is most thought-provoking [i.e., being]. But if we are to perceive what most provokes thought, we must for our part get underway to learn thinking. [. . .] What we can do in our present case, or anyway can learn, is to listen mindfully, properly, authentically [*genau hinzuhören*]" (GA 8: 28/WCT 26). And in "The Turn," Heidegger will even argue that "we do not yet hear, we whose hearing and seeing are perishing through radio and film under the rule of technology" (GA 11: 125/QCT 48–49; BF 72). Somehow, we need to learn how to dwell in this world of ours despite the inevitable, ceaseless noises (*Geräusche*) of urban, industrial, and commercial life. In the context of Heidegger's great project, a compelling argument can be made that we desperately need to be liberated from the commercialization and unprecedented intrusiveness that characterize the *Gestell* constitutive of our contemporary world of sound. This *Gestell* is determining our ontology; that is, it is determining what possibilities there are for the experiencing and disclosing of being. What would be involved in learning the kind of hearing Heidegger would want us to develop?

I suggest that if we attempt to model the development of our ability to hear beyond our everyday ontic way of hearing, we would schematize such development in terms of its stages, as follows:

1. Involuntary pre-ontological, prereflective hearing, passively received: A book falls off the shelf and I hear the sound.

2. Attentive ontic listening: I hear, for example, a voice outside my study, and listen attentively to find out who it is.

3. Consequent ontic hearing: Listening attentively, I either achieve and fulfill that effort, hearing who it is, or else I fail to hear, despite my efforts. If I really want to know, I could try listening even more attentively.

4. Ontologically attuned listening and hearing: In the first stage of hearkening (*das Horchen*), I gather into a fourfold symphony, a *Geviert*, the sounding forth of earth and sky, mortals, and the voices that remind us of our values and ideals.

5. Ontologically attuned listening and hearing: In the second stage of hearkening, I listen away from the sounds and voices of the sonorous beings in the *Geviert* to become more attentive to the background, the auditory field itself, the open clearing necessary for the sounding forth of all sonorous beings. And I listen, too, for the emerging and fading away of their sounds and voices as they echo and finally return to an immeasurably deep silence, hearing within the sounding of that silence the very hum of being—being as such.

6. Thus, in a third stage of hearkening, the sounds fade away into inaudibility, lost, present only in their felt absence as they withdraw into the elemental cosmological dimension, becoming, as our science informs us, mere vibrating pulsations, waves, rhythms, mere perturbations in the abyssal cosmic field of space-time events.

Everything, every being, has its sounds, its distinctive song. And, if we want to listen, we can hear the singing of earth and sky, us mortals and our gods, surrounding all the things we live with. And we can hear, too, the immeasurable silence into which these songs will always ultimately send us. The Fourfold (*Geviert*) that Heidegger wants to *see* surrounding everything can equally be a Fourfold embodied in sound: the ringing of voices, ours and ones that represent the principles and ideals of ethical life, gathered together with the ringing of the elemental sounds that are coming from the earth and the sky, surrounding the thing.

Our seeing also has similar stages of development, passing from (1) involuntary (passively received) sighting; (2) intentional glancing, quickly looking; (3) deliberate, more attentive, focused seeing, that is, looking, gazing, into (4) an ontologically attuned envisioning, welcoming the gathering of the *Geviert* around what is seen; and finally (5) an ontologically attuned envisioning of being itself, gently attentive to the interplay of concealment and unconcealment that is taking place in the gathering Fourfold of the visual field, the clearing that, in *Gelassenheit* (the phenomenologically disciplined attitude in which we let the phenomenon show itself as it is), our eyes have taken part in opening up, experiencing in heightened awareness the immeasurable dimensionality of earth and sky and the vulnerability of us mortals and our values and ideals; (6) but our vision can venture even further, envisioning beyond the edge of its farthest horizon, its farthest gathering ring, the embrace of an infinitely, endlessly vast dimension of cosmological space-time, concealed in the utmost darkness.

§3

Reminding us, in his volume *Against the Event*, of Maurice Blanchot's ruminations on the everyday, Michael Seyeau argued, "The everyday is what we never see a first time, but only see again."[12] In *Being and Time* (1927), Heidegger strongly disparaged the everyday: for him, everydayness is shallow, superficial, life lived inauthentically and without the care for being that thought enjoins. But in the post–World War II years, he began to reconsider that harsh indictment and, looking differently at everyday things, he intensified his critique but now attempted to envision the possibility of an everyday world redeemed by mindfulness (*Besinnung*). It is, I believe, in order to induce us to see and hear again, hence see and hear otherwise, that Heidegger gives thought to perception—and above all, to seeing and hearing. The gathering of the Fourfold, *das Geviert*, is his envisioning of a different way of seeing and hearing things—even the most ordinary things in our everyday world. The key to this different way of seeing and hearing, a way that might begin to redeem things, returning objects to their being as things, is the ontological attitude of *Gelassenheit*, which holds open a clearing for things that, in a guardian care, lets them be what they are.

I suggest that "*Geviert*" ("Fourfold") is the name Heidegger is giving to the possibility of a transformation of the *Gestalt*, ending its degeneration and devastation in the *Gestell* formation.

§4

In his notebook thoughts written during the 1930s, Heidegger, sounding very much like Rilke, observed that "the great joy in learning about small things is the distinctive art of the transformation of human beings into thrown-open clearings [*eigene Kunst der Verwandlung des Da-seins*]."[13]

But what is a thing? What is it for something—anything—to *be* a thing? What stirred Heidegger to raise such a question was his deeply felt conviction, as he expressed it in 1949, that somehow, "the things are as though long gone, gone away"—"and nevertheless they have never yet been *as things*" (GA 79: 23/BF 22). What would it be like for things finally and fully to be things? What would it be like for things to be *experienced* as things? I suggest that Heidegger's answer is—consider the *Geviert*. At stake is an experience that transforms into the *Geviert* what have become reduced to objects, gathering the Fourfold (earth and sky, mortals and their "gods") around the object, in effect returning the object to its "prelapsarian" ontological condition as a thing-that-gathers, a *Ding* that *dingt*.

In this chapter, we will give thought to one of Heidegger's most revolutionary proposals: a fundamental reimagining of the phenomenology of the thing, not only leaving behind all the metaphysical conceptions, but also challenging us to venture into a profoundly new experience in relation to the things with which we live, the things, near and far with which we are surrounded. Briefly stated, what constitutes the thing (*Ding*) according to Heidegger's vision is (1) that its being is inherently conditioned (*be-dingt*), fated to finitude, vulnerable to destruction, dissolution, and nothingness; and (2) that it is the site of a gathering (*Ding*) taking place around it.[14] Heidegger seems to have derived his vision of this new old experience from the etymological origin and history of the Germanic word for "thing," thereby retrieving in recollection (*Erinnerung*) an experience actually as old as the word itself—or perhaps, indeed, even older. This derivation exemplifies the material importance of cultural memory in Heidegger's project. It is always a question of memory for the sake of an ontological disclosure that could profoundly change the future toward which we seem to be irrevocably headed. So, to the extent that, by means of what he calls "thoughtful recollection," we could be brought around to experience the presencing—and the presence—of things in this new old way, a way requiring the phenomenological attitude of *Gelassenheit*, there is some reason to hope that the essential nature of things might be rescued from the catastrophic fate that, with its ever-increasing sway, is awaiting them in the epoch in which the *Gestell* triumphantly dominates our world, our lives.

§5

Arguing that philosophical thought needs to become a negative dialectic, Theodor Adorno observed that, "The means employed in negative dialectics for the penetration of its hardened objects is possibility—the possibility of which the object's actuality has cheated them, yet which gazes out of each one."[15] Heidegger, too, emphasizes possibility; in fact, not only as a way to undertake the work of critique, but also as a way to envision how things could be different (GA 2: 51–52/BT 63).

In "The Turn" (GA 79: 74–75/QCT 45, BF 70), expressing his distress regarding "the neglect of the thing [*die Verwahrlosung des Dinges*]"—and, even worse, the frightening violence to which, in the epoch of the *Gestell*, the thing is increasingly subjected, Heidegger argues that "the impositional ordering belonging to the *Gestell* sets itself above the thing, and leaves it, as thing, unsafeguarded, truthless": "Das Bestellen des Ge-stells stellt sich vor das Ding, läßt es als Ding ungewahrt, wahrlos" (GA 79: 75/QCT 46, BF 71). "Wahrlos" means both truthless and unprotected.

Heidegger was trying to awaken us to a more thoughtful awareness—so that, with the eyes and ears we have been given, we might perhaps find ourselves moved by "the secret sense of things" to envision and hearken to a different world. Might a different experience with things, and, correspondingly, a different philosophical understanding of the thing, be achievable? Might we find a way to break out of the regime of the *Gestell*? Drawing guidance and inspiration, as he so often did, from the etymological history of the words in his language—in this instance, the relationship between

Ding, the word for thing, and the verb *dingen*, meaning "to gather," as in a community assembly, Heidegger undertook to explore what it might mean to think of the thing as determined (*bedingt*) by its being a center, a place, of gathering: a gathering that he imagines as a Fourfold, a round-dance (*Reigen*) gathering earth and sky, mortals and gods into their ownmost modes of ap-propriation (*Er-eignung*): a ring of interacting, reciprocating relationships that would bring each of the four, through and with each of the others, into its own ap-propriation (GA 7: 167–87/PLT 165–82).

§6

In Rilke's *Sonnets to Orpheus*, there are some lines of verse that, posing an urgent question, merit our consideration as a way of continuing this chapter.

> We, with our violence, are longer lasting.
> But when, in which of all lives,
> Are we at last open and welcoming?[16]

The fate of all the familiar things that belonged in his world was for many years a matter of the greatest concern in Rilke's life. But the violence he felt to be threatening the world of these things is something that Heidegger also recognized as defining our time, our world; and it was for him no less of a distress. What will be our answer, our response to the poet's question? In a 1918 letter to a friend, the poet wrote, "I can hardly stand before beautiful old things without being frightened at their forlornness,—how lost they have become, though they still continue to exist."[17] And he deplored the commercial production of so many ugly things—"a shameless sign of their exploitation, their non-reality, their nothingness!"[18] This is not nostalgia. It is dread of nihilism, the nihilism that Nietzsche already warned of. Several years later, in a 1925 letter to another close friend, he returned to this theme.

> Nature, the things of our intercourse and use, are provisional and perishable; but they are, as long as we are here, *our* property and our friendship, co-knowers of our distress and gladness, as they have been the familiars of our forebears. So, it is important not only not to run down and degrade all that is here, but just because of their transience, which they share with us, these things

should be understood and transformed by us in a most fervent sense. Transformed? Yes, for it is our task to imprint this provisional, perishable earth so deeply, so patiently and passionately in ourselves that its reality shall arise in us again "invisibly."[19]

"The *Duino Elegies*," he said, reflecting on these poems, "show us at this work, at the work of these continual conversions of the beloved visible and tangible." And he followed this claim with a compelling expression of his inconsolable despair over what was happening to things—especially the things of the hearth he grew up with and loved.

> And this activity is curiously supported and urged on by the ever more rapid fading away of so much of the visible that will no longer be replaced. Even for our grandparents a house, a well, a familiar tower, their very clothes, their coats: were infinitely more, infinitely more intimate, almost everything a vessel in which they found the human and added to the store of the human.[20]

And rather like Heidegger, Rilke used "America" as a rhetorical figure for the fraudulent materialism in the "utopian progress" he opposes.

> Now, from America, empty indifferent things are pouring across, fraudulent things, sham life. . . . A house, in the American sense, an American apple or a grapevine over there, has *nothing* in common with the house, the fruit, the grape into which went the hopes and reflections of our forefathers. . . . Live things, things that have mattered in our lives, are fading away, vanishing, no longer to be replaced.[21]

Then, expressing himself emphatically, he wrote, in italics, "*We are perhaps the last still to have known such things.*" This dire warning, already a cry of mourning, prompted a reflection on the poet's responsibility.

> On us rests the responsibility of preserving not only the memory of them, [. . .] but also their human and laral value. ("Laral" in the sense of the household gods.) The earth has no way out other than to become invisible: *in* us who with a part of our natures partake of the invisible [. . .]—*in* us alone can be consummated

> this intimate and lasting conversion of the visible into an invisible no longer dependent upon being visible and tangible, as our own destiny continually *grows at the same time* MORE PRESENT AND VISIBLE in us. The *Elegies* set up this norm of existence.²²

The most important thing that we can do, he thinks, is protect the invisible, including the invisible dimension of the things that are visible—and attempt to redeem the promise in familiar things by poetically estranging them, withdrawing them, for a while, from usage, and from the possession of categorial knowledge. Heidegger likewise summons us to safeguard the invisible: it is this realm of the invisible—and the realm of the inaudible—that, surrounding things, protects them and preserves their truth. Unlike the *object*, which resists invisibility and inaudibility, the *thing* gathers and celebrates the invisible and the inaudible. This, in our time, however, is disturbing, because things that emerge from and retain an invisible, inaudible dimension elude our control, our will to power.

§7

In the Summary, or Protocol, of a 1962 seminar concerning Heidegger's lecture on "Time and Being," we find this illuminating evocation of the Fourfold, the *Geviert* which, in this volume, I am attempting to contemplate in terms of the phenomenology of the *Gestalt* that forms in perception as a gathering around the perceived thing.

> What the event of being [*Ereignis*] appropriates [*ereignet*], that is, brings into its own [*ins Eigene bringt*], [is] the belonging-together of being and man [*das Zusammengehören von Sein und Mensch*]. In this belonging-together, what belongs together is no longer being and man, but rather—because of the correspondence, or oscillation, in the appropriation—mortals taking part in the Fourfold of the world [*die Sterblichen im Geviert der Welt*]." (GA 14: 51/OTB 42)

Envisioning the gathering of the Fourfold—earth and sky, mortals and gods—around each and every *thing* our sight and hearing encounters, Heidegger suggests how a certain receptive, welcoming openness to the dimensions constituting our world might turn the perceptual experience that is now determined by the *Gestell* into something entirely different, released from nihilism and the history of violence. However, Heidegger's envisioning of the *Geviert* involves a "Revolution der Ortschaft des Denkens," a "revolution in the topology of thinking" (GA 15: 385/FS 72). Are we capable of such transformation? In the fourth of the poet's *Duino Elegies*, we are reminded that the ego-logical subject, the bourgeois subject, does not easily renounce its will to power. It proclaims, "I remain nevertheless. There is always looking." ("Ich bleibe dennoch. Es gibt immer Zuschaun.") Yes, there is always looking. And hearing. But what is the character, quality, and dimensionality of that looking and hearing?

§8

In reflections written between 1938 and 1940 and published under the title *The History of Beyng*, Heidegger worked to sharpen his critique of the nihilism into which he watched our world falling, calling attention to the ways we human beings have already been reduced to hollowed-out subjectivities and *things* have been reduced correlatively to mere objects, mere items, serving the imposition, the *Gestell*, of the will to power.

> Beings are everywhere abandoned in their being, leaving them to the claws and talons of objectification [*Fängen und Griffen der Vergenständlichung*]. The objective is the spoils of calculation. Objectivity imposes itself in the place of being. "Beings" disintegrate [*Das "Seiende" verfällt*]. And being [that which makes their meaningful presencing possible] has concealed itself. (GA 69: 151/HB 130)

"Nevertheless," he says, "the din and rush of everything imposes itself and denies what has gone before, disseminating the semblance of the new [*den Schein des Neuen*]." Thus, he laments, registering an observation that is similar to those one finds in Adorno's *Minima Moralia* and in some of Rilke's letters.

> Not a trace [*Spur*] leading to being remains anywhere, for even beings have been eroded by use into calculated contrivance [*errechnete Gemächte*]. The latter lays claim to all passion and all meaning.

The critique, reminiscent of Plato's animadversions regarding the popular appeal of what is mere semblance, continues as follows:

> Everything has to be new and ever more rapidly new. [. . .] What is without substance is what endures and has its presencing in the shining of mere semblance. The unconditional character of the shining of mere semblance demands of everyone who does not want to perish here that they "engage" in this process. The shining semblance itself, however, is incapable of acknowledging itself, since before all else it must first of all constantly evade itself, so as not to discover what is behind it. Shining semblance must continually keep itself on track and divert calculation and suffering onto the objective. (GA 69: 151/HB 130)

In his postwar writings from the mid-1940s through the 1950s, Heidegger intensified and developed this critique while at the same time thinking beyond it, as in his vision of the Fourfold surrounding the thing. Can we recover the wondrous facticity of the thing? Can the promise in the thing be redeemed? Can its essential being—the being proper to it—be rescued from our instrumentalizing assault and—as Heidegger expresses the issue in "What Are Poets For?"—from "the still covetous vision of things"—"des noch begehrenden Sehens der Dinge" (GA 5: 317/PLT 138)? Heidegger's envisioning of the Fourfold is an attempt to affirm the possibility of a more hopeful world for vision, hearing, and gestures to bring forth.

His thinking is predominantly in terms of vision; however, when it is a question of understanding the pre-Socratics, Heraclitus in particular, his thinking is absorbed in breaking out of everyday habits in listening and hearing. But although he does not attempt to think the *Geviert* in terms of our hearing, in his 1943–1944 lecture courses on Heraclitus, he does, I believe, come close to schematizing in phenomenological terms an ontologically attuned modality of hearing for which his somewhat archaic-sounding word *Horchen*—"hearkening"—seems to be fitting.

How would hearkening differ from ordinary listening and hearing? Primarily in a releasement of the figure-ground structure, letting the dynamics flow more freely. But consequently, also by becoming more attentive to the emergence and fading away of sounds and voices, following reverberations and echoes into the abyssal realm of a silence where sound and silence cannot be differentiated. This releasement of the figure-ground structure is also crucial in regard to the ontological dimension of our vision.

§9

In his 1931 "Little History of Photography," Walter Benjamin comments on a statement made by a photographer who had argued that "the spirit that overcomes mechanics translates exact findings into parables of life." He wrote,

> The more far-reaching the crisis of the present social order, and the more rigidly its individual components are locked together in their death struggle, the more the creative, in its deepest essence [. . .] becomes a fetish.[23]

Benjamin argues against art that attempts to present our world as unquestionably beautiful, and, as if anticipating Andy Warhol, he urges the unmasking of "a photography that can endow any soup can with cosmic significance, but cannot grasp a single one of the human connections in which it exists." Could we have both cosmic significance and also the human connections? Drawing inspiration from Walt Whitman, I shall argue that we can.

The perception of the *Geviert* that Heidegger envisions in his later writings potentially endows even the smallest, slightest thing, or being, with cosmic and metaphorical significance—but only in terms of its existential relationality, which brings into view the *interdependencies* among the four that require of us mortals the assumption of our responsibility as sole guardians of the thinghood, or being, of all the things that appear in our world.

If, in our time, the thing in its perceptual *Gestalt* is increasingly suffering the imposition of reification and totalization, or closure, turning it into an instance of the *Gestell*, might it be possible not only to resist this imposition and rescue the *Gestalt* from this fate, but actually to transform it—transform it into what, after Heidegger, we might call a *Geviert*, a perception-event that becomes the site for a gathering of the Fourfold? In and for such a perception, each being singled out for attention, be it a tree, a tin of sardines, a light bulb, a river or a human being—would appear as the center of a site for a Fourfold, a multidimensional structure, gathering around it, and into a certain presence, earth and sky, the fundamental elements between which the world we inhabit has taken place, and mortals and gods, the two dimensions of material and spiritual life shaping our world.[24]

It is in his later thinking that Heidegger introduced this thought of the Fourfold; but the presentation leaves it vulnerable to interpretations that assume it is "merely" metaphorical—philosophical poetry. We should, as he insists, take the metaphor seriously, letting it, as the Greek provenance of the word suggests, take us into a very different experience of the thing, or being. What if we attempt to understand Heidegger's thought-image as allegory indicative of a possible transformation in our perceptual experience? Can we take his thought and give it convincing phenomenological meaning: a meaning for perception, and perhaps even a significance that Heidegger himself did not venture to entertain?

My claim in this chapter is that the Fourfold—*das Geviert*—is Heidegger's utopian dream-concept, his envisioning of a world transformed: a world in which everything, each and every being, would be experienced as gathering around it, as if in a dance, a round-dance (*Reigen*), earth and sky, us mortals and our gods. Many scholars seem not to know what to make of the texts in which Heidegger discusses this Fourfold; not sure how to understand it, they regard it as a "merely" metaphorical fantasy or thought-experiment of little significance. I shall attempt not only to suggest and defend its significance, but also to redeem it as a sublime utopian vision—in fact, a vision, a *Denkbild*, bearing truly revolutionary potential—by showing how its cosmic dimensions might be connected to the material transformation of the world we actually live in.

In this redeeming, however, I feel compelled to draw out and unfold implications that take us beyond where Heidegger's vision, as he himself must have understood it, would take us. Nevertheless, I hope that what I am drawing out from his conception—primarily a secular and democratic significance reminiscent of the world evoked by Walt Whitman—will at the very least be discerned and recognized as an appropriate possible extension of the meaning and significance Heidegger gives it, an extension that is a potential genuinely implicit in its very design.

Is this Fourfold merely the wishful thinking of an abstract philosopher? I want us to take it seriously, because I believe that it could be made into much more than a mere metaphorical fantasy. But let us proceed slowly.

†

There is a delightful anecdote told about Heraclitus of Ephesus, the philosopher who believed that the elemental nature of the universe is fire. When some curious admirers sought out the old man in his home, they found him, much to their surprise and consternation, not appearing deeply absorbed in thought or study, as they had imagined, but simply bent over the hearth, serenely warming himself while cooking something to eat. Noticing both their reluctance to disturb him, and also their poorly disguised disappointment, their disillusionment at finding a philosopher, a sage, engaged in something so ordinary, he welcomed them, but he would not forswear reminding them that, "even around the humble cooking stove the divinities are present." Heidegger liked to repeat this story (GA 9: 354–55/PM 69–70). Perhaps it was this story that bestirred in him the vision of a very different way of encountering the essential character of the thing—a vision that finally takes us out of, and beyond, the various metaphysical conceptions that have held sway since the beginning of Western thought. What Heidegger envisions is that the thing—presumably each and every thing, no matter how small—is, as such, a topology for the gathering of a *Geviert*, bringing together earth and sky, us mortals and our gods.

Might we, living in today's world, actually learn to see and hear things—beings—this way? What might that actually mean for the being of all beings?

What Heidegger is suggesting is a transformation from the epoch of the *Ge-stell* into the beginning of the *Geviert*, gatherings of the Fourfold ending the imposition of total reification, in which the being of the human, that is, its thrown-openness, its bodily presence as a clearing, has been reduced to the ontic being of a subject while the thing it apprehends has been reduced to the being of an object, and the prevailing structure of subject-confronting-object would be transformed into the ontological *Da-sein*-being structure, a structure in which the ontological dimension of that relation between the human as *Da-sein* and being itself becomes a vibrating oscillation, a belonging-togetherness constitutive of what Merleau-Ponty would call a chiasmic reciprocity.

§10

In "Fundamental Questions of Metaphysics," a series of winter semester lectures given in 1935–1936 at the University of Freiburg and published in English translation under the title *What Is a Thing?* (GA 41), Heidegger took up for questioning some of the major philosophical and scientific conceptions of the thing, touching on Aristotle, Descartes, Leibniz and Hegel, but concentrating primarily on Kant.[25] This was not the first time that he had lectured on this topic; nor would it be the last time. His questioning of representations of the thing in the history of metaphysics figures prominently in *Being and Time*, published in 1927, and in a 1935 lecture, revised several times in the 1950s in "The Origin of the Work of Art," as well as in "The Thing,"[26] a 1949–1950 lecture first published in 1951, "Building, Dwelling, Thinking," a 1951 lecture first published in 1952, and "The Question Concerning Technology," based on a 1949 lecture that Heidegger continued to work on and revise into the mid-1950s.

In concluding *What Is a Thing?* Heidegger comments that that question ultimately cannot be answered without addressing the question "What is the human being?" And he finishes this thought with a remark touching on the dimension of openness that encompasses us in our relations with things—an openness that becomes increasingly important in the hermeneutical phenomenology of his later thinking: "A dimension is opened up in Kant's question about the thing which lies *between* the thing and man, and reaches out beyond things and back behind man."[27] This dimension that thinking has opened up between the thing and man reaches "beyond things" to being itself and lies "behind" our human existence in our appropriated essence in *Da-sein*. In elaborating phenomenologically what that means, Heidegger takes us deeper into the belonging-together of the human being as *Da-sein* and the thing in its distinctive mode of being—deeper into our experience of appropriation and the responsibility that forms therein. This experience, originating in the belonging-together of *Sein* and *Dasein*, the ontological dimension of our experience, is explicated in his text on "The Principle of Identity," a text that retrieves for our thinking the wisdom of Parmenides.

Heidegger challenges the primacy of the subject-object structure into which the philosophical tradition since Descartes has represented and enshrined the essence of the thing—the thing our untutored experience encounters. First, that philosophical representation distorts our experience, both of ourselves and of things, as they are in the "natural attitude" of everyday life. And second, the structure represented fails to recognize the unifying bond (*Bezug*) that *precedes* the differentiation that emerges and soon develops into that structure. Heidegger also challenges how, inheriting Aristotelian metaphysics, both empiricism and idealism conceptualize the object, either separating the object's posited "substance," its "matter," from its phenomenal "qualities" or predicated "attributes," or else reducing the "substance" to nothing but a gathering of phenomenal "qualities."

Listening to what gifts language grants to those who listen with care to their language, Heidegger hears in the word for "thing" that he inherited from his native language, the Old High German word for a gathering (GA 7: 177ff/PLT 174ff). This etymological "recollection" emboldened him in his critique of all the philosophical representations of the thing since Aristotle. And it inspired him to envision a very different experience and understanding of the thing. Insisting on approaching the thing phenomenologically, taking the thing as it shows itself, just as it is given to our experience, Heidegger insists: the thing is simply a thing. The thing things. That "thinging" is its very essence. The thing is first encountered as a thing, something that is; and it is only for subsequent thought that it can be taken to be *res*, *ens*, or object. As he argues in "The Thing," taking the thingness of an ordinary jug for his theme, "the thingness of the thing has become concealed, forgotten" (GA 7: 172/PLT 170). In the sciences as in philosophy, "the nature of the thing never comes to light, never gets a hearing." In fact, he adds, "not only are things no longer admitted as things, but they have never yet been able to appear to thinking as things" (GA 7: 172/PLT 171). In "Building Dwelling Thinking," he reflects on the thingness of a bridge, and in "The Thing," he reflects on the thingness of a jug, seeing these things as sites for the gathering of the Fourfold (GA 7: 172/PLT 171). Is this poetizing of the thing phenomenologically grounded? To be sure, in our everyday interaction with things, we do not experience them as gatherings of a Fourfold. However, if we give thought to the things we encounter and live with, suspending our habitual ways of thinking about them and interacting with them, it becomes possible to experience these things as Heidegger has described—and, moreover, to see that the thing has *always* been a gathering of the Fourfold, even though we did not recognize it as such.

In the poem "Anecdote of the Jar," Wallace Stevens describes a situation that suggests how something like this Fourfold gathering might occur.[28] Here is the first stanza, the first two lines of the second, and one line from the third and final stanza.

> I placed a jar in Tennessee,
> And round it was, upon a hill.
> It made the slovenly wilderness
> Surround that hill.
>
> The wilderness rose up to it,
> And sprawled around, no longer wild.
> [. . .]
>
> It took dominion everywhere.
> [. . .]

This jar, though, is mischievous. And it is by no stretching of the imagination at all certain that its gathering is, or will be, redeeming. Stevens, I suspect, remains skeptical.

†

In *What Is a Thing?*, Heidegger asks a question reminiscent of Nietzsche's critique of metaphysics, "Has man read off the structure of the proposition [*das Wesen des Satzes*, i.e., the grammatical construct of subject and predicate] from the structure of things, or has he instead transferred the structure of the proposition onto the things?"[29] Manifestly, he wanted to argue that the philosophical representation of the thing in the history of Western metaphysics has been beguiled by the grammatical structure of its languages instead of registering our everyday experience of the thing—and bringing out, by way of a hermeneutical phenomenology, the commonly unrecognized prereflective, preconceptual dimension that underlies and precedes the oppositional (*gegen-ständlich*) moment of structural differentiation, turning the relation between human being and thing-being into an inherently willful relation between subject and object.

The thing can be seen—and heard—*as* a gathering only insofar as we, in relating to it, hold ourselves thrown-open, open to experience the thing in the expanse of its Fourfold dimensionality, deeply connected to earth and sky, deeply connected, also, to a felt sense of our mortality and to a vivid concern for our highest ideals and aspirations as human beings.

†

In an essay comparing Adorno and Heidegger in which she acknowledges the considerable affinities and correspondences between them, despite the magnitude of their political differences, Ute Guzzoni explores what the two philosophers have to say regarding the possibility of "a relation to things no longer corrupted by the spell of identity, on the one hand and by the oblivion of being on the other."[30] This formulation of the matter indicates the direction of her argument, skewed very much in favor of Adorno. However, although it is correct to say that Heidegger was deeply concerned about the oblivion of being (i.e., nihilism), Guzzoni seems to think, incorrectly, that this implies that Heidegger, unlike Adorno, was not concerned about the corrupt, totally reifying imposition of identity on things—that is to say, on their being. This frequent criticism of Heidegger actually makes no sense, inasmuch as the reason why Heidegger felt concerned about the oblivion of being was precisely because he cared about protecting and preserving the being of all beings, among which, all *things*. It was always for the sake of the rescuing and redeeming of *things*—indeed all the beings of our world—that

Heidegger fought against the oblivion of being. Thus, for Heidegger, there is no either/or: to be concerned about the oblivion of being necessarily requires being concerned about the reifying logic of identity imposed on things in the violent time of the *Gestell*.

For the purposes of her comparison, Guzzoni relies primarily on Heidegger's *Being and Time* and on some of his shorter texts, such as "The Origin of the Work of Art" (1935–1936), "*Gelassenheit*: Country Path Conversations" (1944–1945), "The Thing" (1951), and "Building Dwelling Thinking" (1951). Unfortunately, however, there is no consideration of Heidegger's thinking regarding things in "The Age of the World Picture" (1938), "The Question of Technology" (1949), and "Poetically Man Dwells" (1951). But above all, there is no consideration of Heidegger's thinking with regard to identity and difference in "The Principle of Identity" (1955–1957). This crucial text followed many earlier texts, in which he formulated a strong critique of the contemporary character of our relation to things—our relation to their ways of being present and to the conditions that make their presence and absence possible.

What makes "The Principle of Identity" singularly significant is that, in it, Heidegger *opposes* the reifying imposition of categories of identity—the corrupting "spell of identity"—by engaging our attention in the *phenomenology* of the subject-object dialectic: the oscillation, or counterresonance (*Gegenschwung*) operative in the belonging-together of *Mensch* and *Sein*. Moreover, by drawing our awareness back into the phenomenology of this primordial interaction preceding the formation, in extreme differentiation, of the subject-object structure, Heidegger does not only *oppose* the "spell of identity," but he also shows us a way to *resist* its influence, its power. That is because, in returning back into the preconceptual dimension of this interaction, a dimension belonging to repressed nature, wherein structural differentiation has not (yet) solidified, we cannot easily avoid feeling and recognizing that there is no identity without difference. Retrieving from its repression our experience of that dimension in our relation to things ("die Grundstimmung des Bezuges zum Seyn," as he phrases it in his *Grundfragen der Philosophie*, GA 45: 2) thus *begins* the process that Adorno called "reconciliation": the "redeeming" of the *being* of things, freeing them from domination.[31] As Adorno has nicely described it,

> The reconciled state would not, through philosophical imperialism, annex the foreign, but would have its happiness in the persistence of the foreign and the different within the granted nearness.[32]

Returning in awareness to the phenomenology of the preconceptual, pre-ontological dimension could encourage what Adorno characterized as "the long and non-violent look upon the object."[33] Heidegger would have no problem agreeing with this characterization. For him, though, it would be a question of a way of seeing that is grounded in, and emergent from, an *ontological* moment of *Gelassenheit*, the attitude constitutive of the phenomenological method, letting the object, the thing, *be* what and how it is. In regard to our capacity for hearing what gives itself to be heard, be it in sound or in silence, this is precisely how hearkening (*Horchen*) is supposed to work in its opening up of the ontological dimension in the auditory field.

Arguing for the "reconciled state," Adorno will even speak—as Heidegger has also—of learning "the love for things," "nestling near to things" and being "in touch with the warmth of things."[34] And, in an essay on Alban Berg, Adorno, again like Heidegger, urges us to develop an "attuned sensibility," a gentle, caring protection of things—"*eine schonende Liebe*."[35] This mindful protection (*Wahren*) is what Heidegger emphasizes by thinking of perception as *Wahr-nehmung*.

In his "Conversation" on *Gelassenheit*, Heidegger's interlocutors give thought to nearness and farness. Guzzoni is thus entirely mistaken when she argues that, in his commitment to the "abstraction" of an ontological orientation for being, Heidegger *turned away* from the lifeworld of human beings and our relation to things. On this nearness and farness, the thinking of Heidegger and Adorno once again in fact converges. According to Adorno,

> The non-violent observation that generates all happiness of truth is bound to the fact that the observer does *not* assimilate the object: nearness is bound to farness.[36]

This "farness" is not coldness, rejection, or neglect, but recognition and respect for the singularity and otherness of the thing.[37] In the context of Heidegger's project, the phenomenology of this farness-in-nearness and nearness-in-farness is moreover inherent in the emerging and withdrawing of beings; and it is represented in the two axes (earth and sky, gods and mortals) constitutive of the "topology of being" that would form in the Fourfold around each and every thing. "*Geviert*" is thus Heidegger's name for the redeeming of things, a possibility for the things we are living with, requiring, hence dependent on, our caring, our response-ability, releasing things from the tyranny of the reifying logic of identity in the subject-object structure.

†

In "The Origin of the Work of Art," in the course of attempting to understand in what ways the work of art is a distinct *kind* of thing, Heidegger critically examines three different interpretations of the thingness of the thing that, "predominant in the course of Western thought, have long become self-evident and are now in everyday use": (1) the thing as an underlying substratum, a substance around which various properties or qualities have assembled (see Aristotle and the Western philosophers of the Middle Ages); (2) the thing as synthetic unity of the sensible manifold given to the senses (see Kant); and (3) the thing as formed matter, matter informed, or determined, by its ideational form (again see Aristotle and medieval Scholastics). In one way or another, he argues, all three of these interpretations are reflections of an attitude—one might call it the will to power—that encourages what he boldly describes as an "assault" on the thing, an "inordinate attempt" to exercise control over the thing (GA 5: 7–16/PLT 22–31). All three interpretations fail to recognize and understand the thingness of the thing, either reducing its self-containment to subjectivism or reifying it in the objectivism of the natural sciences. And none even begins to appreciate the distinctive way in which this thingness emerges and manifests in the work of art; they all miss the work's relation to the hermeneutics of truth and the way in which, while belonging to the elements, dependent on their materiality, the work of art brings forth a world. "In setting up a world," he says, "the work [of art] sets forth the earth." Thus: "The work moves the earth itself into the Open of a world and preserves it there. *The work lets the earth be an earth,*" "*Das Werk läßt die Erde eine Erde sein*" (GA 5: 32/PLT 46). And it "opens up [*eröffnet*] in its own way the being of beings" (GA 5: 25/PLT 39).

Heidegger thinks that in the authentic work of art, we can experience the "truth," that is, the being, of beings. However, what makes the traditional, representational work of art—at least the work of art from ancient times to the very late nineteenth century—fascinating from a philosophical point of view is that it is at once a thing and not a thing, a thing made of earth, a thing composed of matter, and yet, at the same time, a thing that presents itself in a way that utterly transcends and often conceals its thinghood. As a work of art, it is the mystery of a complete transformation, a thing no longer only a thing that can be weighed, measured, or objectified.

Beginning in the late nineteenth century, though, as representational art yielded to Abstraction, Minimalism, and other forms of intensely self-reflective art that call attention to their material conditions of possibility and question that process of transformation, the mystery in the presence of a representation of the world has been vanquished, so that enchantment has given way to processes of disenchantment, works of art revealing the work in its humble thingly being. As I shall elaborate in chapter 6, the painted cubes and boxes made by Donald Judd in the New York Minimalist movement of the 1960s constitute a serious attempt to destabilize the distinction between thing and art, compelling us to question our assumptions and reflect on our experience. It can be distressing to see what claims to be art reduced to what appears to be mere thinghood. But that, too, can be revelatory, as revelatory as representationalism, whether showing the illusion that art creates to *be* nothing but an illusion, hence showing the work of art in its emergence from, and submergence in, the materiality of the thing, or isolating and showing nothing but the thing itself in its unadorned thingness, as if it could be cut off from all relationality; that too is art opening up a world for us. Discovering how a work of art that looks like nothing but a thing, a simple cube or box, can nevertheless reveal the difference between thing and art is the work's redemption as art.

†

While formulating objections to all three metaphysical interpretations of the thing, Heidegger nevertheless draws on all of them to a certain extent in order to imagine the thing as appearing to our perception in a profoundly new *Gestalt*—that distinctive geometric configuration he calls the *Geviert*. In "The Thing," Heidegger says,

> Earth and sky, divinities and mortals—being at one with one another of their own accord—belong together by way of the coherence of their unifying Fourfold. Each of the four mirrors in its own way the presence of the others. Each therewith reflects itself in its own way into its own, within the coherence of the four. (GA 7: 180–81/PLT 179)

Each thing in its presencing gives us mortals something to think about, something to care about, something that appropriates us, calling us as we are into question. The text continues as follows:

> This mirroring does not portray a likeness. The mirroring, lightening each of the four, appropriates their own presencing into

> simple belonging to one another. Mirroring is this appropriating-lightening way, each of the four plays to each of the others. The appropriative mirroring sets each of the four free into its own, but it binds these free ones into the simplicity of their essential being toward one another. [. . .] This appropriating mirror-play of the simple one-fold of earth and sky, divinities and mortals, is what we call world.

This leads into an illuminating explication of the sense Heidegger wants to make of our "appropriation" as gathered through the thing into its surrounding Fourfold.

> If we let the thing be present in its thinging from out of the worlding world, then we are thinking of the thing as thing. Taking thought in this way, we let ourselves be concerned by the thing's worlding being. Thinking in this way, we are called by the thing as the thing. Thus, in the most immediate sense of the German word *bedingt*, it is we who are the be-thinged, the conditioned ones. We have left behind us the presumption of all unconditionedness. (GA 7: 182/PLT 181)

To be able to see what is visible, we must ourselves belong to the visible. We can relate to things only because we are ourselves be-thinged: in other words, we are beings who are conditioned to perish, made of the same ultimate matter as all the things we live with. Heidegger further explains, then, what this implies, and indeed enjoins, regarding our appropriation as mortals.

> If we think of the thing as thing, then we are engaged in sparing and protecting the thing's presence in the region from which it presences.

At the same time, however, that he wants to emphasize our appropriated responsibility for things and their conditions of possibility, he also wants to deny any suggestion of subjectivism and anthropocentrism.

> When and in what way do things appear as things? They do not appear *by means of* human making. But neither do they appear without the vigilance of mortals. The first step toward such vigilance is the step back from the thinking that merely

represents—that is, explains—to the thinking that responds and recalls [*andenkende Denken*]. (GA 7: 182/PLT 181)

Things do not necessarily appear, or show themselves, to *be* things; they can, instead, appear only as *objects*. And, in the contemporary world, things mostly *do* appear as objects. We do not even realize that they are the constructs of a modern will to power. But, in their truth, things are not reducible to objects: an object is the product of a process of detachment and abstraction, removing it from its referential context; thus isolated, it becomes the product of an imposed meaning and identity. Unlike objects, things are obdurately inseparable from their context, which alone gives them their own proper meaning. Things resist their reduction to objecthood, resist their reduction to our purposes in many different ways; however, we are often insensitive and blind to that resistance, determined to make them yield to our will and serve our purposes. For things to appear, to presence, as things requires not only the *fact* that we, in our thrown-openness, are not encapsulated, thing-like substances, but also that we take a step back (*Schritt zurück*) from the so-called natural attitude (our everyday habits) into the phenomenological. This, he says, is "no mere shift of attitude," because "all attitudes tend to remain committed to the precincts of representational thinking."

> The step back does, indeed, depart from the sphere of mere attitudes. But the step back takes up its residence in a co-responding [*Ent-sprechen*] which, appealed to in the world's being by the world's being, answers within itself [*innerhalb selber*] to that appeal. (GA 7: 183/PLT 181–82)

In the step back into phenomenology, philosophical thinking refrains from taking the contemplative, theoretical position that sees the thing as *vorhanden*, present-at-hand, and refrains as well from the instrumental position, for which the thing is something merely *zuhanden*, ready-to-hand, in order to co-respond as openly as possible to the thing in its gathering of a world. However,

> A mere shift of attitude [*Wechsel der Einstellung*] is powerless to bring about the advent [*Ankunft*] of the thing as thing, just as nothing that stands today as an object can ever be simply switched over into a thing. (GA 7: 183/PLT 181)

It is not entirely clear how we might prepare for such an ontological transformation, returning things to their thinghood and redeeming their historical essence and promise (GA 7: 184/PLT 182). Heidegger quite appropriately does not presume to tell us what to do. He does, however, counsel "pure waiting," which I take to mean finding a way, in the way we live, to make the world more receptive to ontological change without exercising or encouraging the will to power. It would be a question of our being, by virtue of our appropriated mindfulness, more open to the dimensionality of the clearing—the perceptual field—and more vigilant in holding it open for what might come to presence in its field of presencing.

†

In "Building Dwelling Thinking," Heidegger describes how a "thing" such as a bridge is, and could be regarded as, a site gathering the Fourfold, earth and sky, gods and mortals, around itself (GA 7: 154–61/PLT 152–58). Despite a certain formal similarity, this understanding of the perceptible thing in its contextual place greatly differs from the metaphysical conceptions proposed in the past, because its point of departure is not the conceptual and theoretical exigencies of some philosophical system, but *the thing itself as perceived*, and as it figures or functions in all the contexts of our lifeworld. But Heidegger's distinction is to have recognized an implicit logic of *gathering relationality* in all three philosophical representations of the thing.

In the course of Western thought, "the thing has been represented as an unknown X to which perceptible properties are attached." So, he adds, "From this point of view, everything that already belongs to the gathering nature of this thing appears only as something that is afterward read into it" (GA 7: 156/PLT 153). This does not mean that Heidegger rejects the usefulness, hence the pragmatic truth, in the ways that the nature of the thing is treated in mathematics, physical science, and technology. However, beginning his phenomenology, in this text, by observing the ways in which the bridge as a thing serves the life of a community, the ways in which it functions in our lifeworld, Heidegger is not only suggesting a different *understanding* of the thing and of the way we might *think* of the thing; he is also suggesting a different way of *experiencing, and living with* all the bridges and jugs in our lifeworld—and indeed, a different way of looking at, and seeing, each and every thing that presences in our world. At stake in the redeeming of the thing as thing is ultimately an entirely different way of living, building and dwelling. Thus, as Heidegger's description in this text makes clear, even our sense of location, place and space, and nearness and farness can, and would, undergo enormous transformation, were we, in our sensibility and perception, to encounter all things, all beings, as topologies for the gathering of the Fourfold—and correspondingly experienced ourselves as mortals taking part in this gathering.

†

In "Building Dwelling Thinking," "What Are Poets For?," and "The Thing," as well as in other texts, Heidegger explains with philosophical clarity and poetic beauty what "earth" and "sky" can signify, and what our most appropriate, most fitting comportment in relating to them should involve. "Earth" and "sky" are names designating the environmental elements and the natural world they compose—rivers, oceans, clouds, volcanos, stone; but they are names that also call into the gathering all the plants that grow and all the animals that make their way in the nature of these elements. "Sky," moreover, symbolizes, or meta-phors, the sublimity of the depths of the infinite, the immeasurable, granting us mortals a sensible intimation of the measureless by which to take the measure of our humanity as human beings, while "earth" symbolizes, or meta-phors, the dense, the obscure, the limits, or finitude that, even while it grants a certain measure of security, a sense of groundedness, also compels us, as in the emergency of landslides and earthquakes, to recognize the vulnerability, finitude, and ultimate groundlessness of the human condition. For the earth can withdraw its grounding from the world; and in response to the will to power, it can show itself to be a ground from which all final grounding has been withdrawn. The earth is also that to which, in our death, we return. We have an ineluctable responsibility to take earth and sky in our care.

Besides gathering earth and sky, the thing also gathers mortals. But who are the mortals? Because, for Heidegger, we human beings alone can die, we are the mortals. Always already and yet, we are not—or not yet. Not, or not yet, unless we are like Socrates, like Montaigne, individuals who would live their lives with a deep sense of their mortality giving coherence and meaning to even the seemingly most insignificant matters in their lives. This "mortality" that Heidegger ascribes is not simply a neutral empirical fact characterizing all human beings. We are all, as human beings, assigned to death, fated to die, to perish. In that sense, we are all mortals; death in the sense of no longer being alive is inscribed in our very essence. But how we live our lives and how we live our dying and meet our death is up to us. We can evade it and deny it or take it over as the measure of our lives and as giving shape to the meaning of our life as a whole. To be a mortal in that more existentially authentic sense is to live one's life with death as the measure.[38] In his *Essays*, Montaigne remarked that to study philosophy is to learn to die. Hence, as he also said, it is always to live life with the taste of death in the mouth.[39] But death, in our culture, is as much as possible reduced to a mere fact, avoiding the reality, avoiding its fullness of meaning.

If living with a deep sense of mortality is required of us in order to take part in the Fourfold, then most human beings are not yet fully gathered into the Fourfold that surrounds all things. So, while I consider that sense of mortality to be of the greatest importance for living to the fullest and deepest extent what it means to be a human being, I think Heidegger wants to say that *all* human beings, regardless of the depth and extent of their sense of mortality, would be gathered, nevertheless, into the Fourfold that surrounds all things. For all human beings are earth-bound beings already fated to die; all are in that way mortals summoned to acknowledge, and learn how to live from, their mortality. I will now explain why this more inclusive sense of "mortal" should not be neglected.

§11

In Heidegger's projection of the Fourfold, the thing is envisioned as gathering us, as mortals, into our deepest human connections. This gathering that he imagines around the thing certainly makes us see in a new light the things we have reduced to objects. Things once again could possess existential meaningfulness. But we human beings are not only mortals; we are social, cultural, political beings. Hence, I want to argue that, in this projection of the gathering, Heidegger neglected to think what a gathering of mortals should mean in terms of our human connections. Without envisioning the thing in the ethical and political life of human connections, we cannot even begin to reconcile and redeem the promise in the thing—the promise of the thing. The thing will remain a corrupted matter; and it will continue its tyranny as object. That means, correspondingly, that we remain subjects, not only subjected to the tyranny of the object, but imposing that subjection, that oppression, on the lives of others.

So I want to argue, differing from Heidegger, that this gathering must be a *democracy* in that it recognizes the *shared humanity* of all mortals, all human beings, regardless of race, religion, nationality, ethnicity, and other social identities; a *democracy* that recognizes the shared humanity of people in all social and economic conditions, all stations and vocations, all destinies; a *democracy* that recognizes that no one, not even the richest, can enjoy what they have without depending on the consent and contributions of all the others gathered in the social order.

As my grandfather once had occasion to tell me when I was a child, no monarch, no matter how majestic, how well protected, withdrawn into his fortified castle, can escape the ravages of the pestilence, because, in the kitchen, cooking feasts for him, there are impoverished peasants from the nearby village, where the epidemic defiantly reigns. In essence, as the wise saying goes, we are *all* on this same boat—the Earth—hurtling through space and time. Or, as an Italian proverb says, After the chess game, the King and the Pawn go into the same box!

Thinking of Heidegger's Fourfold as the envisioning of a new, universal Humanism, a Humanism recognizing our "true dignity" as human beings, consequently seems to conflict with his exemplary rhetorical images of the Fourfold, which consistently evoke the world of a pastoral, Arcadian community. (At least, it seems that it does not have to be German!) There are no images of a Fourfold gathering human beings together in the context of urban, cosmopolitan life. No images of any gatherings around the things belonging to an advanced industrial society. So, I do not see how it is possible to reconcile his Humanism, which presumably must be universal and democratic in virtue of its recognizing that there is humanity to be found in all human beings, with the world of his rhetorical images. Insofar as all human beings are recognized and gathered, they are recognized and gathered only in their mortality—not in regard to their humanity. In this there is a decisive difference. Hence, in Heidegger's project, the Fourfold is not the gathering of a true democracy. Nor can it redeem the historical fate of the thing, rescuing its promise for the world to come. That process can be completed only when, because of their belonging-together, *both* the being of the thing *and* the being of the human being are released from all forms of violence.

It is imperative that the Fourfold recognize and affirm our deep social and ecological interdependencies—and the corresponding responsibilities we have as individuals and members of various communities. No one can exist in total, absolute isolation and independence. There are many versions of individualism. Some versions are to be celebrated. But the form of individualism that the system of late capitalism and its technocracies encourages today—and even sometimes requires—is in many ways very destructive, threatening interdependencies we desperately need and making very difficult the peaceful reconciliation of differences that is essential for the flourishing of human life on this planet. As Robert Reich eloquently argued in his March 24, 2022 podcast,

> The common good consists of our shared values about what we owe one another as citizens who are bound together in the same society—the norms we abide by, the sacrifices we make. A concern for the common good—keeping the common good in mind—is a moral attitude. It recognizes that we're all in it together. If there is no common good, there is no society, no civilization.[40]

So, I want to suggest, as a way to begin thinking about the achievement of this reconciliation, a very different image for the gathering of the Fourfold. Around even the smallest thing, a thing seemingly inconsequential in the endless cosmic drama—let us think of a tin of sardines—the four are waiting to gather, waiting to be received into the realm of the visible and audible. And that means that, gathered around this ordinary tin of sardines, one should bring into view and acknowledge all those who in any way took part in, or contributed to, the presence of this tin, with its sardines, on my table: all the fishermen, boat builders, longshoremen, miners, geologists, engineers, machine inventors, tin-factory workers, packers and truckers, bankers, lawyers, government legislators, fisheries police, merchants, road builders, bridge builders, traffic light designers, electricians, streetlight manufacturers, olive grove farmers, olive oil makers, and so many others. All gathered, all gathering, whether or not they are visible and audible in the flesh, and even when we have not explicitly recognized their presence. Recognition, or say, rather, acknowledgment, is something that ultimately depends not only on mindfulness, on our giving thought to the appropriation that has brought us into the gathering that surrounds the thing engaging us, but on our kindness, our capacity for sympathy, and our generosity of spirit.

I would argue that it is to give voice and encouragement to just such mindfulness, and just such acknowledgment of our shared humanity, our shared mortality and shared interdependencies, that the American poet, Walt Whitman, wrote his greatest poems, "Song of Myself" and "Salut au Monde!"[41] They are poems of celebration and gratitude that gather *all* of us into the Fourfold of a democracy built by generosity of spirit and mutual acknowledgment. Sadly, though, Heidegger's Fourfold is not Whitman's, because, despite its "Humanism," its solemn invocations of "humanity," the world that the philosopher projects does not seem to welcome all human beings.[42] How can the essence of the thing be redeemed in a Fourfold that still has not brought all human beings together into a condition of reconciliation? I believe that, as participants gathered into the Fourfold, every one of us is bound into the responsibility of a relationship of mutual respect with all the other human beings in the gathering. Thus, the clearings that our presence constitutes need to be hospitable to the formation of public spaces wherein, with a sense of public responsibility, true freedom and democracy can finally really flourish.[43]

We also are bound into a responsibility for the natural world—the environmental elements, earth and sky, and all the things, plants and animals, that those elements make possible. In regard to *this* dimension of the gathering, my thought gladly returns to Heidegger's topology, which makes compellingly clear our role in that relationship to nature: faithful guardianship. We, we mortals, bound as we are to the generosity of earth and sky, and to the plants and animals those elemental environments support, are the ones—the only ones—entrusted with the preservation and truth of nature, hence, too, we are entrusted with a caretaking that calls on us to prepare, as best we can, for a way of bringing forth, letting things presence, whether in perception or in making and using things, that would no longer be in the grip of the technological, military-industrial economy, the encompassing *Gestell* that, in our time, imposes its reified ontology, its essentially nihilistic determination, on the truth of being.

†

But, now, finally, *who* are the gods, the fourth participant, in this *Geviert*? *What* are they? Heidegger does not actually tell us very much. He invokes them with very little explanation or interpretation of their ontological status. The first thing we need to do with Heidegger's invocation of "gods" or "divinities" is to take them out of theology and Romantic metaphor, bringing them into meaningful relation to us mortals as embodiments of utopian challenges to our way of seeing and hearing things, making us responsible for poetically building a more just, more humane world while at the same time caring for and saving earth and sky. That, I think, is how we should best interpret Heidegger's invocation of the gods and his assertion that, between gods and mortals, there is a kind of "mirroring," appropriating each to the other. I suggest taking this to mean that the gods, being exemplary in their embodiment, are projections that reflect, or mirror, our highest ethical values, moral principles, and cultural ideals, appropriating us for their actuality, their realization, the consummation of their embodiment.

In the famous interview published in *Der Spiegel*, Heidegger is quoted as saying, no doubt with Hölderlin's poem in mind, that "Only a god can save us."[44] A god? Yet another god? Might we not have had enough of the gods? Might his disquieting words be simply a way of saying that only something extraordinary—some extraordinary event—he cannot now even begin to imagine what—not necessarily a god as such—might save us? Might his invocation of a god be nothing more than a figure of speech, a dramatic way of saying that our situation is so dire, so grave that it seems hopelessly beyond human powers to turn things around and rescue us from the very worst?

The ancient Greeks eventually abandoned their gods, laughing at their moral failings. Today, the Gods of Judaism, Christianity, and Islam are envisioned as imperiled, suffering, and perhaps dying because of the evils that we humans have wrought, exercising our free will. The Christian's savior passed through this world, but few were the ones who recognized him. The world is destitute; it remains to be transformed. The Jews still hold on to their conviction that the Messiah has not yet come. The time for that transformation has not come. But the Jewish prophets counsel hope in vigilance and spiritual preparation for that coming. The failure of Christ to transform the world seems to confirm the Jewish skepticism, or perhaps rather, the attitude of waiting and hoping, portrayed so compellingly by Kafka and Beckett. More precisely, it is a question of waiting without waiting and hoping without hope. Very much, it seems to me, what Heidegger was getting at.

†

In "The Question Concerning Technology," even in the midst of invocations of the danger of nihilism in our time, a time submitting the *Gestalt* to the *Gestell*, the imposition of reification, Heidegger, like Hölderlin, is not without hope. There is promise of transformation, he says, because, "wherever man opens his eyes and ears, unlocks his heart, and gives himself over to meditating and striving, shaping and working, entreating and thanking, he finds himself everywhere already brought into the unconcealed" (GA 7: 19/ QCT 19). Might we not, in such mindfulness, such openness of heart, find ourselves enabled to perceive "the secret sense of things"?

†

It is appropriate that the gods, interpreted metaphorically as embodiments of our highest, most cherished values, principles and ideals, should be projected in the sky, signifying that they are as insubstantial as air if not materially actualized on the ground where we dwell.

†

As we noted, in the interview published in *Der Spiegel*, Heidegger voiced his concerns regarding the present and future of the contemporary world and opined that "only a god can save us."[45] Years earlier, in the 1930s and 1940s, years when his thinking seems to have been influenced with exceptional intensity by Nietzsche, Heidegger brought his thinking to bear on the question of "the last god." In *The Event*, texts written during the War years 1941–1942, Heidegger said,

> The last god is the oldest, most inceptual god, the one that is determined in regard to his essence in the inceptuality of the beginning, the one that could *be* more eminently only if the truth of beyng were inceptually grounded in him, which is not something in his own power. (GA 71: 229–30/E 197)

In his *Contributions to Philosophy*, texts written during the years 1936–1938, Heidegger had written the following:

> "Dasein . . . hat sein Wesen in der Bergung der Wahrheit des Seyns, d.h. des letzten Gottes in das Seiende." ["*Dasein*'s essence lies in its care, its protection and preservation, of the truth of beyng—that is to say, the last god—in the realm of beings (the realm of what-is).''] (GA 65: 35/CP 29)

And again:

> "Das Wesen des Da-seins [. . .] ist die Bergung der Wahrheit des Seins, des letzten Gottes, in das Seiende." ["The essence of

Da-sein (. . .) is taking the truth of being, the last god, into its care, its protection, in the realm of beings."] (GA 65: 308/ CP 244)

According to Robert Calasso's study of Greek and Roman mythology, it was to attend the marriage of Cadmus and Harmonia that, for the very last time, the gods descended from Olympus to take part in the human life-world. Reminding us of Calasso's account of that mythic event, Salman Rushdie conjectures that, "perhaps, it's only when people stopped believing in the literal truth of their myths, stopped believing in an actual Zeus hurling actual thunderbolts, that they, we, were able to start believing in them in the way in which we believe in literature—that is to say, more profoundly [. . .]. It was only then that these myths began to give up their deepest meanings, meanings previously obscured by religious belief."[46] And, perhaps even more importantly, I would say, ceasing to believe in these archaic gods, the Greeks and Romans could finally begin to believe in themselves.

If "the last god" is, as Heidegger says, "the truth of beyng," then it is an unnecessary way of invoking the fundamental ontological openness with which we should take part in the historical conditions by which we find ourselves challenged. The "last god" appears only to disappear, leaving behind "the truth of beyng," which it is then our responsibility to keep open for the sake of world-transforming possibilities. I suggest that the "last god" is a way of referring to a momentous time of transition, an event (*Ereignis*) of history-breaking, history-making significance, when, at long last, we human beings, recognizing and understanding our essence as *Da-sein*, would finally authentically "enown" it and begin to enact it, and, no longer appealing to deified forces to explain and justify the way things are caused to be, we would begin to take responsibility for the conditions of the world. The future for us depends on our taking into our care the openness of the world that our existence (*Da-sein*) opens to. "The last god" symbolizes—metaphors—the god of the moment when, at long last, we *cease* depending on a god to take care of what needs to be done, understanding our existence in the light, and truth, of being.

†

In concluding his short text on "Logos (Heraclitus, Fragment B 50)," Heidegger draws, as he so often did, on the metaphors of visual perception to assert his unshakable conviction that "thinking changes the world." However dark our future appears, he believes, no doubt inspired by Hölderlin, that, paradoxical though it might seem, it is precisely when our situation seems darkest that it can "offer promise [*das Versprechen*] of a greater brightness" (GA 7: 234/EGT 78). At the heart of this promise, today, must be a new, more mature humanity, ceaselessly building toward a better democracy, to be founded in mutual goodwill, mutual respect, and the openness of mutual sympathy. What would be the appropriate development of our capacities and capabilities in this regard? In question is the character of our responsibilities as human beings building a world of ethical life on this Earth. In Heidegger's critique of our way of life, I have found indications and implications suggesting how the development of our capacities and capabilities in regard to the character of our seeing, hearing, and gesturing could contribute to the emerging of a body of ontological understanding.

As Walt Whitman says, in his *Leaves of Grass*, as if anticipating Heidegger's redeeming of the thing in its reticent truth, making visible and audible the gatherings of the Fourfold, already waiting, needing only to be recognized: "All truths wait in all things."[47] Unfortunately, however, the Humanism of democracy, where the principle is the identity, in reconciliation, of identity and nonidentity, will be waiting in vain for proper recognition from Heidegger's conception of the Fourfold. But reading Whitman after Heidegger, we can imagine the democracy that could gather in a Fourfold around all things, transforming each thing, however small and insignificant it may have seemed, into something to be in some way acknowledged, possibly bearing the secret of a redeeming promise.

Chapter 5

The Incarnate Dialectics of Aesthetic Hyper-reflexivity

Within broad historical epochs, the mode of sense perception [*die Art und Weise ihrer Sinneswahrnehmung*] changes with the overall mode of being in the world [*Daseinsweise*] of the historical collective.

—Walter Benjamin, "The Work of Art in the Epoch of Its Technical Reproducibility"[1]

In *The Origin of the German Mourning Play*, Benjamin states that the meaning of an original work of art is apparent only in a dual insight, which discerns in a work not only the traces or scars of history, but also intimations of a future history that will change both the work and the traces of history already discerned in it.

—Howard Caygill, *Walter Benjamin: The Colour of Experience*[2]

The more horrible this world (as today, for instance), the more abstract our art, whereas a happy world brings forth an art of the here and the now.

—Paul Klee, *Diaries*[3]

We always want to see what is hidden by what we see.

—René Magritte[4]

113

> I wanted to make paintings that were a celebration and that revealed something and obscured something at the same time.
>
> —Damien Hirst[5]

> I came to painting at the time of its death, not to breathe its last breath, but to caress it in its lifelessness [um *mit ihrer Leblosigkeit sanft zu spielen*].
>
> —Steven Parrino[6]

> What haunts the twenty-first century is not so much the past as rather all the lost futures that the twentieth century taught us to anticipate.
>
> —Mark Fisher[7]

§1

I would like to argue that, beginning in the paintings of the Italian and Northern Renaissance, not only with regard to perspectivism, but also in regard to forms in which painting exhibited itself in the mirroring and hermeneutical circle of hyper-reflexivity, and then increasingly, especially in the nineteenth and twentieth centuries, works in painting began to entertain a Modernist self-reflection, a certain self-absorbed turn of attention to themselves, and in particular, to the contingency of their historical "essence." At the same time, these works dialectically engage the vision, the gaze of the viewers, in a corresponding hyper-reflexivity, re-turning the gaze in a way that invites the viewers to reflect on themselves in regard to their visual experience, thereby setting up a vibrant, oscillating reciprocity of benefit both to the work of art, which is revealing more about itself, and to the gaze of the viewers, who are encouraged by the work to learn more about their own ways of seeing. In this dialectic, painting and gaze co-respondingly reflect one another, as if they were mirrors, engaging one another in processes of critical aesthetic hyper-reflexivity.

In his writings on modern art and society, Walter Benjamin argued that the increasingly intricate, fraught relationship between word and image is indicative of much broader tensions and struggles within modernity. The images created in modern art, he thought, should be understood as a technology for questioning experience, a way to reflect critically and speculatively on the limits of experience from within it. Increasingly liberated from representation and its normative paradigms, modern art from the late nineteenth century on has taken advantage of the new technologies and new materials, experimenting with them together with hitherto denied subject matter and new, sometimes shocking ways of presenting familiar subject matter. Sometimes now, the image does not even remain merely visual, but instead engages the beholder's experience of embodiment—as when, for instance, the flat picture-surface is broken up and reconstructed on different three-dimensional planes. And the pictorial line becomes writing—or a traumatizing cut and tear.

In putting new technologies and new materials into play in works of art, artists have challenged the inhumane ways these technologies and materials are being used by our economic, political, and social system; and they can inspire or suggest ways to change the ontological paradigm that, in the epoch of the *Gestell*, is nothing but malevolent and, ultimately, nihilistic.

Hegel saw in the representational forms of his time the historical end of art, failing to consider that, out of that death, new forms could—and would—emerge, far more challenging to the life of the spirit than the art of the past he knew. Thinking about the ancient Greek temple, Heidegger understood how a work of architecture could serve to gather a community around its religious vision; but, perhaps because of very limited exposure to works of visual art, he failed to understand the profoundly reflexive, critical social role that late modern and contemporary visual art can take on. Much more of ourselves and our world is engaged and at stake in today's art than Heidegger was able to see or imagine.

Much of the late-nineteenth-century avant-garde art, and much more of twentieth-century art, in its very form and structure, that is, in its various ways of drawing the viewer into a loop of hyper-reflexivity that calls into question the ethical character—and not infrequently, the political disposition—of the viewer's habits of looking and seeing, bears on Heidegger's critique of the West's ocularcentric will to power. Although he deliberately abstains from moralizing, his critique nonetheless implies both (1) a critique of looking and seeing, hearing, and listening in our ethical life and (2) a certain visionary projection of a better life more befitting our shared sense of humanity.

And in this regard, Heidegger's critique does not spare our habitual ways of touching, holding, carrying, and handling things—ways that embody the two reigning ontological modalities, *Zuhandensein* and *Vorhandensein*, in terms of which Western life relates to the being of beings. So, it should not be surprising that our contemporary forms of art—painting, sculpture, and installations—get us to reflect on the ontology and ethical character secretly at work in our gestures, perhaps even getting us to change how we engage with things. Our bodies are not only endowments of nature; they are also informed by culture and altered by individual life. The arts speak to our bodies—to the memories and dreams and traumas they bear and express.

And there is a deep and fundamental connection between our experience of art today and our corresponding understanding of ethical life: what brings them together, as Kant's *Critique of Judgement* and Friedrich Schiller's *Letters on the Aesthetic Education of Mankind* have argued, is sensibility. In art, it is a capacity to be moved by the beauty in the free expression of human experience, be it joy or suffering. And in ethical life, it is our capacity to be open, exposed, and sympathetic to the experience of other, seemingly very different human beings and other very different ways of living.

§2

According to Merleau-Ponty, attention "is not merely to elucidate further objectively pre-existing data, but rather to bring about a new articulation of it."[8] In this way, attention may be said to inaugurate the primordial reciprocity by which we come into existence as so-called embodied "subjects." Finally, in the twentieth century, as representation in art lost compelling truth and its magical power to captivate waned, it is increasingly this postmodern Modernist art of self-reflection that challenges its historical essentialism and, correspondingly, what is demanded of the viewers in regard to their experience of looking at the work of art.

And as I shall argue, this dialectic can also be operative in sculpture, art installations, and architecture, engaging us not—or not only—in the realm of vision, but perhaps in a more elemental way, in our felt sense of embodiment, our sense of the tactile, and our sense of spatiality, challenging, with Heidegger, the long-reigning philosophical interpretation of embodiment that persists in thinking of it as an encased substance and encouraging, instead, an experience of ourselves as *Da-sein*—beings thrown-open into the situations of a world.

Hyper-reflexivity involves both epistemological and ontological changes, which phenomenology can bring to light. Considered in terms of its ontological dimension, the experience of this dialectic, drawing attention to itself, reveals the oscillating reciprocity in the belonging-together of viewer and painting, art lover and art, *Dasein* and being. And it reveals the fact that what we think of as "the painting" or "the sculpture" is always being made anew in every dialectical encounter, just as, because of the reciprocity in their belonging-together (*Zusammengehörigkeit*), the viewer is always undergoing questions, solicitations, and challenges that can reveal within vision some of its heretofore unrecognized possibilities—new ways of looking and seeing and feeling what there is to see and be with, and indeed, new understandings of being.

This dialectic of hyper-reflexivity in Post-Modern art deconstructs or abolishes the subject-object relation that, enshrined in modern philosophy since Descartes, has determined the habitual character of most of our experience in the Western world. Breaking through the subject-object structure to engage the prior and underlying relation to being, the dialectic releases both the artwork—the painting, the sculpture—and the art lover from the restrictions inherent in that structure, engaging and enriching the deeper dimensions of the aesthetic experience and, correspondingly, letting the work of art not only reveal much more of itself, but reveal what could only be experienced if we are no longer fixating it in objectification.

In *Sense and Non-Sense*, Merleau-Ponty argued that the relationship between subject and object is no longer to be understood as

> that *relationship of knowledge* postulated by classical idealism, wherein the object always seems the construction of the subject, but a *relationship of being* in which the subject *is* his body, his world, and his situation, as by a sort of exchange.[9]

This is also Heidegger's position. Thus, in "The Principle of Identity," he argues that *Dasein* and *Sein* belong together in a dynamic, oscillating ontological relationship prior to, and underlying, the ontic relationship of knowledge, where there is a subject-object structure. Some years later, Merleau-Ponty will describe as a dynamic relationship of chiasmic reciprocity what in this passage he referred to as "a sort of exchange." This description gives further phenomenological concreteness to Heidegger's representation of the ontological connection to being. In this way, phenomenology sets the stage for interpreting the hyper-reflexivity already happening in some of the innovations appearing in late-nineteenth century modern art: a hyper-reflexivity that increasingly seems to engage the viewer's felt embodiment, and not only the process that engages seeing in an optical interplay of concealment and disclosure.

In my way of thinking, "Modernity" begins with the Renaissance and enters its final moment near the end of the nineteenth century, as painting announces its Post-Modern revolt in Cubism, Surrealism, and Dada. (See my chart in the Notes,[10] briefly showing how I am interpreting the different movements in the history of art.) But the self-conscious *Modernist* art appearing at the very end of modernity and the hyper-reflexive art now flourishing in the postmodern world are not only playfully disrupting and deconstructing the subject-object structure that governed the aesthetic experience of art, especially the art of painting, during the modern period; it has increasingly challenged perspectivism, subverted the viewer's bodily felt sense of positionality and spatiality, erased the figure-ground structuring in the perception of the painting, and dissolved the solidly "objective" nature of the painting into pure opticality or tactility. All of these procedures problematize the tradition of representation that goes back to the cave paintings left by our earliest genealogical ancestors. At the beginning of the twentieth century, representation is increasingly broken up, fragmented, reorganized, emphasizing shapes, colors, patterns, textures. With hyper-reflexivity, forms of abstraction begin to prevail.

As abstraction abandons representation, it contests and abandons the logic of identity; it increasingly works according to the logic of difference, nonidentity. And even as it deploys the calculative, technological, technocratic reduction of Enlightenment rationality, it also shows its resistance to that very rationality—the Enlightenment paradigm and its metaphysical assumptions.

Abstraction in art is *both* a reflection of, and a response to, the fragmentation and alienation taking over our world, our lives, overwhelming changes seemingly beyond our control; *and it is also*, at the same time, an expression of our freedom from that traumatizing reality, the realm, we might say, of imposed necessity: it is freedom from fixed concepts, freedom from representation according to a concept, freedom to alter our reality. So, it is, in a way, a manifestation of the will to power. Abstraction in art is an expression of the subjective, reflexive turn that began with Descartes and found its completion in the Kantian turn, the Post-Modernism of a certain transcendentalism: a Modernist self-critical illumination and questioning of "essentialism," exhibiting, in and as the work of art, its own conditions of possibility. Abstraction is a reflection on our time and of our time, a way of acknowledging, mastering, and creatively using the breakdown of the traditional forms of perception, meaning, expression, and identity. Abstraction calls for hyper-reflexivity.

Despite emphatically asserting the belonging-together of *Sein* and *Mensch*, Heidegger does not seem to recognize the operation of this dialectic in our encounter with works of art. Consequently, he does not see in art its enormous potential for deconstructing the subject-object paradigm and returning us to the prereflective, pre-ontological dimension of experience, so that we would be able to encounter the artwork from within the vibrantly dynamic configurations in our belonging-togetherness with its emerging contingencies of being. The work of art thereby would become, in effect, a performance; and its very identity only begins to emerge in a finely attuned collaboration: painting and vision, sculpture and felt embodiment. The sway of the subject-object paradigm induces us, however, to overlook this collaboration, for which Heidegger uses words such as *Schweben* and *Schwingen*, suggesting a vibrant bodily felt oscillation: instead, we recognize only the painting or sculpture as an inert fact and remain satisfied with our own merely "subjective" projection. I want to show the significance of aesthetic experience for informing our awareness of the dynamic belonging-together of *Mensch* and *Sein*—what in Merleau-Ponty's later phenomenology of perception is described as a chiasmic reversibility and reciprocity. Much Post-Modern art assumes this phenomenological understanding of perception as the basis for its playful subversions of our perceptual and bodily habits.

§3

Heidegger wrote very little about individual works of art; his writings tend to concentrate on larger historical, cultural and ontological matters—questions in and for a *philosophy* of art. After finishing *Being and Time* (1927), Heidegger began, in the 1930s, to turn his thought to some major texts in the history of the philosophy of art, giving lecture series on Hölderlin, Schiller, Kant, Schelling and Nietzsche. Heidegger's most significant contribution to the philosophical understanding of art is perhaps in his 1935–1936 text, revised again in 1950, on "The Origin of the Work of Art" (GA 5: 1–74/PLT 17–87). In this text, in order to get at the essential way of being (*Wesen*) of the work of art, he asks us, first of all, to consider what it is that we call a "thing." This ontological question is addressed in a survey of the history of philosophical interpretations of the thing, wending its way from the ancient Greeks and Romans through the medieval philosophers and the British empiricists, concluding with Kant and idealism. He then asks us to consider whether a work of art is or is not a thing, concluding with the recognition that it is, paradoxically, both a thing and not a thing. It is a thing in the sense that, like all things, it has size, weight, and other sensible properties, a volume always occupying a certain space-time location. And yet, insofar as what is in question is a work of art, none of these properties defining a thing essentially matter. The work of art is something that appeals to a heightened, educated sensibility and stimulates a lively exercise of the capacity for imagination. Post-Modern art in particular defies the logic of determinate identity. Even Minimalism defies it—but in a paradoxical, uncanny way, seeming to reduce the work of art to bare facticity, sheer being, yet compelling an attentiveness that frees its thing-like presence from all normal contexts, radically estranging it from any fixed, substantive identity.

It is unfortunate that, in reflecting on the thing and its essential difference from the work of art, Heidegger did not know about what was happening in the revolutionary movement in art called Minimalism. There was, for instance, Donald Judd's plain, unadorned wooden boxes and cubes, some painted, some not, elegantly geometrical, which profoundly questioned, challenged, and destabilized that fundamental difference of essence that the Western world had always taken for granted. Requiring a reflexive turn, these boxes and cubes could be seen as mere things or they could be seen as historically revolutionary art. They compelled viewers to reflect on their shifting ways of seeing, because the objects remained materially unchanged throughout the perceptual shifts. But who knows what Heidegger would have thought if confronted with Judd's works? Would his notion of art have changed? How would he relate Judd's boxes to his reflections on the thing? Are the boxes so thing-like that they cannot be art? How does the difference between work of art and thinghood depend on our vision, our bodily engagement with them? How does recognition of that ontological difference affect the experience of looking and seeing?

For the artist, that engagement is what was being sought. For the thought behind Heidegger's project, at once critical and visionary, that engagement is one that could eventually, perhaps, inspire and generate significant changes in the cultural reproduction of our ways of seeing and living our sense of embodiment—for instance in the *Mitsein* of our gestures. And if such changes were to extend their influence beyond the world of art, they could conceivably liberate us to some extent from the *Weltbild* that imposes its will, in this time of the *Gestell*, through our perceptual faculties and gestural dispositions.

One of the two works of art that Heidegger contemplates in "The Origin of the Work of Art," however, is not a painting or a work of sculpture, but a Greek temple. What draws him to this kind of art, a work of architecture, is its relation to earth and world: manifestly grounded in, and on, the earth, and moreover built from the very substance of the earth, the temple asserts its belonging to a community, a cultural world, that its presence gathers to celebrate and commemorate. But in this assertiveness, the temple inevitably sets itself in the midst of a ceaseless strife between earth and world, each of these claiming predominance. The temple is, in effect, the center of a *Geviert* that it has gathered: it speaks to the earth and the sky, mortals and their gods. The temple forms a clearing in the larger world for the gathering of a community devoted to a deity; it rises from the earth as a place connecting human beings to their gods in the sky. But the earth remains powerful; and ultimately, it will reclaim the stone of the temple.

Now, as the title of Heidegger's text indicates, the philosopher's concern, stimulated no doubt by Nietzsche's essay on *The Birth of Tragedy*, is ultimately for the origin (*Ur-sprung*) of the temple as a work of art. "Origin," for Heidegger, is not ordinary history; rather, it is what makes the history of art possible. In this text he explains his word *origin*: "Origin here means that from which and by which something is what it is and as it is. What something is, as it is, we call its 'essence.' The question concerning the origin of the work of art asks about its essential source." That "source" is its mode of being, hence the ontological conditions behind the being of the work of art. That, for him, introduces the question of truth in art, which is not a matter of correctness, accurate representation, but rather, instead, the work's disclosiveness—*aletheia*. Drawing on other texts by Heidegger, I suggest that, in regard to the temple, this "origin" is twofold: it not only springs forth out of the earth; it also springs forth into a world, the world that its being-there gathers. It is not something natural, a creation of nature, like a stone or a seed; it is something made by human hands, but it is also not an instrument, not something made for practical use, like a bowl, a fork, or a bread.

In its gathering of the Fourfold, the temple engages the earth in its strife with the world it represents. But it does much more than that, for it reveals to us the earth *as* earth and the world *as* world. It reminds us of our dependency on the earth while commemorating and celebrating the cultural world we have built on it.[11]

Although this text is illuminating with regard to the Greek temple, it does not offer much illumination in regard to the ontological condition of the other arts: music, dance, sculptures, paintings, and literature. The question of "origin" is also not really very useful for understanding art. And indeed, despite giving his text a title that emphasizes "origin," Heidegger quickly dispatches the matter in the first page, turning to the ontological difference between art and thing. In an "Epilogue" (GA 5: 69–70/PLT 81), Heidegger has nothing more to say about "origin." Instead, he connects art to the happening of truth, concluding with the thought that "The history of the nature of Western art corresponds to the change in the nature of truth"—that is, its reduction from disclosiveness (truth as *aletheia*) to truth as correctness (*orthotes*). Moreover, except for the art of theater and perhaps also the choral dance, it is not at all obvious how the question of origin would even bear on the being of these other arts. The word *theater* of course derives from the Greek *theaomai*, meaning to receive and behold the (female) deity (*thea*). This explains the earliest historical forms of theater, especially the Greek tragedy.

The other work of art that Heidegger discusses in this text is a painting by van Gogh showing a pair of old, muddy shoes. Again, what draws Heidegger's attention is that these shoes disclose their ontological dimension of truth—*aletheia*: the inherent strife between world and earth.

The phenomenology of disclosiveness (truth as *aletheia*) soon replaces reflections on the "origin" of the work of art. "Art," says Heidegger, "is the setting-into-work of truth" (GA 5: 65/PLT 77). Art "lets truth [i.e., disclosiveness, *aletheia*] appear" (GA 5: 65/PLT 77). That means, he says: "Truth happens in Van Gogh's painting [of the two old work-shoes]" (GA 5: 43/PLT 56). "The art work lets us know what shoes are in truth" (GA 5: 21/PLT 35). It reveals the shoes we normally and habitually fail really to see, letting us see them as if for the very first time. "This does not mean that something is "correctly" portrayed, but rather that in the revelation of the equipmental being of the shoes, that which is as a whole—world and earth in their counterplay—attains to unconcealedness" (GA 5: 43/PLT, 56). That is a thought that can be used to comprehend all of the arts, not only Greek theater; not only Greek temple architecture; not only an old pair of shoes. What draws Heidegger's attention and stirs his thought are works of art in regard to which he can weave an interpretation that supports his philosophical project: in this case, an argument concerning truth in art and the relation between earth and world. He has little or nothing to say about these works of art as unique identities. What matters is the disclosiveness of the work of art: a matter of getting to the essence—whatever that might be—and revealing its being.

There is compelling evidence, in texts and testimony, that Heidegger liked works by Paul Cézanne, paintings evocative of the southern France that he knew and enjoyed because of his visits. But there is nothing especially illuminating about those works in the reflections and comments that are available.[12] We also know that, in 1956, he saw an exhibit of Paul Klee's drawings and paintings in Basel, and that he liked what he found there. But, once again, what stirred his thought were entirely matters manifestly connected to his much larger philosophical project, for instance Klee's determination, expressed in his wonderful 1925 colored drawing, *Crescent Moon over the Rational*, to challenge and somehow transcend Western rationalism and its metaphysics. But Heidegger seldom discussed individual works of art. And he never really elaborated an aesthetic theory, believing such theory to emphasize private sensory experience—*Erlebnisse*—and consequently support philosophical subjectivism; nor did he develop a comprehensive philosophy of art, such as we find in Plato, Aristotle, Hegel, the early German Romantics, Kant and Nietzsche. In 1959, he reportedly remarked—cryptically—that, "in Klee something has happened that none of us grasps as yet." Klee's abstract representations and purely fanciful figurations, which he apparently liked more than Picasso's, got his interest; but it seems that he was pretty much at a loss to understand and illuminate them in terms of his philosophical project. Unfortunately, he was stirred to significant thought only when he could interpret works of art in a way that would serve to instantiate and exemplify the arguments constitutive of the project. Klee's later works, involving lines and colors delineating recognizable forms, patterns, and shapes, often geometric, as well as lines and colors that vibrate like musical tones, expanding and contracting, receding and shifting forward, show that he was working with the figure-ground *Gestalt* in ways that exhibited both the tension and the free flow in the emerging and withdrawing of figure-and-ground constructions. In terms of Heidegger's project, this is art manifesting the phenomenology in a dynamic interplay of concealment and unconcealment. After looking at a number of Klee's geometrically patterned works, Heidegger was reported to have declared that Klee depicts no object, but instead "the nothing comes to presence [*Nichts anwesendes*]."[13] He naturally would like this effect, since it fits nicely into his project; but in fact, much, if not most, of Klee's drawings and paintings do depict recognizable shapes, objects, patterns, and stylized characters and do not suggest that what is primarily to be experienced is the manifest presence of absence as such or the abyssal as such. However, Klee's paintings and drawings on paper do make visible the process of making visible. "Art," the artist said, "does not reproduce the visible: it makes the visible visible": visible, that is, in its coming into visibility.[14] Klee suggested, therefore, the recognition of a distinction between the traditional art of "optical seeing" and the kind of seeing he wanted his art to provoke and induce: a "penetrating and morphological gaze."[15] His was not to be a superficial art gathering mere fleeting impressions for the eyes, but an art for aesthetic hyper-reflexivity: the more the viewer's response is reflexive, turned back on itself, the more it could enjoy the richness awaiting discovery in the work—above all, what Heidegger wants us to think of as an experience of *aletheia*, a hermeneutics of truth-coming-into-being.

What is to be said about the lines and figures, background and figuration in some of Klee's art could also be said about many of Wassily Kandinsky's works, for instance his 1920s *Composition 8*. There are so many possible events that can occur for the viewer of this work, who must finally renounce trying to make "rational" sense of it in order to enjoy the free play in reconstructing the pre-objective rhythms and melodic patterns of the work, letting new configurations appear and vanish in reciprocating attunement with the activity, the movement, of the viewer's attention.

†

In his later years, Heidegger found considerable pleasure and inspiration in some impressive sculptural works, notably by Ernst Barlach, for whose exhibition catalog he contributed an essay; by Bernhard Heiliger, for whose gallery exhibition he gave a speech; and by Eduardo Chillida, with whom he engaged in some lengthy and lofty conversations. In a brief text, "Art and Space," Heidegger asserted, but without much elaboration, that sculpture is "the embodiment of the truth of being [*Verkörperung der Wahrheit des Seins*]."[16] But he said the very same thing about the Greek temple. What differentiates architecture and sculpture? He noted, still rather abstractly, that works of sculpture transform their space in ways that cannot be understood with the concepts of science and technology.[17] But that is also to be observed in regard to the Greek temple. What does "*Verkörperung*" mean when it is supposed to "embody" the truth of being? How does a viewer's embodiment affect the viewer's experience of the work as exhibiting or manifesting the truth of being? And how does sculpture affect the viewer's (felt sense of) embodiment? Heidegger leaves the embodiment in a very abstract formulation. It almost seems necessary to interpret "*Verkörpereung*" as nothing more than a figure of speech. His abstract interpretation of "embodiment" makes it virtually impossible to appreciate the experience of encountering a Rodin or Giacometti sculpture. How do these works *embody* "the truth of being"? This is a question that could challenge not only our sense of physical materiality, but also our sense of how truth is disclosed.

John Chamberlain's large sculptural works, assembling reshaped automobile parts in a multitude of twisted combinations and creating a multitude of oddly shaped interior and exterior spaces, so many secretive nooks and crannies, invite us to engage with our eyes and bodies, as in a kind of primordial contact bonding the viewer and the aesthetic object, bringing into felt experience the emergence of what Merleau-Ponty would call pre-objective spatiality and compelling the viewer to connect what is visible and what is invisible with what the body, denied tactility, nevertheless viscerally feels. These nooks and crannies block, turn and twist vision, making the viewer reckon reflexively with hiddenness and the defeated urge to see everything.

Something similar occurs in beholding Paul Cézanne's very expressive Post-Impressionist paintings, which deny sharp differentiation between figure and ground and often merely give a mere hint, trace, or suggestion of something—a terrace, a garden of flowers, an apple, a smile. Visiting Cézanne's homeland in the 1950s, Heidegger is reported to have said, "If only one could think as directly as Cézanne painted!"[18] What would "directness" in thinking be like? Heidegger certainly does not seem to have made such directness a *desideratum* in his own thinking. As Merleau-Ponty observed in "Cézanne's Doubt": Cézanne "did not want to separate the stable things which we see and the shifting ways in which they appear."[19] In effect, Merleau-Ponty's phenomenology returns intellectual consciousness to its roots in prereflective experience, fleshing out the meaning of Heidegger's "embodiment of the truth of being."[20]

What Heidegger argues in "The Principle of Identity" regarding the intimate immediacy of our connection to the being of the world gets explained in more experiential terms in Merleau-Ponty's phenomenological project. The phenomenology that he brings into articulation "re-achieves a direct and primitive contact with the world."[21] "Radical reflection," he says, "amounts to a consciousness of its own dependence on an unreflective life, which is its initial situation."[22] In painting that encourages this hyper-reflexivity, Cézanne draws us into an awareness of the conditions for creating meaning while we are in the very act of re-creating it. Hyper-reflexivity does not necessarily mean more intense cognitive work; in the experience of Cézanne's paintings, it means instead a much more intense engagement of sensibility and its felt vibrancy, aliveness, and richness in sensation and perception. What exactly was it that Heidegger admired in Cézanne's paintings? The way the image coalesces and emerges in response to the attunement of the gaze? He does not tell us. I suspect a Romantic sentimentality.

What seems to have really drawn Heidegger's interest, though, was, as Andrew Mitchell convincingly argued, how works of sculpture can challenge "a traditional view of space as an empty container for discrete bodies."[23] That very old philosophical view of space and our bodies falls away before the phenomenological truth of which we are sensible, sensing and feeling our embodiment as *Da-sein* in our living. In his conversations with the sculptor Eduardo Chillida, Heidegger also seems to have realized how poorly many of the traditional philosophical concepts for understanding sculpture fitted the revolution that the late-nineteenth-century modern and contemporary artists, from Auguste Rodin and Alberto Giacometti on, achieved, moving from realistic representations into experiments in Abstract Expressionism along with Cubism and its various permutations. When Heidegger turned to thinking about sculpture, what also stirred him, besides how such art challenges philosophical representations of space and bodies, was how sculpture prioritizes sensuous tactility, rather than the estranging visual experience into which Post-Modern painting, and some Late Modern painting, draw us. This is of importance because he had strongly argued against the prevailing disposition of our vision in today's world, namely, its reifying, nihilistic character—the Gorgon stare in the will to power. In encountering works by Rodin and Giacometti, as well as works by the three sculptors with whom Heidegger personally is known to have engaged, the art lover is drawn into an exceptionally keen sense of tactility and a surprisingly new sense of embodied spatiality.

Rodin released sculpture from representational realism and truth as correct correspondence; and he created figures with rough tactile surfaces, creased, folded, tortured, molding depths that are intricately expressive, independent of their visibility, tangible yet inaccessible: sculptures, in short, that bring forth a new and unfamiliar awareness of the ontological interplay of presence and absence, unconcealment and concealment. And as the artist Thomas Housago noted, "there is in Rodin a very pagan concern for the life-death continuum: clay as a manifestation of life and death [. . .]. It is a way of reminding us about the complexity of being a body, being alive, inevitably fated to die."[24] The common visceral response to the sculptural works by Rodin, Giacometti, and the three sculptors with whom Heidegger engaged in dialogue manifests a hyper-reflexivity taking place—not in thoughtful reflection, however, but, more immediately, in the bodily felt sense we have of sharing our belonging to the spatiality of the sculptures, taking part in an event forming what Merleau-Ponty would call a "universal flesh."

§4

We will now begin reflections on paintings that go into more elaboration, because in Western history, and perhaps especially in our time, this art has had a singularly important role in the formation of our ways of seeing and our relations to the visible and the invisible. But since the "origin" of the artwork as an ontological phenomenon engaging Western history was Heidegger's primary concern in the 1930s, it is understandable that he would choose to think about a Greek temple. However, other types of artwork—painting, for instance—also need philosophical interpretation. Paintings, too, come from, and eventually return to, the substance of the earth; and they, too, gather a world within our world. Paintings also, as Heidegger recognized in his comments on the van Gogh painting of a pair of old peasant shoes, take part in a hermeneutic phenomenology of revelation, disclosing to us the nature and character of our perception, while also disclosing something of the distinctive world they are evoking or creating. We will accordingly venture outside the textual contexts of Heidegger's thought to illuminate, though only briefly, but in a way that is still in keeping with ontological matters at the heart of his hermeneutic phenomenology, movements in painting that have excited philosophical thought in the twentieth century.

One of those Post-Modern movements is what I will recognize as *Modernist*, following the bold and insightful writings of Clement Greenberg and Michael Fried.[25] The definition of Modernist painting that I find most compelling interprets the works belonging to this movement in Kantian terms. The paintings contributing to this movement explore and exploit the hyper-reflexive possibilities in that art in order to reflect on, illuminate, and throw into question the historically traditional attributes necessary for a painting *being* a painting—*being* a work of art. Strictly defined, Modernist paintings are designed to address in ontological terms a Heideggerian question: What *is* a painting? What is involved in something *being* a painting? *We* can always ask that question of any painting. But paintings that *themselves* ask and answer that question constitute a singular Post-Modern category. In regard to their meaning and significance, even if the paintings are at all representational, they do not primarily refer to whatever it is that they are representing; in a crucial difference from representational art, they are primarily turned on themselves, interrogating the painting itself. What is the "essence" of a painting? Must the painting be framed? Must it be a certain shape? Must it be paint on a flat surface? Must it be recognizable as a representation of something either belonging to the world we live in or belonging to the projective imagination? Must it be put onto the surface by a brush? Modernist works in this Kantian sense insist, among other things, on making manifest the two-dimensionality of the picture surface. They compel the beholder to see the painting first as a flat painted surface, and only later as a picture; in other words, they expose *as illusion* the illusion of a three-dimensional space in traditional representational painting. According to this definition, Georges Braque, Piet Mondrian, and Frank Stella are, at least in some of their major works, paradigmatically Modernist painters, making works of art expressly created to raise questions in one way or another about themselves as paintings. Braque challenged the illusionism; Mondrian's spectral lines, floating shapes and odd geometry challenged the implications of framing and set in motion ambiguous figure-ground relationships; and Stella's oddly shaped painted canvases challenged the conventional framed shape. Stella's later works, involving the intricate construction of different intersecting colored planes, even challenged the old distinction between paintings and sculptures.

I want, however, to *extend* the Modernist terminology to include paintings that do not, strictly speaking, make it their very (Kantian) essence to reflect on and question that "essence," their defining attributes, but do nonetheless challenge in some visibly significant way our assumptions about painting, for example, its representational faithfulness, its perspectival accuracy and lucidity, the dimensionality of its representation of space, the figure-ground formation, and the spatial location of things, works of art, and the people looking at them.

Considered in this larger context, Modernist paintings, and other representatives of Post-Modern painting, raise such questions either by manifestly defying the historical conventions or else by in some other way calling our attention to the presence or absence of the conventional attributes. Paintings can defy the conventions in many different ways: by abstractions that resolutely deny pictorial, illusionistic, and fictive representation, as in the monochrome and color-field canvases of the 1950s and 1960s, or by shapes that abandon the square or rectangular canvas for an irregular, undefinable shape, or by painting not only with brushes but with squeegees (Gerhard Richter), or by dripping paint onto the canvas (Jackson Pollock), or by letting a very liquified paint flow as it will (Richter), or by introducing writing into the representational space (René Magritte, Jean Dubuffet, Jean-Michel Basquiat, Cy Twombly). Another one of the ways that painting can call attention to the conventions, and indeed to the very definition of a painting, already appears in some Late Modern works, rendering the application of paint especially manifest by applying it thickly and massively, as by "painterly" gestures that leave behind noticeable traces of the intensity of the gesture itself (van Gogh). And in the excessive Expressionism of Ben Benn's *Street in the Jewish Quarter, Montmartre* and Oscar Florianus Bluemner's *Evening Tones* and *Little Falls, New Jersey*, where the sharp contrasts of intensely pure color defining everything in the painting compel the beholder to acknowledge the enchantment of the paint as such. In the profusion of intensely Expressionist colors, and in that alone, representational realism is subverted, creating a dynamic aesthetic tension, as the dazzling colors draw attention to themselves. But the gaze is released, invited to play in pure *jouissance*. This is a freedom that challenges the gaze that imposes its will to power on things in the world of the *Gestell*. As Merleau-Ponty observes in his *Phenomenology of Perception*, "Learning to see colors is the acquisition of a certain style of vision, a new use of one's own body; it is to enrich and reorganize the body image" (117).

Another way for a painting to call attention to itself—to its way of being—as a painting, as something painted, is demonstrated by virtually all of Francis Bacon's mature paintings, for instance, in his engaging 1967 portrait of *George Dyer Staring into a Mirror* and his 1969 *Self-portrait*. In one of the 1944 *Studies for Figures at the Base of a Crucifixion*, we see from the side a woman seated in a chair. Bold brushstrokes elongate her neck and deform her face and torso; and her legs, instead of being completed, end about halfway between her knees and the floor: they end where the jagged, blurred, gradually fading brushstrokes make visible the fact that the brush that was painting them has arbitrarily been lifted off the canvas, leaving the legs dangling unfinished. Grief and mourning cannot alone explain the distortions—nor this strange abandonment of completeness. By prematurely ending the painting of the legs before they are completed, showing that what we are seeing are mere brushstrokes, Bacon compels us to recognize our visual expectations for what they are. The painting returns our gaze by painting in a way that compels us to question ourselves, our gaze. But, moreover, the painting is painted in a way that, before our very eyes, questions and subverts its own original claim to veracity or verisimilitude. In his paintings of people, the extreme distortions of their bodies and faces, many absurdly grotesque, serve to proclaim not only the brutal facticity of paint but also the absolute freedom of the painter's brush. Sometimes, though, it seems that the sweeping curves distorting faces and bodies are intended to show the subject in actual or possible motion, instead of being fixed into a position, defying thereby the "still life" convention defining the art of painting in contrast to the motion pictures of cinema.[26]

In Henri Matisse's *The Piano Lesson*, almost nothing about the accurate representation of space is respected; walls are rendered by colored vertical rectangles; a shadow on the boy's face appears as a black triangle cutting into his face; rays of sunlight appear as a large pale-green triangle. Although the presence of rooms behind the boy at the piano is implied, the forcefulness of the variously colored geometric shapes around him belies that assumption, flattening the spatiality of the setting, reducing it to a design of colored geometric shapes. This oscillation between flat design and three-dimensional realism plays with the spectator's vision. Confronting that painting, we begin to recognize that the character of our seeing is not determined by nature—the neurophysiology of the eyes. And in such experience, we begin to learn of what our seeing is capable, beyond what nature and social culture have so far validated.

Pablo Picasso challenged many of the conventions: with paintings that are representational but present their subjects in multiple simultaneous perspectives; with paintings that make their representations ambiguous by delineating them in ways that readily reduce them to appear as if they were almost nothing more than a flat design, portraits composed in a pattern of fanciful lines and colorful shapes; and with paintings that are representational, but oscillate between flat two-dimensional configurations and hints of three-dimensionality. These works remind us that the character of our vision is not predetermined, and that there are ways we can change how we see the world. They open up new possibilities for us that might serve to get us out of the spell of the *Gestell*.

Jasper Johns, going beyond the paradoxical matter-of-factness in paintings such as his famous presentations of the American flag, challenged conventions in representation and framing while also renouncing the expressive gesturing in Abstract Expressionism. Later, however, in a large gray-toned canvas titled *In Memory of My Feelings* (1961), he allowed himself to make expressive gestures; but these gestures were not only free of representation but also defying the formation of a figure-ground structure, giving the eyes of the beholder no possible perspective to see with. Moreover, attaching hinges to the quadrants of the canvas and hanging a fork and spoon from the top of the painting, the artist compels the beholder to disengage and remain "outside" the work, acknowledging its inhospitable flatness and materiality despite the seductive warmth of the predominant gray.

Foremost among others, Mark Rothko intensified these attributes, creating surfaces with solid regions and bands of color that completely exclude any expressive gestures. And yet, the regions of color have a vibrancy that draws the viewer into an interactive relation with the work in which there is a hyper-reflexive oscillation and reversibility engaging viewer and painting. Commenting on the deep affinities between Rothko's color-field paintings and Morton Feldman's music, critic Alex Ross noted that, "around 1950, both turned toward an ethereal form of abstraction, avoiding the more hectic modernisms of the period. The painter applied himself to opaque fields of color, windows to otherness and nothingness. The composer reduced his language to isolated notes and chords, letting one sound die away before the next arose."[27] In their works of interpretation, Abstract Minimalism can actually become all the more evocative, all the more expressive, by renouncing and abandoning the traditional forms of expressiveness. Eliminating all distractions, it is an art that cuts to the essence. In the beholder's engagement with the Minimalism of color-field paintings, that engagement, deeply affecting the beholder's sense of bodily presence, can dissolve the structural separation that normally exists between the painting and beholder's embodiment, reducing it to the oneness of a pure feeling of encompassing color—a new experience of color beyond subject and object.[28]

The subject and object structure can also be challenged by paintings that radically deconstruct traditional forms of representation. Willem de Kooning painted a series of works representing his spouse; but by the time he transformed her in the style of Abstract Expressionism, she was not only virtually unrecognizable; she was no longer an independent being: her being, her bodily presence, had been fragmented, deconstructed, and dissolved, distorted and broken up by the willfulness of the painterly gestures in order to invite us, the spectators, to reconstruct her visibility, compelling us to engage with the resistant facticity of the paint. She disappears into the chaos of shapes and colored patches. It is the artist's way of involving us in the process of painting. The work invites us to struggle ourselves with the paint and its tracing of the brush's gestures, attentive to the surface of the canvas as the movements of our gaze gradually let the woman in her integrity emerge into visibility from the agitation and contingency of the paint. It is only in this hyper-reflexivity that the image appears, as if miraculously coming to life out of the paint. There is here not only an *ontic* disclosure in the moment of recognition, when the woman emerges from the puzzle of fragments; there is also an *ontological* disclosure, as the essence of painting itself and as such comes to light, to be seen as indicating, or intimating, beyond the ontic disclosure, the truth of being: disclosiveness as such.

Another Post-Modern device creating visual hyper-reflexivity involves collages, photographs, and paintings in which there are discernible traces of layers of meaning-formation, pictorial meanings superimposed on or subordinated to other pictorial meanings, as in the hermeneutics of a palimpsest, obscuring or resisting clarity and certainty in the experience of vision, while enriching the event of meaning even in the presence of absence. I have in mind here works by Gerhard Richter, Anselm Kiefer, Robert Rauschenberg, Cy Twombly, and Julie Mehretu. Such works of art conceal more than they freely reveal, compelling viewers to question their engagement of vision and struggle with the urge to know and understand, recognizing their own role in the visual construction of an interpretation making sense of the pictorial configurations.

In keeping with Heidegger's deeper, ontological conception of "truth" as *aletheia* underlying, or grounding, truth-as-correctness, according to which there is an inevitable interplay of concealment and unconcealment, the inseparability of presence and absence, I am reminded of Walter Benjamin's deeply insightful essay on Goethe's *Elective Affinities*, in which he says,

> If one views the growing work as a burning funeral pyre, then the commentator stands before it like a chemist, the critic like an alchemist. Whereas, for the former, wood and ash remain the sole objects of his analysis, for the latter only the flame itself preserves an enigma: that of what is alive.[29]

One of the strategies that artist Alberto Burri, a major poet in the *Arte Povera* Movement in Italy, deployed in some of his works involved setting a controlled fire to the art, burning a part or parts of the surface: reminding us not only of the vulnerability and concealment of the material, the substance of the art, but also of our own limitations and vulnerabilities, while at the same time exalting, and symbolically purifying, the work of art, preserving the sublimity of the enigma—and, as Rilke perhaps would have understood it, a terrible, tragic beauty.[30]

In Burri's abstract compositions, some using collages of burlap pieces attached to a wooden support, others using thick applications of paint, the burnt material is the trace, the vestige, of the flame of creative inspiration, redeeming, as it were, what our eyes do not want to behold: the world's enduring poverty and destitution, violence and war, that the work refuses to ignore. These traumatized works, with their burns and cracks, are like a cracked mirror, drawing vision into a process of hyper-reflexivity, imparting a sense of the trauma.

§5

Venturing back into historical time, we will discover, perhaps with some surprise, that there are some important historical precursors that likewise challenged habits and conventions in quite Modernist ways, making that challenge to the truth of painting in the painting itself. We can find irrefutable versions of hyper-reflexivity in both the Italian and the Northern Renaissance. One version involves playing with the frame and its peculiar duplicity. Thus, for instance, some of the essentialist challenges in Modernist art already appeared, though more playfully than challenging, in Sandro Botticelli's *Young Man Holding a Roundel* (late 1470s) and Michel Sittow's *Portrait of a Gentleman* (ca. 1520), where the frame appears as both frame and window, and in Frans Hals's *Portrait of a Man* (1614–1615), where the painter positions the man inside an oval frame, but paints the man's right hand extending outside that frame, creating thereby a certain paradoxical play ambiguating and challenging the enframing and our assumptions about the difference between reality and representation. The man that we thought was a representation in a painting suddenly breaks out of the frame as if he came to life. A similar play for the eyes appears in Philippe de Champagne's *Portrait of Arnauld d'Andilly* (1650), in which the artist paints a wooden frame around the man and places the man's right hand outside that frame. These paintings *play* with the convention of framing; but this play is mere play: it is not taken seriously as a *challenge* to enframing. That is the difference between then and now.

Equally fascinating is a different version of hyper-reflexivity, this time in the intricate dialectic of mirroring taking place both within the painting itself and in relation to us, its viewers. Well-known, of course, is *Las Meninas* (1656) by Diego Veláquez: a painting in which the artist has not only painted himself looking out at us, but has pictured the infanta looking at us with guileless curiosity while the dwarfen lady-in-waiting on the right is also looking at us; and, as if that weren't enough to capture our attention and gaze, the artist shows a courtier standing in a doorway far in the background, looking into the room. A metaphor he is, too, as a reflection of our own curiosity. Finally, there is, on an easel in the background, a mirror image of the king and queen as they appear in the painting, looking directly out of their position in the mirror. So many crossings and double-crossings of curious, inquiring eyes looking at us, the viewers of the painting, questioning our attention, our motives, our perception, the character of our gaze. What do we see? What do we imagine *them* to see in *us*? In a historically singular way, the painting pulls us into a complex dialectic of hyper-reflexivity.

In the Renaissance of Northern Europe, as in Italy, there are some truly wonderful instances of the dialectic involving the presence of a mirror that complicates the viewer's experience. In Lukas Furtenagel's *The Painter Hans Burgkmair and His Wife Anna* (1529), currently in the Kunsthistorisches Museum, Vienna, we see the couple looking out at us. Anna is holding up a mirror that reflects two skulls, not Anna and her husband in the flesh of life. The mirror, though, is just a creation in paint. Everything in this painting reminds us that we are seeing only a painting, only an interpretation, while at the same time claiming to present the truth in, and of, that couple. On the side of the mirror there is written a maxim: "Erkenn dich selbst" ("Know thyself"). But the significance of the maxim only becomes manifest when we read the words written at the top-right corner of the painting: "Such were both our forms; in the mirror, nothing but this." Nothing but skeletons: Being unto death, Heidegger's interpretation of human existence as *Sein-zum-Tode*. The gazes of this couple are asking us whether we really know ourselves—know ourselves, that is, in our vulnerability and mortality.

The dialectic of crossing and doubling of gazes can be experienced in the paintings of some other Northern painters: Jan Gossaert and Rogier van der Weyden come to mind here. In the latter's *Saint Luke Drawing the Virgin* (1435–1440), kept in the Boston Museum of Fine Arts, we glimpse from a side angle a sheet of paper on which St. Luke has sketched the head of the Virgin. But Mary's actual presence is testified to only by the painting—a painting which makes it necessary for us to recognize that her presence for the painter is only taking place in the fiction of a painting. Our trust in the truth of the image, the representation, is compelled to come into question. *Our* trust—not, of course, that of the painter's own time. In Post-Modernism, this "truth" is problematized in a way that it was not in the world that originally received the works of painting. And yet, for the painters themselves and their patrons, the play of mirrors in their paintings was hardly a mere mannerism. In Jan Gossaert's very mannered, almost baroque version of *St. Luke Painting the Virgin* (1515–1525), kept in the Kunsthistorisches Museum, Vienna, we see the artist, St. Luke, drawing Mary and the baby Jesus. Again, a painter is staging the scene of his painting. But his eyes are almost closed, and Mary and Child appear enveloped in a cloud. Behind him an angel hovers, suggesting his divine inspiration for evoking them in imagination and reproducing that inner vision on paper. But the actual artist here is not St. Luke but Jan Gossaert, painting both St. Luke and Mary with Jesus. There is, in this staging, both arrogance and humility: arrogance in painting into visibility what has withdrawn into invisibility and cannot be made actually present, humility in showing an angel guiding his hand. Gossaert is not claiming to be painting Mary, but only copying St. Luke. There is, therefore, a certain turn in the history of painting, whereby the painter puts himself in the painting, showing himself in the act of drawing and painting. This revolutionary turn, breaking away from the Byzantine period and the Middle Ages, where the painter behind the art never appears to spoil the illusion, shows itself to be a significant moment in the historical development of subjectivity, akin in a way to Cartesian subjectivism. But paradoxically—from a philosophical point of view—these Renaissance paintings, both North and South, are not shy about painting human and divine bodies: the body that appeared in its sensuous glory in ancient Greek statues has finally reemerged, after ages of repression, in the Humanism of Renaissance art.

Let me mention now another instance of Late Modern art, also from a period well before Modernist art as a movement challenging the inherited conventions. We cannot neglect here the great artist Édouard Manet, who painted a number of canvases, notably *Le Déjeuner sur L'herbe* (1863) and *Olympia* (1865), works that, although representational, unnervingly emphasize, using unnaturally sharp delineation, the flatness of the representation on the canvas, depriving our gaze of the expected illusion of three-dimensional reality. This was, historically considered, a stunning revolt. But although his contemporaries were shocked and disconcerted, the significance of the flatness was not understood and appreciated at the time of its first appearance.

In the strictly Modernist works, the hyper-reflexivity initially turns the work on themselves, making themselves the content, as in the Kantian paradigm of self-interrogation and self-exploration; but, as I have tried to show, in many Modern-period works, and even some from much earlier centuries, there is at least a certain degree of reflexivity: paintings directed toward an exchange of gazes with the spectator, inviting us to get in touch with the nature and character of our vision—what we see and how we are seeing it. What habits, what assumptions, are we bringing into the encounter with paintings intended for our experience—our adventure—with vision?

§6

Minimalism, rebelling against representational art and all painterly effects, the corresponding artifice in painting, working mostly on the creation of objects—things—such as we encounter, or could encounter, in the course of our everyday lives, works in its own way through hyper-reflexivity. Reduced and simplified though it is, eliminating all distractions, it is a form of art that does demand our lingering presence with it, and a rigorous, concentrated attention—an attentiveness (not only *Aufmerksamkeit* but also *Besinnung*) that normally such seemingly self-evident "things" do not receive. Instead of exciting and agitating vision, overloading our eyes with things to look at, as in representational art, or stirring and demanding endless exploratory movement, as in Abstract Expressionism, Minimalism offers a minimum of provocations and distractions, encouraging a serene gaze, a slowed-down, more meditative approach, letting the beholding open up to receive and absorb what presents itself. In Minimalist color-field paintings, the coloring is simplified, intensifying the vibration and resonance to be felt in the presence of color; and in the objects Minimalism makes, our attention is concentrated on the ordinary things of our world that, since we habitually take them for granted or reduce them to their utility, their functionality, we never really look at and see. Judd's Minimalist cubes and boxes, basic in their simplicity and purity, can cleanse and refresh our vision, encouraging an ontological experience in terms of the truth of being. And the attentiveness into which such art draws us can become an overwhelming experience of longing—a longing for something as yet unknown, but conveying the sense of clearing out the unnecessary clutter in our lives, making way for a redeeming of the promise in human existence.

Did you ever look at a box and find yourself gazing at it in a contemplative mood, so that you began to see the box *as* a box, taking in its what-it-is and getting a vividly lucid sense of its essence, its very being? For all its literalism, its reduction to bare particularity, even Minimalism can encourage a dialectic of hyper-reflexivity. What do we see in a thing? How do we look at a box by Judd differently from how we look at a box that held apples from the orchard?

Marcel Duchamp's 1912 copy of a urinal, which he called *Fountain*, was the work of a true iconoclastic revolutionary, determined to end the domination of art intended solely for the eye's entertainment, it could be said to have inaugurated Minimalism and served as the inspiration for Andy Warhol's reiteration of Campbell Soup cans and Donald Judd's meticulously crafted cubes and boxes.

Minimalism also emerged in what we could still call "paintings," despite their radical break, not only with representation, but with all the conventions involved in traditional painting. I am thinking, for instance, of Sol LeWitt's *Wavy Lines in Black* and the numerous color-field paintings: Ellsworth Kelly's *Red Yellow Blue II*, Robert Ryman's *Untitled (Orange Painting)*, Barnett Newman's 1951 *Cathedra*, Mark Rothko's 1954 *Royal Red and Blue* and his 1956 *Orange Red Yellow*, and Ad Reinhardt's 1963 painting covering the entire surface of the canvas in an abyssal black. In Rothko's two canvases, almost translucent washes of color seem to float in the air, as if detached from the canvas, teasing the viewer's eyes. The Minimalist color-field movement really began much earlier, though, with the paintings of Kazimir Malevich's 1915 *Black Square* and *Orange Square* and his 1918 *White on White*. These colored paintings eliminated the painterly gesture so powerfully present, for example, in van Gogh; and they eliminated representation, compelling full, lingering attention to the phenomenology of vision.

In *Mountains and Sea* (1952), a historically important painting, Helen Frankenthaler used the color-stain technique she invented and continued to experiment with in making other color-field paintings, sometimes with abstract traces of figuration and landscape. See, for example, her increasingly effective movement, from the glorious Abstract Expressionism of *Painted on 21st Street* (1950), using oil, sand, stain, and plaster of Paris and combining stain effects with applications here and there of thick heavy dabs and strokes of paint, to *Barbizon* (1971), *Sentry* (1976), and her powerfully evocative *Shippan Point: Twilight* (1980). These works, creating startling interactions among loosely formed colors, shapes, and textures, encourage attention to the vibrancy and vitality of color, changing before one's very eyes from moment to moment as our gaze, in belonging, interacts with them. If a box is not just a box, and a soup can is not just a soup can, so black is not just black and red is not just red. We are learning to look and see in new ways—and to see familiar things in unfamiliar appearances. This deliberate attempt to *avoid* hyper-reflexivity is nevertheless far from innocent, uncanny enchantment, since even an all-over black canvas compels a hyper-reflexive challenge to continue looking, but now with a heightened awareness of one's looking, as different shadings of black slowly begin to reveal themselves to the lingering eyes. If they do nothing else, at least these canvases of pure color teach one the rewards of patient gazing. And the ultimate reward is, I suggest, the experience of the hermeneutical phenomenology, as the different tones and shades of color appear and disappear, vibrating and shimmering in tune with the tension and movement in the viewer's eyes.

In "A Child's View of Color" (1914), Benjamin reflected on the difference between how children and adults experience color.

> The colorism of children's drawings proceeds from brightness. The particular and highest transparency of color is pursued, and there is no relation to form, surface or concentration of space. Pure seeing is not directed toward space and the object, but to a coloring that appears in the highest degree objective, but not spatially objective.[31]

And, as Howard Caygill notes,

> The concentration of seeing in colour dissolves not only the opposition between form and matter, but also the collateral distinction between a formative subject—the one who forms and inscribes—and that which is formed or inscribed. Benjamin puts this dissolution of the subject and object opposition in several ways: "I see" is to say I perceive and also "it looks" and "The look of colours and their being seen is the same: that is to say, the colours see themselves."[32]

Damien Hirst's recent very large flat paintings offer similar rewards. I have in mind his series titled *Veil of Hidden Meaning*, and in particular, a 2017 work to which he gave the intriguing title *Veil of Logic*. His project began with very large dots of many colors seemingly positioned at random, though intricately interacting with one another in ways that do create some figuration; but as the project developed, the dots got smaller and smaller, eventually becoming an animated scattering of mere dabs of color with flakes of gold brilliantly vibrating here and there and defying any attempt to impose a perspective on them. Would Heidegger, recalling Hegel's words about the death of art, have been appalled, lamenting in melancholy nostalgia what the history of painting had come to? Or would he have been intrigued and pleasured, looking at paintings intended to give viewers a vigorous hermeneutical experience of color and figuration?

Commenting on Klee's paintings, Heidegger said, "Darkness is something that in a quite specific way, lets things be seen."[33] This is, I suggest, an allusion to the figure/ground *Gestalt*, as well as to the dynamic interaction, or *aletheic* interplay, between concealment and unconcealment that is involved in the presencing, the appearing, of all beings that enter the field of our clearing. In the context of visual perception, "being" would thus refer to the clearing, the dynamic ground that surrounds the thing in focus, giving way to its figurative sway while also receding and withdrawing into the darkness of self-concealment. In references interpreting Heidegger's invocations of "ground," too many scholars have neglected embodied perceptual experience, seeing and hearing, thereby unnecessarily promoting lofty metaphysical interpretations. The importance of recognizing the figure/ground *Gestalt* is that, following out the implications of Heidegger's critique of our contemporary Western world as a world in which the *Gestalt* in perception, in seeing and hearing, has suffered the imposition of a process of reification and degradation that he calls the *Gestell*, the historicity of our perception, hence its contingency, its mutability, becomes manifest, overcoming any lingering sense of fatalism. Heidegger struggled to overcome (*überwinden*) or deconstruct the metaphysics of transcendental grounds; but the modest source of inspiration for such grounds, unrecognized and unacknowledged, namely, the figure/ground formation in perception, gets compellingly deconstructed in Jackson Pollock's revolutionary canvases, with paint dripped, spattered and poured, creating amorphous stains and lines crossing and swerving and encircling, and where, in consequence, the ground is repeatedly destabilized, suddenly shifting in keeping with the solicitations that engage the viewer's attention.

In Merleau-Ponty's phenomenology, the *Gestalt* is shown to emerge from a primordial, prereflective experience in which the ground (background) has no objective identity apart from the figure that eventually comes into the focus of attention. Thus, the metaphysics of transcendental groundings gets no validation from Pollock's art, or from Merleau-Ponty's phenomenology of perception. Neither familiar with Pollock's revolutionary canvases, nor with Merleau-Ponty's phenomenology, Heidegger missed a way to interpret his bold, but still very abstract philosophical formulations, observing their operation in the sensuousness of paint playing with the visible and the invisible, and in the very concreteness of the flesh, where a dynamic oscillating reciprocity and reversibility is always taking place in the intertwining belonging-together of *Da-sein* and being, a relationship that is originally pre-ontological.

§7

A very different dialectic of hyper-reflexivity is at work in many art installations: Richard Serra's monumental rusted steel structures; Louise Bourgeois's strangely cluttered "rooms"; Rachel Whiteread's various structures and installations; the stuffy attic "collection room" in Oslo, created by Ilya and Emilia Kabakov, who filled display cases with obsessively collected detritus from daily life; and Doris Salgado's long and deep crack made in the concrete floor of the Tate Modern in London. These creations speak to our eyes; but more significantly, as we interact with them, and in some works actually immerse ourselves in them, or enter into them, they address our bodies—and our *sense* of embodiment, making us aware, for instance, of our spatial presence, our smallness or heaviness or balance or disorientation or claustrophobia or vulnerability. In these installations, we find ourselves questioned, challenged, undergoing experiences that are felt in our bodies, but in which the source of that experience can be located neither in the subjectivity of the body nor in the objectivity of the work of art, because it is the effect of a site-specific dialectical interaction in which the so-called properties of the work of art are emergent, hence also contingent and variable, in correspondence to the singular response that they happen to solicit in the individual engaging with the installation at a certain moment. These installations make us take part, with and through our embodiment, in the *event* of their presence. Installations are events, performances in which we become participants. They *become* events of art when we get dialectically engaged with them. In *our* presence, the installations come alive, so to speak: they are no longer merely inert things; they become hyper-reflective, somewhat like mirrors or thermometers, engaging our hyper-reflexive bodily response-loop. Emerging from an immersive experience with some installation art, our bodies—and our felt sense of our bodies—can undergo astonishing felt transformations, reminding us that what we take to be solid, permanent, and necessary might not always confirm the assumptions we depend on in everyday life. Installations play with, or perhaps wrestle with, our bodies, the sensations and feelings we are accustomed to; they compel us to shift out of the detachment of vision and get in touch with our experience of embodiment. Such experience refutes the representations—mind and body, subject and object—argued for in rationalism and empiricism; but it confirms Heidegger's "existential" representation, in which the human body, no longer the enclosed substance of metaphysics, its ontological "intentionalities" extending out like the roots of a tree, no longer living in the peculiar solitude and detachment of vision, is thrown-open, exposed, living interactively and interdependently in the world. In such experience, something of the body of ontological understanding can emerge.

§8

Bearing in mind Heidegger's scattering of reflections on phenomena of light and the clearing that opens a space for light to make things visible, I want to call attention to two outstanding artists working with phenomena of light: Dan Flavin, whose early work, *Diagonal of Personal Ecstasy* (1963), and later mature work, a 1992 installation at the New York Guggenheim Museum, use light as both medium and meaning-content of the art; and James Turrell, whose works include *Light Projections* (1967) and *After Effect* (2022), exploring at once the materiality of light and its evanescence, its shimmering evasions of objectification, destabilizing the "enduring presence" that metaphysics has always idolized. These works attempt to show us that our ways of perception, hence too the very *being* of the beings we perceive, always involve historically acquired cultural habits that can be questioned and changed. How might the human species need to reform and adapt in order to continue surviving on this planet? As the electric lights of our cities increase and expand their reach, the light from the stars becomes invisible. But these artworks can remind us not to take for granted our lights and the natural lights of the cosmos; and they can encourage us to contemplate the character of the clearing (*Lichtung*), the ontological dimension of being that makes room for such light.

Heidegger unquestionably wanted us to experience the belonging-together of *our* being and being itself, *Sein* and *Mensch-sein*. One might consider thinking of the relation (*Bezug*) as a collaboration, but without attributing agency to being. I can think of no better way to experience that phenomenology than to encounter paintings and installations that demand reciprocal performative hyper-reflexivity in order to understand them or appreciate their play with the conventions that govern our sense of reality—of being.

By undertaking a critique of the ontological consequences of the psychosocial pathologies in our habitual ways of listening, looking at things, feeling and handling them, Heidegger was implicitly encouraging us to reflect critically on these ways. Modern, Modernist, and Post-Modern paintings offer a rich resource for engaging in such reflexivity. But he did not recognize this resource in the visual arts. Regarding these arts, Heidegger was surprisingly silent. Van Gogh's Post-Impressionist painting of the old peasant shoes did stir him to talk about earth and world. And he apparently liked what he saw of the paintings by Paul Cézanne. But we have no significant commentary on Cézanne's innovative variation on Impressionism; and it is not surprising that there is nothing from his pen on Jackson Pollock,[34] though in different ways both artists painted with a deep, bodily felt attunement to a dimension of bodily experience—in Merleau-Ponty's phenomenology it is called "the pre-objective"[35]—that challenges the philosophical paradigm that recognizes in worldly experience only a structure of subject and object: precisely that stable, solidified structure against the primacy of which Heidegger vehemently and persistently argued, for example, in "The Principle of Identity." In viewing with genuine attention works by Cézanne, Matisse, Klee, Kandinsky, Pollock, and others, the experience does not bear the sense of something already given, objectively given, but rather has the felt sense of something in the process of being achieved—something coming forth, as if for the first time, into visibility.[36]

§9

Lest we lose our sense of what is at stake in this brief summary of art and its historical adventures, I would like to say in conclusion that, in the light of Heidegger's critique of the *Gestell* that, imposing its regime on our experience of being, is increasingly drawing our life-world into a time of inhumanity, distress, and devastation, my primary concern was (1) to observe how our art is challenging the prevailing character of our perception, and challenging also the prevailing character of our embodiment in touching, handling, moving about, and spatializing, and accordingly, (2) to argue that this reflexivity in art gives us some reason to hope for a future different from the present, insofar as this future for which Heidegger wants us to prepare is one that would require a great transformation, not only in our understanding, but in our lives in regard to being, and the being of beings. This new future is possible only if our ways of looking and seeing, listening and hearing, touching and holding are transformed. Art is crucial for showing a way to such transformation.

As we change, our relation to being changes; and that means changes in our world. However, despite so many changes taking place in our world, everything we cherish in our world is haunting, since things bear, even in their corruptness, the message of a lost future: ghostlike traces of the ancient promise of a worldly redemption that is still lost. And some of our most engaging contemporary art and literature will remind us of all that remains to be achieved. I experience Paul Klee's enigmatic work *Tod und Feuer* (1940); Anselm Kiefer's *Merkaba* (2010), with burned books, ash, and a crashed airplane; and Alberto Burri's *Combustion* series of traumatized artworks, skillfully exposed to fire, to be very much in this spirit. Uncanny forms of iconoclasm dedicated with the deepest love to the redeeming of life in all its manifestations.

§10

I would have enjoyed knowing Heidegger's thoughts about the paintings and woodcut prints of Albrecht Dürer, the Isenheim altarpiece by Matthias Grünewald, *Adam and Eve* by the Elder Lucas Cranach, the Romantic paintings of Caspar David Friedrich, and the paintings of the Blaue Reiter and the Vienna Secession. However, he gave us no philosophical ruminations to illuminate them. He seems to have had a livelier attraction to some contemporary works of sculpture: somewhat surprising, I think, inasmuch as such works demand a full-bodied response to their presence. And I would especially have liked to hear him discuss the two outstanding contemporary German painters, Anselm Kiefer and Gerhard Richter, both of whom, not well-known during his lifetime, worked though hermeneutical palimpsests in paint and other materials to register, among other events and themes, the ultimately unrepresentable horror and trauma in Germany's embrace of war and genocide. I think it is unfortunate that Heidegger's engagement with the arts was so strongly influenced by Nietzsche and his own deeply irresistible metaphysical impulses. With more sustained exposure to art, and more felt reflection, especially on late modern and contemporary art, Heidegger might perhaps have recognized in some of that experience with art the emerging of an ontological understanding of our existence for the possibility and enactment of which he dedicated a lifetime of extraordinary thought.

§11

As long as we human beings survive, there is still some promise and hope to be sustained by contemporary works of art that, in their various enigmatic and disquieting forms of conscience and revolt, compel critical self-reflection and remind us of our troubled, languishing aspirations. And it is ultimately from the socially shared felt sense of these aspirations that the body of ontological understanding must find its way to emerge. For the sake of our humanity. And for the sake of this planet Earth.

Chapter 6

Insight into Being

On Heidegger's "Einkehr in das Ereignis"[1]

Though the time be long, / that which is true / will come to pass.
(Lang ist / Die Zeit, es ereignet sich aber / Das Wahre.)
　　　　　　　—Friedrich Hölderlin, "Mnemosyne"

One's destination is never a place, but a new way of seeing things.
　—Henry Miller, *Big Sur and the Oranges of Hieronymus Bosch*[2]

§1

I am venturing here a substantially new interpretation of Heidegger's key word *Ereignis*, frequently translated as "event" and interpreted either as (1) an "event of being," or as (2) an "event of appropriation." Both interpretations are in fact needed; each one, I suggest, contributes something crucial to our understanding in regard to the conduct of our lives. (1) As an event of being, the *Ereignis* is an experience of the that-there-is (*das "Es gibt"*). Consequently, the *Ereignis* in this sense is an experience of being as setting the conditions of meaningfulness that make possible the appearing of what is, hence an experience of being as what Heidegger will call the clearing. Thus, for instance, it is an experience of being as the ground or field of perception that makes possible the presencing and absencing, visibility and invisibility of beings, the figures that appear in the perceptual *Gestalt*, emerging from and withdrawing into a context or ground (GA 9: 337/PM 256). But (2), the *Ereignis* is also an experience of being that appropriates us, stirring us to get in more intimate touch with the nature of our connectedness to being and with what that singular disposition of connectedness demands of us, namely: (1) work on ourselves in a process of *propriation*, or self-understanding, in the course of which (2) we come to understand that, and how, our connectedness to being constitutes, as Heidegger argues, our imperative "responsibility for being." *The Principle of Identity* (GA 11: 40n53). Such is the interpretation for which, in this chapter, I will be elaborating an argument. What this responsibility for being means, what kind of engagement it calls for, needs to be made clear and convincing.

†

When Heidegger writes (GA 14: 49–50) of "that which sends" as "the *Ereignis*" (*das Schickende als das Ereignis*), he is giving us a very abbreviated, condensed formulation that can be very misleading. What makes possible all forms of appearing is the clearing (*Sein, Seyn*). And that occurs through the appropriation of our ex-istence, by and in the experience of the event of being: an appropriation challenging our ex-istence to become what it in essence already is, namely, a thrown-openness for clearing. So, what our ex-istence (*Da-sein*) as the clearing makes possible ("sends" or "gives") is the appearing or presencing of beings within the world of our experience. The *Ereignis* is an *event* of being that appropriates us *Dasein* (takes hold of us and lays claim to us, calling us) to become aware of what we are in our deepest, most fulfilled nature (hence are already and yet also, not yet), namely, *Da-sein*, thrown-open situating sites, openings, clearings, for the presencing of beings that are then able to appear in those clearings, "sent" or "given," so to speak, by, in, and through those clearings our presence opens in the world. In our experiencing of this appropriation, the event of being claims (summons) us not only to become what we are in a process of propriation, but also to take responsibility for maintaining the openness of the clearing as its only guardians—the sole guardians, that is, of being, that is, the being and meaning of beings. The *Einkehr in das Ereignis* therefore refers to our entering into the experience of the event and taking up its appropriation, its call and claim, in a process of propriation that, in disclosing the nature of our connection to being, enables us to recognize and take on our responsibility for being.

I argue that, in the history of philosophy, the event, understood as an insight into being itself, set in motion the inception of a philosophical discourse within which we are still thinking, and that, inspired and guided by his philosophy of history, Heidegger was hoping our own reflections on being itself could likewise set in motion preparations for another inception. I maintain the claim that, whereas, for the early Greek philosophers, their insight was an experience of awe and wonder, for us of today that insight sets in motion a turn "inward" that puts *us* in question and stirs us to acknowledge our responsibility for being in a time when being is under assault. At stake, for Heidegger, is the destiny of our humanity and our world. Hence, our highest appropriation to responsibility.

> In the age of history in which beyng illuminates its more original beginning, the selfhood of the self of historical mankind is the responsibility [*Verantwortung*] of the response [*Antwort*] which prepares the word of language [*das Wort der* Sprache] for the claim [*Anspruch*] of the event. "Responsibility" is meant here not in a "moral" [*moralisch*] sense, but rather, with respect to the event [*ereignishaft*] and as related to the response. (GA 71: 155/E 134)

We human beings fully and properly belong (*gehören*) to the event of being insofar as we *enter* into our experience (this is the *Einkehr in das Ereignis*), responding and thereby corresponding (as in an *Entsprechen*) to the claim (*Anspruch*) we experience of the event. This claim is an appropriation we would experience as coming from our own nature (our *proprium*, as Thomas Sheehan calls it), an enowning of our essential nature as thrown-open. But in entering into the experience of our relation to being, we learn that the appropriating claim comes from our *being in that relation*. Heidegger argues that each of us, as a *Da-sein*, bears a responsibility (*Verantwortlichkeit*) to answer (*antworten*) that claim, even though it may unsettle us, challenging us to question, in light of our recognition that we have necessarily, and always already, belonged in relation to being, just who in truth we are as *Da-sein*. Two years earlier, in his 1955 text "What Is Philosophy?" (GA 11: 5–26), Heidegger already made this argument quite clear and compelling, moving from (1) our intimate relation to being, which he describes as a vibrantly oscillating belonging (*schwingende, schwebende Gehörigkeit*), and which can actually be seen and heard (*gehört*) to (2) *our responsibility for being*. But the phenomenology needs some further elaboration in regard to this *ability* to be co-responsive. And that, in turn, should draw us into reflecting on the nature of "our most fundamental [bodily] disposition" (GA 20: 209) and the "gentle law" (*Ge-setz*) of ontological correspondence and attunement that it carries (GA 12: 248/OWL 128). More on this matter later.

Responsibility for being presupposes an understanding of what is at stake. In *Between Past and Future*, Hannah Arendt praises Herodotus for his sense of historical responsibility and his courage to say, of what is, that it is, and of what is not, that it is not.

> No human world destined to outlast the short lifespan of mortals within it will ever be able to survive without people willing to do what Herodotus was perhaps the first to undertake consciously [in the recording of historical truth]—namely, λεγειν τα οντα, to say what is. No permanence, no perseverance in existence, can even be conceived without people willing to testify to what is and what appears to them because it is.[3]

In his final poetic work "The Golden Dot," Gregory Corso attempts to think the event of being as inception,[4] finding simple words to evoke, beyond our experience of a reification and reduction that ends in nihilism, the unfolding of the cosmological mystery.

> *This is how it happened:*
> *At the end*
> *everything that was*
> *dwindled into a dot;*
> *the dot exploded into the void*
> and the beginning began again—

Like Rilke, he understood the poetry of being, fearlessly saying what is and what is not, to be a dangerous art. In Heidegger's thought-poems and philosophical meditations, courageous ventures of insight into the event of being, its history past and its endless promise are gathered into words that challenge us to assume responsibility for the conditions that we have wrought.—If only, after the fact, *nachträglich*, he had been moved by empathy and remorse, and had found the courage to acknowledge—and take responsibility for—his egregious moral errancy in supporting Hitler's National Socialism!

§2

Using Heidegger's words, what is proposed for thought in this essay is the "Einkehr in das Ereignis" (GA 14: 51/OTB 42; GA 14: 50/OTB 41; GA 15: 390/FS 75): our entering, as in a flash of insight, into an ontologically significant experience, an experience of the very facticity of being; an uncanny experience of being itself, being as such, that also, at the same time, should engage us in a reflective return to ourselves, a process of *propriation*, or enownment, and dedication, or commitment (*Zu-eignung*), in which, in the most fundamental way, we question who we are and need most deeply to become, and find ourselves called to recognize the essential nature of our relationship to being as a relationship of belonging-together (*Zusammengehören*), hence mutual appropriation (*einander übereignet*), so that we are accordingly called to take on responsibility for the historical and contemporary character of that relationship (GA 11: 37–42/ID 29–33). If we care about the beings in our world, beings that include us humans, then we must care about their being, and for that reason we need to protect and preserve being itself, which is today the object of neglect or denial.

The *Einkehr* that takes place in the *Ereignis* is thus in two ways a "return": it is, first of all, a return in the sense that we are returning from our engagement with beings in the world to attend to ourselves, questioning and examining ourselves; but it is also a return from beings to being, a return to the primordial difference between beings and being, retrieving our pre-ontological, preconceptually *embodied* experience and understanding of being, an experience and understanding that we lived in during our infancy and blocked and forgot as we entered the adult social world. Returning to retrieve this *pre-ontological* understanding gives insight into that which *is*, revealing the truth about our inseparable relation to being.

For the early Greeks, the experience of being was one of wonder and awe—but also dread. They only began to understand that what stirred them to these overpowering emotions was the fact that this experience *exceeded* the bounds of the sensible: being is not intelligible in the terms we use to make sense of the beings we encounter in our world. Understanding the significance of that dimension of excess (*Übermaß*) in regard to being is, for Heidegger, a crucial step beyond the Greeks. That step is what he calls "entering into the Ereignis": entering into the event that is the experience of being in its difference from the beings that figure in our world.

Being, in each of its four senses, involves a dimension of excess. (1) Understood as that-being (the "it-is-something-that-is" and the "that-it-is"), "being" involves recognizing the changes and contingencies occurring in the world. (2) As reflectively emergent and projected in the *what-being* or essence (*Wesen, Wesung*) of beings, "being" keeps open its radical version of empiricism, emphasizing our interaction with the world. For Heidegger, "essence" is not a noun referring to an eternally immutable state of being; it is instead a verb referring to an ongoing interaction with a changing world. The *event* of being as such is inherently excessive, inherently unsettling, even capable of causing us to tremble in shock and dread, in regard to sedimented systems of sense. (3) Understood as the ecstatic presencing of things (beings) in the temporal inflections that constitute the dimensions of their temporality as past or future, "being" recognizes that presencing always takes place in an interplay of concealment and unconcealment, according to the grammatical inflections that designate forms of temporality. We never see the whole of a thing in all its temporal moments, nor in their absolute unity. We never can claim a final meaning. (4) And understood as necessary condition for the very *possibility* of such presencing, that is, as necessary condition for the very intelligibility or meaningfulness of what presences, "being" takes us beyond the situational event, the taking place of beings; not into an abstract transcendentalism, but rather into the larger context, to give thought to what Heidegger calls *Die Lichtung* (clearing), that is, the fields or contexts of intelligibility and meaning constituting the world, including its sensible, perceptual fields, in the immeasurable dimensions (*Übermaß*) of which such presencing can take place: "Being" in this sense takes us *beyond* the situational given, beyond what actually presences in such a way that we can experience the utmost *contingency* in terms of which the world itself, the *Lichtung des Seins* (GA 9: 326/PM 15–16), with its perceptual fields and situations, is given; and we can also experience concealed dimensions that expose our limitations, finitude, endings.[5]

Trying to understand this givenness of being—why is there a clearing, a world of sense and sensibility of being, why is there anything at all?—we inevitably encounter the abyss of nonbeing, an endless dimension haunting our world-order. "Being" is a summons to enter into the deepest dimensions of being in our thinking. (See GA 9: 326: "The clearing of being, and only it, is world." Also see GA 79: 51–52: "The world is . . . being itself.") The world is a theater, providing not only the given conditions and contexts of intelligibility and meaning for whatever presents itself to experience, but also a dimension of possibilities; it is the given (*geschickt*) conditions and possibilities into which every *Dasein* is thrown open and its own clearings occur. The experience of being returns our thought to ourselves in and as our vulnerable, thrown-open situated *Da-sein*: In *Walden*, Henry David Thoreau muses: "As I sit at my window this summer afternoon, hawks are circling about my clearing."⁶ In this thought, he recognizes himself—his being, his ex-istence, as a clearing. That is what he is as interactively and co-respondingly embodied in a context of meaning, vectors, and relations.

In the *Zollikon* seminars and conversations with Medard Boss, Heidegger provides further illumination on the question of the *Mensch-Sein* relation. To be sure, he says, the clearing is not possible without human ex-istence. Moreover, the human being *is* the guardian of the clearing (*der Hüter der Lichtung, des Ereignisses*), sole guardian of the event that is "the truth of being," but the human being "is not the clearing itself, not the entire clearing; nor is he [*sic*] identical (*identisch*) with the totality of the clearing as such" (ZSG: 223/ZSE 178). I *am* my essence, but I am also *other* than my essence: in some ways, more than it, in other ways less; but always other, never reducible. Phenomenologically considered, I *am* the clearing, *am* the openness my sheer presence has opened and in which I stand. But the clearing, the opening, is not reducible to me, is not related to me in the strict sense of logical identity. And that is so, even when "the world" is understood to be "my world," "my own personal world" (my *Eigenwelt*): because even then, there is an openness, hence a dimensionality of concealment, an excess of meaning, a contingency over which I can have neither knowledge nor power. Thus, the structural configuration resembles, *mutatis mutandis*, the figure/ground *Gestalt* in perception, in which the ground recedes, withdrawing into concealment as the figure of attention comes forth.

As *Da-sein*, then, that is, as thrown-open, we *are* clearings. Structurally considered, we are pre-ontologically *always already* clearings; but in terms of our lived-in experience, our self-awareness and self-understanding, we may *not yet* be—that is, may not yet experience and live ourselves as—clearings. We stand *in* these clearings, these conditions for the appearing (*Anwesung*) of that which, in some way, and to some extent, will be meaningful to us. But, although clearings *depend* on our presence, the dimensions of these clearings *cannot be reduced* to my experience, knowledge, and understanding. Hence the clearings emerge from, and cannot be totally wrested from, their dimensions of concealment; they are always open to events and entities that could exceed and distress the bounds of our understanding—perhaps to the extent of trauma. The clearings are always formed within the dimensions and conditions of a historical world: a historical world that we always find ourselves having been already given (*geschickt*), a world of clearings within which we have only very limited control. Thus, bearing this surpassing in mind, we are not, and can never be, even in our thrown-openness as *Da-sein*, in a relation of identity to the clearing: not even in control of an identity with the *meaning* of being, reducing it to a mere projection of our subjectivity. The essence of the clearing is fundamentally constituted in—that is, occurs in—the dynamic eventfulness of an inseparable togetherness connecting *Menschsein* with *Sein*, that is, with the meaning of being as it figures in the conditions necessary for experiencing the appearing, or presencing, of beings.

In "Moira" (GA 7: 257/EGT 97) and in "On the Essence of Truth" (GA 9: 194/PM 148), as well as in other texts, Heidegger needlessly turns a perfectly natural, easily recognizable phenomenon into a profound "mystery." He argues in these texts that the clearing (i.e., being understood as *aletheia*) is intrinsically hidden (*verhüllt*). This is at the very least misleading, missing the phenomenology that instantiates the figure-ground *Gestalt*. The clearing is indeed "hidden"—but in three distinctly different senses, only the first of which recognizes that the clearing is, in a way, a "mystery," "intrinsically" hidden.

> 1. We do not know why *Dasein* is thrown open, why our existence occurs as clearings. We do not know why there are clearings, conditions that make appearing, or presencing, possible, any more than we know why there is anything at all rather than nothing—or why human beings exist. We might wish, as Heidegger does, to think of this "intrinsic hiddenness" as a mystery.
>
> 2. However, the clearing is only structurally "hidden," in just the same way that the ground, or context, for the emergence of a figure in the perceptual *Gestalt* is "hidden," namely, it withdraws and recedes from focal attention as the figure emerges into attention. It is in the very nature of the clearings that our presence in the world opens and in which we stand that they cannot be made totally visible, totally present, totally known. Thus, if a clearing is made totally visible or known, it will always be a clearing taking place as a figure in a larger clearing that is not totally visible or totally known.
>
> 3. But we might also think of the clearing as we think of the ground in a *Gestalt*, namely, as a phenomenological process of

which we are commonly unaware or unmindful, until it is called to our attention.

In his eagerness to evoke an unfathomable mystery, Heidegger completely forgets the *Gestalt* formation manifest in perception, but which in fact occurs in all human experience, hence in all our clearings. The concealment that occurs in the experience of "the truth of being" is only an *epokhe*, not metaphysically absolute; it always appears in the light of unconcealment. (See GA 5: 337/254; GA 6.2: 337, 347; GA 14: 62/OTB 52.)

Perhaps nothing in Heidegger's phenomenology confirms our limitations more poignantly than the experience of hearkening, following echoes as they fade away, vanishing into the abyssal dimensions of silence. In "The End of Philosophy and the Task of Thinking," Heidegger tells us that "the clearing, the opening, is not only free for brightness and darkness [*Helle* und *Dunkel*], but also for resonance and echo [*für den Hall und das Verhallen*], for sounding and fading away of sound [*für das Tönen und das Verklingen*]" GA 14: 72/ OTB 65). In "Nature," Ralph Waldo Emerson recognizes this immeasurably vast dimension in evoking the stars of the night sky: "The stars awaken a certain reverence, because though always present, they are inaccessible; but all natural objects make a kindred impression, when the mind is open to this influence."[7] With these words, he is urging us to be open, as if in reverence, to the inaccessible, that event of being which, as Heidegger has argued, will draw us into the abyssal dimension of concealment. Hearkening to the receding of echoes slowly withdrawing into silence is one of the ways that entering into the event of being can teach us that the proper measure of our humanity is to be found in humility. There can be no safeguarding of being, hence no safeguarding of the dimension of concealment, and no appropriate responsibility for being, without that humility.

The character of the responsibility that this *Einkehr* calls for emerges from Heidegger's critique of philosophical thought, together with his corresponding critique of the modern world. It is essential to his project as I understand it that his history of philosophy be much more than historiography and much more than a logic of concept-formation; because this history is inspired and guided by a philosophy of history that, although not a teleology, onto-theology, or eschatology, is nevertheless committed by faith and hope to a redeeming of the promising historical possibilities and potentials that we find ourselves given as human beings, understanding our building and dwelling, standing on this earth under the expanse of the sky. Behind Heidegger's critical reading of the history of philosophy and his critique of our modern world, there is, especially in his postwar and later thought, a poetic vision of a better world, a better humanity, a more demanding Humanism—and a method that connects this vision to a philosophy of history that summons us to the achievement of the great task it brings to light. So "history," for Heidegger, is neither empirical (a finite succession of factual events) nor metaphysical (transcendent, transcendental): it is, rather, a narrative interpreting events in the light of faith and hope in the ongoing task, never completed, of a promising vision.

I am venturing here an interpretation of Heidegger's project. It is not my intention to claim for this interpretation that Heidegger himself would necessarily have recognized it as expressing and representing the project and task he was engaged in working out. All interpretations, like all translations, are merely hypotheses, adventures in language and thought. All that I would like to claim is, as I have indicated, that I can make good sense out of the project and convincingly defend the merits in my interpretation. I believe, moreover, that this interpretation is a reading that usefully shows the historical and contemporary significance of the *Einkehr*, the distinctive reflective turn and return that, after the 1927 publication of *Being and Time* and during the years 1936–1938, Heidegger believed it necessary to make in order to continue the bearing of his project.[8]

However, we cannot avoid noticing that Heidegger leaves his key word, *Ereignis* in considerable indeterminacy and unclarity, causing much confusion and controversy. What kind of event is it? And what is its relation to the question of being? Is it referring to a unique singular historical event, namely the pre-Socratic recognition of being itself, being as such? Is it necessarily always an inceptual event? Is it the inception of philosophical thought or an event that refers solely to a philosophical understanding of being? Does it represent a distinctive category of events, namely, events in which thought turns away, or is turned away, from beings to contemplate, or actively engage with, the fact of being? Is it an event that needs to be understood in the context of historical life in the Western world? Is it an event that only some privileged philosophers could experience? The German language requires that Heidegger speak of "*das* Ereignis." But should we, or must we, translate that into English as "*the* event," suggesting a singular, one-time event? Might we not, instead, translate his German as "event"? Might there not be *many* ontologically revelatory events? And if the ontological revelation is to determine, or attune, an entire world-epoch, must it not be an experience available to many individuals and communities?

Heidegger does tell us, however, that "the 'event' is not a simple occurrence, but that which makes any occurrence possible" (GA 14: 24/OTB 19). The event in question here, sheer happening, sheer eventfulness, is an event of givenness and withdrawal, phenomenality itself: being, presencing, itself (GA 14: 26/OTB 21; GA 65: 30/CP 24–26). The event is nothing but this eventfulness, the very essence of being. Being happens. Formulated in other terms: the *Ereignis* is the *Es gibt*, the fact that there is being, a world, rather than nothing. The ontological event that eventuated in the inception of metaphysical thought in Greece was thus an experience of being itself. But Heidegger sometimes formulates his thought in a way that is misleading, seeming to be suggesting not only that being is absolutely independent from our experience as the "It" ("Es") that "gives" or "sends" ("gibt" or "schickt"), but also that the "It" is a source and agency distinctly separate from the experience of the "giving" or "sending" (GA 14: 8–13/OTB 5–9). Richard Capobianco is one of the scholars who holds to this interpretation. But I am convinced that that is not Heidegger's position. In my understanding of Heidegger: What "gives" or "sends," making presencing—the presencing of entities, beings, entering into the field of our experience—possible is the clearing that we as thrown-open *Da-sein* are: "das Da-sein ist das je vereinzelte 'es,' das gibt, das ermöglicht, und ist das 'es gibt' " (GA 73, I: 642). Our bodily presence as *Da-sein* opens into a clearing, an open field of meaningfulness within which we experience the being, or presencing, of beings. The "giving" or "sending" refers to the fact that it is *the clearing* that does the "giving" or "sending," making the appearing of beings possible; but the particular conditions constituting the situations in which we find ourselves inform and form *how* the clearing makes our experience possible, *how* it "sends" or "gives" phenomenality, experiential presencing, to entities, beings. In its fourth sense, "being" is neither the cause of beings nor their underlying essence, but figures rather as that clearing which *enables* beings to emerge from concealment and appear for a while in some modality of presence in contexts of meaningfulness that are inherently open.

Heidegger's key word *Geschick*, the common meaning of which is "destiny," together with its various cognate and related words, all pertaining to a dispensation, a sending or giving, inevitably takes on a crucial role in Heidegger's elaboration of the history-making significance of the ontological "event" in which being itself is taken up for thought, engaging the process that, in my interpretation, is characterized as entering into the unfolding of an experience in regard to the meaning of being that summons us to come around to recognizing and understanding ourselves, and above all, our responsibilities, in terms of the dimensions constitutive of our relation to being. But the full significance of the *Einkehr* comes to light only when it is interpreted in relation to the *Geschick* that represents the destiny to be achieved, though never absolutely fulfilled, by our thoughtful exercise of freedom in the theater of history, retrieving and redeeming to some extent the promising possibilities and potentials we left behind, for the sake of a new ontological epoch in the experience and understanding of being and a renewed inception in philosophical thought.

The meaning and significance of the *Ereignis* cannot be considered apart from its relation to the *Geschick* that figures in Heidegger's philosophy of history. First of all, Heidegger's interpretation of the history of philosophy, and also his critique of the modern world, are both guided by his philosophy of history, at the center of which is his idea of the *Geschick*, a concept that oscillates irreconcilably, in this context, between suspenseful foreboding and a commitment by faith to the emerging, from within the conditions of history, of that which is promising. Second, understood as an ontological event, an event concerning the meaning of being, carrying great historical significance, the *Ereignis* concerns our appropriation of the destiny the achievement of which would most fulfil our life, dwelling on this earth as human beings. Third, working with the double meaning of the idiom "Es gibt" ("It gives . . ." and "There is . . .") which commonly asserts existence, or presence, Heidegger takes the words to refer to a "giving" or "sending"—a "dispensation" and "gift." What, then, makes this *Schickung* or *Geschick*, this "giving" or "sending," possible? The idiom suggests that an otherwise unnameable "It" ("Es") is behind what is. The appropriating event (*Ereignis*), in which the meaning of being is taken up for thought, necessitates a reflection not only on this "giving" or "sending" but also on the question of this "dispensation" itself—the world situation we are given, or granted, to live in. Can we discern, within this dispensation, that is, in the "Es gibt" of the history we are given, the possibilities for the appropriation and achievement of our destiny? What possibilities are to be discovered, retrieved and revived in the situations we are given to live in and work through? Only time will tell!

Unfortunately, Heidegger's use of the word *Geschick* lets it hover ambiguously between a philosophically innocent sense and a problematic onto-theological or metaphysical sense. (For a striking example of the latter, see GA 94: 304.) Because the German locution "Es gibt," which literally translated means "It gives," carries an idiomatic sense meaning "there is . . . ," recognizing the existence or presence of something, as in, for instance, the assertion that there is a beautiful lake nearby, Heidegger's word *Geschick* can figure in his thought not only to refer to destiny, but also simply to recognize what is given or sent (*geschickt*), namely, the given historical situations in which we find ourselves. In this second sense, merely invoking the givens of our historical situation, nothing occult or metaphysical is necessarily involved—although it could still be the case that, in what we are given to contend with, a destiny is at stake. What is problematic, however, is the interpretation that suggests or implies that a theological or metaphysical source or agency is behind the givens of history, sending or dispensing events—or perhaps giving, or sending, *the* event, *das Ereignis*. I suggest that what "gives" or "sends" is always "merely" a clearing (*Lichtung*): the opening of a world into which our presence, our ex-istence as *Da-sein*, opens. The world into which we are cast constitutes the necessary condition for the possibility of experiencing the presence of beings that engage us. (Memory and imagination can also open "worlds," clearings, within which beings can appear, "given" or "sent.")

Because of its dispensation, its givenness, the fact that it has been given (*geschickt*), the extraordinary event in which being as such is experienced needs to be thought in terms of a *Geschick*. The *Ereignis*—understood as an event of being—is a *Geschick*. But what does that mean, considering that the word refers, ambiguously, to (1) something as given or sent and (2) something to be understood as destiny? Avoiding Heidegger's temptation to think of the *Geschick* in a way that seems to invite, or at the very least, not to exclude, a theological or meta-physical interpretation, I shall argue for a reading of *Geschick* that removes it entirely from possible theological or meta-physical interpretations. Destiny does not require interpretations that transcend the world we live in. Later in this essay, we will return to think about the *Geschick*.

However, for now, I will say only that our realization and fulfilment of the *Geschick*—the meaning of our humanity as ownmost destiny—is in turn possible only insofar as we recognize, acknowledge, and understand the uncanny truth—the true nature—of our own being, namely, our thrown-openness, our situated situatedness in a world that our presence, our embodied existence as *Da-sein*, opens into. In Heidegger's terminology: Our *Befindlichkeit* as *Da-sein* is our *Geworfenheit*. And in this thrown-openness, we become, and are, sites of openness, opening into the world—its *Lichtungen*. The *Einkehr* is thus as much about who we are as human beings, that is, the character of who we are in our humanity, as it is about our experience and understanding of being, being itself, being as such, and about our experience and understanding of our *relation* to being, and consequently, too, about our *role of responsibility* in that relation. That is my argument.

§3

The word *Ereignis* is commonly understood to mean, simply, "event." But I am going to argue that, in the context of Heidegger's project, this word takes on multiple meanings. And Heidegger, I believe, was counting on our understanding this. When, in his project, the word is understood as designating something in the category of an event, *Ereignis* refers, first of all, to a singular, momentously significant history-making event, namely, the event in which, suddenly, for the first time, as with a flash of insight, some pre-Socratic philosophers ventured to turn their thought away from all the beings in their world and attempted to question and contemplate being itself, being as such. This extraordinary moment in the historical experience of thought constitutes what Heidegger will describe as the "inception" of meta-physical philosophy. But Heidegger wants to believe that another inception, another epoch in the historical experience and understanding of being is possible. So, for him, the event of being remains as the possibility of a future-making opportunity to experience differently what it means to be. In his project, the *Ereignis* is considered only as an event of being that pertains to the history and future of philosophical thought regarding the meaning of being. Richard Polt, however, extends the meaning of *Ereignis* as an event of being even further, arguing that traumatic experiences in which our settled sense of what and how things are as they are is exceeded and unsettled can, and do, often happen to us in our everyday life. This challenge to our mind-set is not necessarily history-making, ontologically inceptual experience, but it is a phenomenon we need to recognize.

In his *Tractatus Logico-Philosophicus*, Ludwig Wittgenstein argued that, "Not *how* the world is, is the mystical, but rather *that* it is."[9] Philosophy in the Western world, as Heidegger noted, began in an extraordinary experience of astonishment and wonder—that there is (*daß es gibt*) being rather than nothing. And we, too, can still experience in wonder the fact that there is a world of beings instead of nothing. Why are there beings, why is there a world, a cosmos, rather than nothing? What *is* being? What do we mean when we say of something that it *is*, attributing being to it? What are we thinking about when, in a comprehensive gaze, we consider, by itself, the *being* of all the beings in our world? Why is it not only important but timely and urgent, as Heidegger argues, that we recognize and give thought to the *ontological difference* between being and all these worldly beings? Why is it critically urgent to protect and preserve this difference, both in philosophy and in the world of our experience? As Heidegger tries to explain, the nihilism that imposes the denial of being on our time threatens with total reification, standardization, and reduction the very being of all the beings in our world. If we care about the fate of these beings, care about whether they are (to be) and what they are (to be), then we need to care about the fate of being itself. *Ethics depends on ontology,* on how we experience and understand being, the being of beings; but *the ontology that is actually operative in our everyday lives depends, in turn, on the character of our ethical life*—depends, in other words, on how we relate to the beings, the things, with which we are engaged. How we look at things, how we listen, how we touch and handle things determines what for us they are and are not. Every being, every entity, in every epoch in the history of the world is determined by the contingently prevailing experience and understanding of being: what it means for something—anything—to be. But Heidegger maintains that, in the centuries of the modern world, the dominant experience and understanding of being—our unacknowledged ontological commitment—is increasingly inimical to life on this planet: in its rationalized commodification, identity standardization, and imposed totalization, nihilism prevails, reducing everything our civilization has valued and cherished, above all, human life, to nothingness. So, if we are to rescue our civilization and begin in significant ways to redeem its potential, its promise, we need, before it becomes too late, to recognize how we are abandoning being to a catastrophic fate. This is Heidegger's most important, and most urgent, message. For the sake of our planet Earth; and for the sake of the flourishing moral and ethical life that civilization claims to make possible.

Now, before we advance any further, I want to emphasize here that, although Heidegger argues that we need to give thought to being itself and should not be distracted from this undertaking by our everyday involvement with the world of beings, he is not arguing, as some of his readers have supposed, against worldly engagement. Critics such as Theodor Adorno and Richard Rorty, who accuse Heidegger of turning away from the world for the sake of an empty abstraction, have woefully misunderstood Heidegger's argument. First, his argument for giving thought to being is for the sake of getting into a fitting relationship with beings—getting that involvement right. And second, he makes it abundantly clear that mindfulness (*Besinnung*), or attentiveness (*Beachtung*) should guide the way we relate to the beings in our world. What he wants is a "free relationship" to the beings of the world instead of a totally instrumental involvement with them: a relationship that frees them as well as us. Thus, in fact, he laments how distracted and inattentive, how indifferent and careless, and how obsessed with utility we have become, in our everyday engagement with things—beings. Rilke called that engagement brutal; in his texts on technology, Heidegger called it an "assault."

Retrieving in recollection the archaic historical inception, the extraordinary beginning for philosophical thought, Heidegger hoped to encourage among his contemporaries a renewed questioning and thinking in regard to being. We too can temporarily turn our thoughts away from all the beings of our world to question and reflect on being itself, being as such: How we, living in today's world, are understanding what it means for something—anything—to be. And how we are relating nowadays to threats to the very being of beings. But the intention behind this dedication of thought to being is always, for Heidegger, a more fitting relationship to the beings in our world: a relationship more befitting our shared sense of our humanity. There is so much unnecessary human suffering and so much wonton environmental devastation that remains disregarded, neglected, as if unseen, despite happening in plain sight.

Heidegger was hoping that, in the course of reflecting on the question of being, we of today might prepare for the possibility of another history-making event of inception, another radically different experience and understanding of being, bringing to its end the destructiveness of the modern epoch, in which the reification, standardization, and constant availability of being is imposed on the totality of beings, including us human beings. Heidegger calls our modern epoch the time of the *Ge-Stell*, defining it as naming the *total imposition* of an order, or regime, that ultimately reduces the being of beings to nothing—nothing, that is, to preserve and protect. In his 1969 Seminar in Le Thor, France, Heidegger suggests that,

> In an event of being [*Ereignis*], the history of being [*Seinsgeschick*] does not so much arrive at its end [*ihr Ende gelangt*] as that it now shows itself [in its truth, its use] *as* history of being. But there is no epoch of being inherently bearing destiny [*Es gibt keine geschichtliche Epoche des Ereignisses*]. Rather, what grants destiny is, conversely, what comes from our own appropriation

of the experience of being [*Das Schicken ist aus dem Ereignen*].
(GA 15: 366–67/FS, 61)

Destiny is a question of our own interpretation of the historical givens and the consequent history-making actions that we engage in the world, affecting, even if only in some small way, the epochal meaning of being. And that meaning is constitutive of our ethical life: our way of relating to all beings. Heidegger stresses the importance of the question of being because he recognizes that how I understand being (i.e., the being of beings, what it means for something to be what and how it is) invariably affects how I will relate to beings—to their way of being; but he gives insufficient attention to explaining the existential, ethical importance of being (in all four of its senses) as more than a purely abstract and theoretical philosophical matter.

Thus, as David Wood argues, in "Some Questions for my Levinasian Friends": "How we understand the other is essential to our capacity to honor, respect and protect them. [. . .] The implication of all this is that we cannot separate ontology from ethics."[10] "But," he adds, "just having an ontology does not alleviate blindness. We need to recognize the ways in which one's ontological commitments and prejudices can inform the kind of respect and response proper to different kinds of beings, and where missing, can limit one's capacity for responsiveness." Now, this means, as Wood says,

> My capacity for responding to the other's needs will depend to a considerable extent on my understanding of myself, and also what it is to *be* a human being.

What Wood states in regard to Levinas is what I want to argue in regard to Heidegger. I think Heidegger would appreciate this argument. He came near to formulating it in *Being and Time*, when he briefly invoked an "originary ethics," but he was somehow not able, or not ready, to develop with phenomenological concreteness the significance of the relation between the ethical and the ontological.

Nevertheless, for Heidegger, our self-understanding is inseparable from a responsibility for being. And, although unfortunately, Heidegger never is sufficiently clear, it is for the sake of our ethical and moral life among other beings that this responsibility for being matters.

Now, as I want to argue, in the context of Heidegger's project, *Ereignis* does *not* refer only to an extraordinary history-making, inceptual *event*.

The event implies, hence also refers to, a *process* taking place in our own present-day experience and philosophical reflection. How can this be? In German, the word *Ereignis* suggests another constellation of meaning: the adjective *eigen* means proper, own, ownmost; the verb *eignen* means to be appropriate and fitting; the noun *Eignung* refers not only to an eventuation and a coming to pass, but also to a proper aptitude, what is fitting or appropriate; *Eigentum* means property and propriety, the domain of what is proper; *Eigentlichkeit* refers to what is genuine and appropriate; and the adjective *eigentlich* means authentic, genuine, and in that sense true.

Moreover, "bei sich einkehren" can mean to search one's soul. In the event (*Ereignis*) that is of concern in Heidegger's project, the *Einkehr* is not only an insight into being, into "that which is;" it is also an event, an experience that claims or appropriates us, calling for a *process* of self-examination, a searching of one's soul, one's way of being, the character of one's way of living in the world. And above all, according to Heidegger, it calls for a process of *propriation* in the course of which we come to understand *our relation to being* and the responsibility that corresponds to this relation. (By the way, this "calling" is nothing mysterious: the event of being calls upon us in the same sense of "calls" that figures in our use of that word when we say that the toast calls for butter, the sight of a wildfire in the forest calls for action, and a child's proximity to an open well calls for restraining him. It is not *being itself* that is calling, but our situated-*experience*-of-being that is calling us. But the phenomenology of this phenomenon should not be represented in terms of the traditional subject-object structure, because that misses the nature of the connection between *Dasein* and *Sein*. The call comes from experiencing that connection, that *Bezug*.) For us living today, the event in which we find ourselves turning away from beings to contemplate being itself is experienced very differently from how the pre-Socratics experienced it.

Thus, the ontological event, an experience in which a momentous, consequential shift takes place, drawing our attention away from the beings in our world to the contemplation of being itself, is a leap of thought, a discovery, that is not the end of thought, but only its very beginning. For the pre-Socratics, Plato, and centuries of philosophers after them, the thought of being would set in motion questions and answers for the discourse of metaphysics. What is the meaning of being? What is it for something to be? And why is there being—why any beings at all? These questions gradually entered into the cultural life of the Western world—into its literature, painting, music, and dance.

For the premodern philosophers, these were challenging questions, generating much thought. But they never explicitly and methodically turned that thought back onto themselves, to reflect on the history of the question of being and on their position and role *in relation to* that history and its questioning. The possibility of such a philosophical turn in reflection could only come to light, it seems, in the modern epoch, beginning with the reflectively constituted subjectivity discovered by Descartes and continuing, in many different versions, until taken over by Husserl in the idealism of a transcendental phenomenology.

But Husserl's reductive transcendentalism prevented him from recognizing the need to question and ponder the distinctive historical nature and character of the *relation* between being and human being. When Heidegger returns to the pre-Socratics' inception and retrieves their thought of being, he finds that, although they did bring being as such into disclosure, they did not make the reflective phenomenological turn, to give thought to their *relation* to being, as thinkers, and as human beings. The relation itself remained hidden. It remained for Heidegger to bring it to light in his elaboration of the "Einkehr in das Ereignis." Undertaking that reflection in "The Principle of Identity" (*Der Satz der Identität*) and in *Time and Being*, Heidegger inaugurated a thinking that he hoped might prepare for another event of inception, the *Ereignis* opening up another, hopefully very different epoch in the unfolding of the history of being, an epoch in which beings would no longer be ruled by the ontological regime of the *Gestell*. In *The Event*, Heidegger describes this regime as "the compulsion toward totality" (GA 71: 86/E70). Reductionism, reification, and standardization are also characteristic pressures of this regime.

The *event* in which being itself comes to light is therefore no ordinary event. It is, rather, an event that, insofar as it is understood as calling into question our fundamental *relation* to being, can set in motion a prolonged *process* of deep reflection and self-examination. What is the nature and character of this relation? For Heidegger, this is not only a question that challenges philosophical discourse, the conceptual constructs of metaphysics; it is equally a question that calls for individual, personal self-examination. Moreover it calls, correspondingly, for a critique of our contemporary world, which, in our epoch in the unfolding history of being, that is, in the history of what it means to be a being in our world, is under the sway, and indeed the total imposition, of the *Ge-stell*. Thus, Heidegger's philosophical project is oriented toward the possibility of another extraordinary ontological event—another inception, another very different epoch in the unfolding of the meaning of being, hence what it means to be. That possibility, though, is by no means certain.

§4

It is at this point that the constellation of secondary meanings for *Ereignis* that Heidegger draws out from that word must *eventuate*, coming into consideration. What *is* the process? As being itself comes to light in the *Ereignis*, so too does our *relation* to being. One way of interpreting our experience of the ontological event connects with the ideal of *authenticity* for which Heidegger argues in *Being and Time*. In a deeply reflective experiencing of the ontological event, that is, the event in which we recognize and contemplate being itself and as such, we could find ourselves confronted with questions regarding who we are and want to be as human beings in our relation to being. And in examining ourselves in that relation, we might also find ourselves confronted with questions about our ontological responsibilities. For Heidegger, it is manifest that, in our present ontological epoch, being is considered to be nothing meaningful and the being of beings is under constant assault. Should we not consequently *care* about being, protecting and preserving it? If so, how? For now, my brief answer, with which I presume that Heidegger would concur, is that protecting and preserving being is a question of maintaining our *Geworfenheit* as *Da-sein*: living our lives in the world with deep awareness of the ontological dimension of openness. He will call this openness *Gelassenheit*: releasement.

There are quite a number of textual passages in different texts, wherein *being* is actually identified as *world*, the world that our presence, which I interpret to be our bodily situatedness, that is, *Da-sein*, opens into (GA 79: 51–52/BF). What, then, is our responsibility to care for the world itself—the world as world? For Heidegger, it is a question of challenging nihilism, the negation of being, in all its forms: reification, reductionism, standardization, the imposition of identities and differences.

§5

That there is being rather than nothing is a mystery (*Geheimnis*) that we will never be able to penetrate. No matter how much we struggle, no matter how deeply we press our thinking, we will never totally possess its meaning, secure in its intrinsic dimension of hiddenness. However, Heidegger never abandoned his project, thinking toward being, nor did he ever abandon phenomenology; but he did, more than once, change his approach. He never completed *Being and Time* because he gradually realized that approaching being in terms of the structural properties of human existence set conditions that precluded letting the phenomenology of being show itself as it is.

And in this regard, I suggest that, going beyond thinking of the "Geheimnis" of being as invoking some "mystery," we should understand this term to be a way of thinking of the "Einkehr in das Ereignis." The word *Geheimnis* is metaphoring that *Einkehr* as involving a return, not so much to a grandiose mystery as rather to ourselves, to what needs to get our attention: an ontological dimension of our being and its corresponding responsibility, hiding from our reflective awareness, as if a *Geheimnis*, a secret belonging to our ownmost nature but kept from our mature consciousness, abandoned as we leave infancy behind and enter into the ontic world-order. Heidegger speaks of "das vergessene Geheimnis des Daseins" (GA 9: 194–97/ PM 148–51). The *Einkehr* is a *Heim-kehr*, a returning home, a home-coming in the sense of our going, as it were, "into" ourselves to retrieve the structurally hidden *Ge-heim-nis*: the *pre-ontological* understanding of being that has always already appropriated and enowned us, claiming and attuning the very nature of our embodiment (GA 79: 70/BF 66). In this "home-coming," we return to retrieve our situating presence as a thrown-open situated clearing, this "forgotten" preconceptual understanding of being carried by the very nature of our embodiment; and, in this process, we experience ourselves in our bodily presence as *Da-sein*, as opening up for a clearing; and we get in touch with the belongingness that is constitutive of our embodied relationship to being. The *Geheimnis*—understood now as that which is *contingently* hidden from our awareness—thus comes to light in a *process* of recollection (*Er-innerung*), a process of getting in touch with ourselves, whereby we retrieve from its hiddenness, or from our ontological "forgetfulness," the true nature of our engagement with the meaning of being as it figures in the dynamic, interactive, oscillating relationship we have with beings.

"Geheimnis" accordingly refers to (1) the *contingent fact of hiddenness of being*, due to our ontic-stage repression or forgetfulness of our pre-ontological *experience* and our pre-ontological, preconceptual *understanding* of that relationship (a relationship of mutual "need"), and also (2) the *process of appropriation*, whereby we *come back home to ourselves* from our lostness in ontic life to take up into heightened awareness our hidden pre-ontological, preconceptual *understanding* of that relationship (a relationship of mutual "need"), so that it will guide our way of life. Hence, *Geheimnis* (interpreted now as designating something "secret") thus refers to (3) the hiddenness of the clearing that we are and that we retrieve, entering into the appropriation of an event (*Ereignis*) in which a pre-ontological intimacy (*Innigkeit*) with being, a connection (*Gehörigkeit*) borne by our bodily nature as thrown-open clearings and deeply hidden from habitual ontic awareness, finally comes into singular awareness, compelling reflective recollection, retrieval, and mindfulness.

This "home-coming" is a Hölderlinean inspiration that Heidegger misses, even though he devoted much thought to the poet's works. But, in *Fundamental Concepts of Metaphysics*, it is to Novalis that Heidegger briefly turns, quoting his aphorism.[11] The first clause reads thus: "Philosophy is really a homesickness (*Heimweh*)." But, lest we miss the ontological purport, the subordinate clause explains that this means "an urge to be at home everywhere" ("*überall zu Hause zu sein*"). So, it is not a question of nostalgia, or of nationalism, but of the dream of a homecoming (*Heimkehr*) that would make the entire world congenial. Returning home is possible—but only insofar as we own up to our responsibilities, making our own the great task of creating a better world. And this involves our entering into the appropriating event of being: the *Einkehr in das Ereignis*.

I suggest that the translation of *Geheimnis* as designating some mysterious "mystery" is an unfortunate—and serious—errancy. To be sure, it is a mystery why there is anything at all rather than nothing. We do not, and cannot, have an explanation for this fact: no more than we can step outside ourselves to check on whether the world we see is "in reality" as we are seeing it. Unfortunately, some scholars want to make something much more metaphysically grandiose and dubious of this insightful and extraordinary experience of being, which provokes us to feel awe and wonder as we realize the limits of our powers of conceptual understanding.

The home-coming, a return to oneself, which the ancient Greeks mythopoetically narrated in terms of a dangerous ocean voyage, should be understood as an interpretation of what Heidegger means by invoking the "Einkehr in das Ereignis": our appropriation, bestirred through an experience of being, to take responsibility for becoming the *Da-sein* that we in essence already *are* in our relationship to being. We need to get in touch with ourselves. That means, understanding ourselves as *Da-sein*, as thrown-open in our being, and thereby living in our belonging-together with being. For Merleau-Ponty, this belonging-together is, first and foremost, a bodily felt sensory connection. Thus, it is, at first, pre-ontological as well as prereflective, calling for its retrieval in a genuinely ontological understanding of being and our relation to being. In his *Prelude*, William Wordsworth evoked this belonging together, our primordial bonding (*Bezug*) with being, in this lovely verse (lines 262–64).

> Along his infant veins are interfused
> The gravitation and the filial bond
> Of nature, that connects him to the world.[12]

After *Being and Time*, Heidegger forgets about the pre-ontological, prereflective dimension of human life. To have continued thinking *from* it, he would have had to delve into the phenomenology of our embodiment, where the bonding constituting our belongingness with being is always already functioning. Merleau-Ponty does that needed delving, fleshing out the belonging-togetherness of *Sein* and *Menschsein* that Heidegger briefly describes in words that are already performative (*Schweben, Schwingen*), giving descriptions of that dimension of experience that are not commonly and readily experienced, hence not experienced as true, in order to encourage a radical process of reflection that could eventuate in making our experiencing confirm the deeper truth in what he is describing. Here is Merleau-Ponty's rendering of that pre-ontological connectedness.

> We have the experience of a world, not in the sense of a system of relations that fully determines each event, but in the sense of an open whole whose synthesis can never be completed. We have the experience of an I, not in the sense of an absolute subjectivity, but rather one that is indivisibly unmade and remade by the course of time. The unity of the subject or of the object is not a real unity, but a presumptive unity within the horizon of experience; we must discover, beneath the idea of the subject and the idea of the object, the fact of my subjectivity and the object in the nascent state, the primordial layer where ideas and things are born.[13]

Beneath and before the emergence of the subject-object structure into the realm of truth, there is a preflective, pre-ontological togetherness that forever makes that truth tremble.

As a home-coming bestirred by the ontological event, the *Einkehr* is a return to one's "secret," ownmost self, the beginning of a process of propriation: a coming back to oneself from one's absorption in the ontic, everyday world. It is a process that leads us, beyond experiencing the unfathomable mystery and wonder of being, into examining the essential nature of our relation to being, the event of a two-way belonging-together-with-being (*Zusammengehörigkeit*) that summons us to take on a responsibility for the being of beings, hence for being itself, the world itself: a responsibility for the way we experience, understand, and get engaged with the beings belonging to our given world in the still unfolding epoch in the history of being. The *Ereignis*, understood as ontological event, stirs us and takes hold of us, summoning and appropriating us *through that relation* of belonging-together.[14] Our entrustment and responsibility turn in a historically consequential way on what Heidegger will call our "most fundamental [pre-ontological] dis-position," that is, our situating thrown-openness, as well as turning on the character of our abilities to be appropriately responsive to all that we find we have been given by the contingent circumstances and conditions constitutive of our historically shaped world.

§6

Because of the constellation of secondary meanings, all centered around the word *eigen*, that Heidegger hears and draws out of *Ereignis*, the ontological *event*, in which being itself emerges for thought, has been translated as "event of appropriation," or "appropriating event." Being itself is *not* a process; but the meditative, reflective *experience* of being itself is indeed, as I shall argue, an *event* of appropriation, an event, that is, in which we are called to undergo our appropriation. Insofar as the experience of the event of being appropriates us, it summons us to initiate a process of self-questioning: a process of self-discovery and self-development that can engage one's entire life. It is a question of taking one's life seriously as it passes through this world. So, we might say that, for Heidegger, authenticity describes the life of those who endeavor to actualize, or enact, our potential as beings endowed with the humanity of a distinctively human nature: that which is most *proper* to us, most befitting, most deeply enowned, as human beings. In a more poetic rendition, Heidegger describes appropriation as granting to mortals their true "home," their stay [*Aufenthalt*] within their nature [*Wesen*], gathering and sustaining mortals in their essence" (GA 12:248/ OWL 128–29).

As an *event*, then, the experience of being calls for a *process*—none other than a *process of appropriation and propriation*: deepening our understanding of being, of what it means to be, the experience stirs us to enter into a process of becoming what we most authentically, most properly are as human beings. According to Heidegger, if we are ever to escape the regime of the *Gestell* and redeem in our world something of its promise, then we need to find, in the pull of our relation (*Bezug*) to being, our historical responsibility for being, the being that we attribute to all beings. Thus, to the strange ontological *event* "outside" us in the world, namely, an experience in which find ourselves encountering something that somehow provokes us to give thought to being itself, there should *correspond*, awakened and bestirred "inside" us, a *process* of *propriation* in which, decisively appropriated, we would recollect and retrieve our potential as *Da-sein* and accordingly undertake in earnest to achieve what we take it to call for: a responsibility to develop the humanity in ourselves, a responsibility in our being-with-others, and a responsibility for our role in determining what it means for beings (anything) to be—be present and absent—in our world.

There are times when the English language has far more to contribute to philosophical thought than the German language is able to propose. And I submit that this is the case regarding the English translation of *Ereignis* as "event of appropriation." I propose to distinguish three connected senses of appropriation (*Ereignis, Ereignung*) engaged by the ontological event as we experience it.

1. "appropriation" as summoning and making a claim on us;
2. "appropriation" as Übernahme, as our taking on what it is that this summons and claim calls for; and
3. "appropriation" as propriation, the task of authenticity, becoming true to our existence as human beings—a task that *necessarily* involves understanding and taking responsibility for our relation to being.

We are the only beings for whom our being is in question. And we are the only beings on whom a responsibility falls for the being of all beings. The ontological experience is an event that sets in motion a process of appropriation in sense (1) and sense (2). (See, e.g., "Der Satz der Identität," GA 11: 40n53: "Verantwortung des Menschen für das Sein," and GA 11: 45: "Vereignung und Zueignung.")

Heidegger hopes that the experiencing of this ontological event of disclosure, revealing the meaning of being, being itself in its difference from beings, is one that will make us aware of the ontological claim on us, whether it happens in wonder and awe or in anxiety and dread. That is, the disclosing of the truth of being is an *event* that summons and claims us, appropriating us for a *process of propriation* in which we come to recognize and understand ourselves in our belonging to, and our role in, the disclosing of this facticity of being, and accordingly begin taking on responsibility for the historical character of our disclosive relation to being, and, too, a responsibility for the future in regard to what beings there are in our world and how they can, or must, be present.

So, what Heidegger calls our "entering into appropriation" (*Einkehr in das Ereignis*) is not only a question of our taking on responsibility for the truth of being; it is inherently also, therefore, a question of our being true to ourselves, true to our potential as human beings. And that means it is a question of becoming who we are in essence, namely *Da-sein*. In *Being and Time*, Heidegger thinks of this primarily in terms of existential authenticity. With *Ereignis* and related words, *Er-eignung*, *Ver-eignung*, *An-eignung*, *Zu-eignung*, *Eignis* and *Enteignis* (see "Satz der Identität" GA 11: 40–46 and "Zeit und Sein," GA 14: 28–29, 33, 47, 115, 119), Heidegger refines and develops this existential notion of authenticity, arguing for an understanding of what it means for us, as human beings, to actualize the potential in the essential nature of our humanity. This "authenticity" is not at all the narcissism and individualism that prevails in our world today; on the contrary, it belongs in Heidegger's interpretation of humanism as the commitment to developing and achieving our (most deeply shared sense of) humanity—the sense of humanity constitutive of our *Mitsein*.

In his Summer Semester 1944 lectures on Heraclitus, Heidegger acknowledged that, in our everyday life, we act as if we need not concern ourselves with the fact that beings *are*, and are determined in and by their being. We live with beings all the time; but the being of these beings remains unthought. Consequently, he argues, we neglect our historical *responsibility* for the *being* of beings: for *what* beings *are* and for *how* they are (GA 55.2: 322/H 241). Neglecting their being, we abandon them to their vulnerabilities, their fate in an epoch that imposes total reification on all beings, reducing everything to commercial availability—and the will to power.

The *Ereignis* is an event in which *being itself* breaks through our lethargy, and thus it is—and should be experienced as—a challenge to our way of living, indeed reminding us that caring about being constitutes the very essence of our dignity as human beings, our distinction from all the (other) animals (GA 55.2: 375/H 280). So, this event, in which we finally "discover" being, is an experience that summons us to begin a process of critical self-examination and propriation: to work on ourselves. This includes thinking critically about the categories in terms of which we experience the being of beings.

§7

This ontological event (*Ereignis*), the recognizing and contemplating of being itself, which, I would argue, contesting Heidegger's elitism, could happen to anyone at any time, apparently took place, or was recorded in writing, for the first time in archaic Greece, breaking into the thought of some pre-Socratic philosophers like a flash of lightning. For them, the event was an experience of wonder and awe. However, it is only in modern times, and fully only in Heidegger's thought, that this event of experience gets interpreted, understood, in the overwhelming dimensions of its essence, as appropriating, summoning us to recognize in ourselves, as thrown-open *Da-sein*, an intimidating but imperative ontological responsibility, that is, the *Wächterschaft der Wahr-heit*, caring for the truth of being (GA 65: 240–41/CP 190). For the pre-Socratics, this awesome experience, decisive though it was for their thinking, was not an event that made them look into themselves to recognize their own role and responsibility for being. They did not make the phenomenological turn. Our situation is different. Compelled, today, to give thought to being is to confront something traumatic that requires courageous self-reflection. It is that self-reflective turn, with its self-recognition, and its recognition of a corresponding ontological responsibility, that is, a responsibility for being, that Heidegger brings to the fore, retrieving and interpreting anew Parmenides' saying that mind and being are "the same." For Heidegger, what Parmenides is getting at is the belonging-together of man and being.

Reading and interpreting the history of philosophy, Heidegger was hoping that remembering and understanding the pre-Socratics' experience of this ontological disclosure could become a world-changing, history-making event, bringing forth a new humanity and a new world. But that transformation could happen only through a process of appropriation, in which we human beings, living today, having attained an understanding of the disclosive nature and character of our relation to being (a relation of interaction and belongingness), begin to take responsibility not only for beings, but also for the very being of these beings. To change the world, we need to change ourselves. *Da-sein* (with the hyphen) names that change in ourselves.

If *Dasein*'s "power" to be disclosive of being is constitutive of its essence (*Wesen*), then we need to give thought to that disclosiveness and its potential, for instance, in our experience of perception. Appropriation is also, therefore, about *Dasein*'s self-understanding, its commitment to questioning and realizing what that potential, that essence, demands. In *Being and Time*, this commitment of responsibility is thought primarily in terms of authenticity (*Eigentlichkeit*): being true to oneself, hence committed to developing one's ownmost (*eigenste*) disclosive potentialities.

In the years following the publication of *Being and Time*, the word *Ereignis*, together with its constellation of connected words, assumed an increasingly important role in Heidegger's project, more or less replacing "authenticity." Scholars, however, have not found this key word—*Ereignis*—easy to interpret and translate. Besides interpreting it as referring to an *ontological event* of singular historical, indeed history-making significance, scholars have taken it to refer to our *appropriation* because of the *eigen* (own) and *eignen* (enown) implicit in the key word. Reconciling and deploying *both* these interpretations, I want to connect the word's meaning to the Socratic practice of self-examination, an ongoing process of self-questioning constitutive of a certain "steady moral seriousness."

For Heidegger, human existence is first and foremost a question of authentic resolve: not merely determination, steadfastness of purpose, but what—despite Heidegger's reluctance to engage in thought about "ethical life"—I would characterize as "steadfast moral seriousness," meaning commitment to a ceaseless Socratic process of self-questioning in regard to the ethical character of the life each of us makes—not only for ourselves, but for our communities, our world, and indeed for all creaturely life on this planet. This essentially ethical commitment, and a willingness to change our ways, which Socrates and later Hellenic philosophers called "care of the soul," is both a response to the moral demands of social existence in the world *and* a response to the claim that summons us from deep within ourselves to attend to our *propriation*: a claim that summons us in the very *disposition* of our bodily nature, ex-posing us to questions that address us in our existential condition as thrown-open, disclosive beings: not only questioning how we have lived our time and who we are becoming, but questioning who we are and what we aspire to achieve in our life and time. Although Heidegger refrains from a substantive phenomenological inquiry regarding the good and refrains from characterizing the living of an ethical and political life, nevertheless, in *Being and Time*, he remarks that, implicit in the ontological interpretation of human existence, is "a definite ontical way of understanding authentic existence, a factical ideal of *Dasein*" (GA 2: 310/BT 358). For Heidegger, *propriation* is a process of learning that necessarily involves, as he thinks it would for Parmenides, the character of our disclosive relation to being, the event by which a world, or context of meaning, opens up and gathers together to enable things—beings—to appear for a while in the proper truth of their presence. In the ontological event, we find ourselves learning that it is not only an appropriation calling us to be true to our being, our authenticity; it is also an appropriation summoning us to attend to our relation to being—a relation of co-respondence. Our stewardship of being is at stake (GA 65: 23/CP20).

The words *Er-eignis* and *Er-eignung* refer to the claim that appropriates the essence (*Wesen*) of the seeing of our eyes and the essence of the hearing of our ears, calling into question the character of their disclosive disposition and dedicating them to an ontological responsibility—a steadfast responsibility for the being and essence of beings, not only protecting and preserving beings from reification and other forms of violence, but protecting and preserving the clearings, the contexts of intelligibility or meaning, and the fundamental condition of possibility for experience, within which all beings appear and depart. The *Ereignis* is unmistakably an inspired inheritance from Socrates; but it is also *much more* than a summons to authenticity, much more than being true to one's potential, connected as it is to a critique of our contemporary experience of being and the being of beings, and to a vision of the transformation of humanity that would fulfill the promise in our being, dwelling on this earth in an authentic form of human existence: an existence that would serve the flourishing of life and nature. We need to understand ourselves in our percipience, need to understand what it means for our lives that, in the ways we see and hear, we are not only determining how we are standing on the earth and under the sky, but determining the very conditions of earth and sky, now deteriorating in a planetary emergency. Learning to see and learning to hear are necessary, never-ending processes of ap-propriation (*Er-eignung*) and transformation—processes that are bound to be decisive for the future.

If recognizing and understanding ourselves in the process of propriation involves recognizing and understanding our relation to being, and recognizing and understanding this relation means taking on responsibility for being, then, as Heidegger argues, we need to take on stewardship—*Wächterschaft*: responsibility to maintain and protect the openness of the clearing as the absolutely necessary condition of possibility, and context of intelligibility, for the "Es gibt," unconcealment, the presencing, of being. The clearing in its openness—the clearing that we *are* as embodied *Da-sein*—is the necessary condition of possibility that lets-appear everything in its presence and absence (GA 14: 80–81, 84, 87/OTB 65, 68, 71). Unable to think of any better words, I am obviously using a Kantian phrase to describe the functioning of the clearing; however, this functioning is radically different from Kant's "necessary conditions for the possibility of experience in general," because the clearing is not the a priori projection of transcendental subjectivity; rather, it is an *aletheic* dimension or context for the interplay of meaningful concealment and unconcealment, laid out through our bodily thrown-openness as *Da-sein*. Heidegger seems to have alluded to this difference from Kant when, as the protocol of his seminar indicates, he repeatedly reminded us to think about *aletheia* and the self-concealment of being (GA 14: 56/OTB 46). As that which is *letting*-appear or *letting*-presence (Anwesen-*lassen*), the clearing is what "gives" or "sends" beings, that is, makes their presencing in our experience possible: the clearing is, in one of the two senses of the German word *Geschick*, the "source" of what we find ourselves "given," or "sent"—*geschickt*. (I am using scare-quotes here because I am not philosophically comfortable using those words.) In regard to the "Es gibt," which means both "There is" and "It gives," the clearing is the "Es" that "gives," or "sends," but *only* in the sense that it is the ground or field or context *within which* beings can come to be present and absent. And what "gives" the clearing itself—or, as I prefer to say, what makes it possible—is simply the appropriated nature of our existence. (However, as Sheehan has pointed out,[15] Heidegger does not decisively distinguish between what "gives" or "sends"—that is, makes possible—the clearing and what the clearing itself "gives" or "sends." That creates unnecessary confusion and unnecessarily encourages metaphysical explanations regarding the origin of the clearing.) But Heidegger elegantly explains the *aletheic* functioning of the clearing as "the open for everything that is present and absent" in "The End of Philosophy and the Task of Thinking" (GA 14: 81/OTB 65). (For the phenomenological explication in its entirety, see GA 14: 80–88/OTB 64–71.) According to Heidegger, Western life, and its reflection in philosophical thought, have neglected to recognize and understand the crucial role of being itself, attentive instead only to the beings that appear within its compass (GA 14: 80, 81, 87/OTB 65, 68, 71). Being itself: this could be the field of perception, the context, the background, the situation, the universe of discourse, the conditions of intelligibility or meaningfulness, the world—the opened clearing. If we think of this phenomenology in terms of the figure-ground *Gestalt* in perception, what is ignored, neglected, suppressed, or taken-for-granted is the functioning of the ground, which, like being, must withdraw, must recede to *let*-presence (*lassen*-anwesen), as attention concentrates on beings present and absent (on the functioning of the clearing, see "The End of Philosophy and the Task of Thinking," GA 14: 84, 87/OTB 68, 71). The clearings that our spatiotemporally *ek-static* presence opens are *not* mysteriously hidden, impossible to access, as some scholars maintain, but merely contingently withdrawn: "hidden" only in the same way that the ground or context in the *Gestalt* is said to be hidden (GA 9: 187–200/PM 143–53). Heidegger's distinction between *Anwesen*-lassen and Anwesen-*lassen*, marking the two different emphases, permits him to differentiate (1) what presences (presencing as either present or absent) and (2) the clearing that, in its openness, provides the necessary condition for the possibility of such presencing. However, he still leaves an unnecessary confusion in his texts, since *Sein* is used to designate both phenomena. It is therefore useful to write *Seyn* when referring to the Anwesen-*lassen*; but unfortunately, Heidegger's use of that spelling is not consistent. It must be remembered that in Heidegger's writings, *Sein* (*being*) can assume four distinct meanings: (1) signifying the fact of existence, the *sheer fact* that something is, (2) being as the essence of something, that is, *what* the being is, (3) being as appearing, that is, coming into presence (*Anwesen*), and (4) being as the opened clearing, the context of a "world," constituting the conditions of disclosedness that make such presencing possible. These four senses of "being" can unfortunately create considerable confusion and misunderstanding. But they all have a bearing on our lives—our ways of life.

In *On Time and Being*, Heidegger seems to be recognizing the two senses of the word *Geschick*: his use of the word in its common sense, which signifies historical destiny, and his use of grammatical forms of the word (*Schicken, Schickung, geschickt*) to introduce a *phenomenological* sense (GA 14: 22/OTB 17). "Both," he says, "belong together": "giving as destiny, giving as an opening up that reaches out" (GA 14: 24–25/19–20). Destiny (*Geschick*) "lies" (*beruht*)—is to be sought—in what is given (*geschickt*) in, and by, the clearing (GA 14: 25/OTB 20). Our *Geschick* in the sense of "destiny" is not something given, as if it were an ordained fate or dispensation; rather, it is something to be achieved, though always incompletely, by the exercise of our finite freedom, retrieving promising possibilities and opportunities from the world we are living in—the world as we find it "given," "given" (*geschickt*) in the common sense of that word, merely signifying the facticity of our situation.

§8

Considered as an ontological event, the *Ereignis* is an appropriation that is not only received by consciousness; it also has corresponding resonances in the body. We have noted that Heidegger argues that the *Ereignis* is an experience in which one contemplates and questions being itself, and that this experience is one in which we are claimed and summoned—appropriated—to take being itself into our care, recognizing that the human being and being are in a dynamic relation of belonging-togetherness, and moreover, that in this relation, we are summoned to a responsibility to take being into our care. In other words, this responsibility appropriates us, demanding that we undertake a process of propriation, not only enowning this responsibility, but also experiencing and understanding ourselves differently in the light of the truth in our relation to being.

Despite all that Heidegger says regarding the importance of this appropriation and propriation, he nevertheless has left the phenomenology of the process in considerable obscurity. What is awakened, aroused, and stirred by the ontological experience of something we commonly take to be "outside" us is, I submit, something we commonly locate "inside" us: a disposition of our nature that, as Heidegger will say in his 1925 *Prolegomena to the History of the Concept of Time* (GA 20: 209), constitutes our "most fundamental disposition" (*Fundamentalbestimmung*). And, though he does not say so, it is of course carried by our embodiment as *Da-sein*, our thrown-open way of being.[16] Also left in unnecessary obscurity is, in consequence, the *connection* between this fundamental disposition—our *Da-sein*—and the appropriation (*Ereignung*) that summons and guides us into the process of our propriation. Manifestly, we need to get in touch with this disposition. As Merleau-Ponty observes, "At work in my organs of perception there is something [i.e., a disposition] older than myself of which those organs are merely the trace."[17] We need to retrieve that.[18] The ontological event that takes hold of us works its appropriation through our most fundamental bodily disposition. Heidegger leaves this process—*how* an experience of the *Ereignis*, an event of being, can lay claim to us—in obscurity because he neglects our embodiment. Invocations of "attunement" are not very helpful.

Heidegger refers to this "fundamental disposition" as "the gentlest of laws" (GA 12: 248/OWL 128). But he does not explain why. This law (*Ge-setz*), I suggest, is deposited (*ge-setzt*) in our embodiment. And it is the *gentlest* of laws, because its "incorporation" (*Einverleibung*) is constitutive of our ownmost incarnate nature, summoning us to recognize, take up, and develop ourselves, not only as the thrown-open, hermeneutically disclosive beings we are, but also, therefore, in our role as the guardians of being. This fundamental bodily disposition of law lays a claim to our embodied nature (see GA 11: 30–40/ID 31; GA 70: 9–10). As such, it is radically dis-positioning. Why? Because recognizing ourselves in the dis-positioning thrown-openness, the *ek-stasis* of embodiment that is our *Da-sein*, can be profoundly unsettling, disquieting, even unnerving: *ent-setzend*. We do not commonly experience ourselves as opening clearings. It requires that we experience ourselves and think of ourselves in such a radically different way. In fact, the more we get into the process of propriation, our enowning of ourselves, the more we are susceptible to feeling estranged, strangely inhabiting our own bodies, which we tend to think of as solid, encapsulated substances with an impermeable boundary separating our being from the being of the world. Heidegger challenges this separation, arguing that phenomenological reflection reveals that our embodied relation to being is actually a dynamic interaction, a chiasmic oscillation, and—as Merleau-Ponty understood it—a bodily felt sensory connectedness temporally prior to, and also structurally underlying, the formation of the subject-object structure. Heidegger suggests a vibrating *Gegenschwung, schwingend, schwebend* (GA 11: 46–48/ID 37–39).[19]

This is a good beginning. However, what still needs to be recognized is the role of the body. This would be, I suggest, a necessary supplement, not only to Heidegger's project, but also to the contributions of outstanding scholars such as Richard Capobianco, Richard Polt, François Raffoul, and Thomas Sheehan, who, having come after Heidegger, were able to interpret and illuminate the key words—key terms—to his great project. After all, it is in the phenomenology of our felt embodiment that we experience what Heidegger says more abstractly, namely, the oscillation, the *Schwingen* and *Schweben*, in our interaction, our belonging-together, with the very being of beings.

The phenomenology of our belonging-together (*Zusammen-gehörigkeit*) with being is for Heidegger of the greatest importance (GA 11: 39–41, 45/ID 30–33, 36). But I think he arrived at an understanding of its full significance only in such later works as "The Principle of Identity" (1957) and "Time and Being" (1962). Whereas the Husserl of *Ideas* (1913) and *Cartesian Meditations* (1929), and the Merleau-Ponty of the *Phenomenology of Perception* (1945), were, despite their major differences, still under the influence of Cartesianism, making the percipient subject the philosophical starting point for understanding the perceptual engagement with being,

Heidegger questioned the subject, starting instead from the perceptual *situation* as a whole—the *belonging-together* of subject and object, *Mensch* and *Sein*. This belonging-together is the source of our responsibility for the being of beings, hence for being itself. Husserl's starting point was the *transcendental* ego-subject and Merleau-Ponty's was the *embodied* subject; but both philosophers adopted the subject as the starting-point for their philosophical ruminations. However, in *Being and Time* (1927), Heidegger made his point of departure the thrown-open, disclosive *situatedness* of *Da-sein*, our being-in-the-world.

§9

The ontological event that figures in Heidegger's "Einkehr in das Ereignis" is also our appropriation for the work, the task of destiny. This is how the two senses of *Geschick* work. The task is to prepare for a new epoch in the unfolding history of being. Insight into our relation to being reveals our role of responsibility in the emergence and givenness of historical conditions favorable to a transformative possibility for humanity. Understanding the dynamics constitutive of our engagement with being—what Heidegger calls a relation of "Zusammengehörigkeit"—could serve to guide us out of this epoch of spiritual destitution. The historical conditions that we have been given to live in are contingencies obviously not entirely of our making, not entirely the effect of our will; but it would be an error to suppose a hidden metaphysical, world-transcending source for the historical "dispensations" we must work with. How our situations come about is nothing mysterious; but they cannot be reduced to any simple explanation. Heidegger's philosophy of history thinks of our historical task in terms of a destiny in regard to the meaning of being (*Seyns-geschick*) that, because of the idioms in the German language, is all too readily thought of as a sending (*schicken*) of the world's "given" conditions. And these idioms all too easily suggest a metaphysical source and agency beyond our world.

At stake is the possibility of a new experience and understanding of being. However, I submit that there is no way to use Heidegger's word for destiny, namely, *Geschick*, without raising countless very troubling questions. Sometimes, it can seem as if he is assuming or positing some transcendent metaphysical agency—some *theologoumenon*, mysteriously at work in the course of history. And yet, I think that preparing for a future, a destiny, in which our relation to being is properly grounded is a concern too fundamental in Heidegger's project to be dismissed. We cannot simply ignore the question of destiny. The rhetorical role of the key word *das Geschick* in Heidegger's philosophy of history, hence its role in his reading of the history of philosophy, is ultimately too important in his great project to be neglected. Can it be rescued for a redeeming task?

Taking us beyond the metaphysical understanding of being, Heidegger proposes introducing a new key word: *Seyn* (*beyng*), though unfortunately his use of this variant is not consistent and consequently creates some unnecessary problems. Beyng is the *Da-sein*-appropriating event in which there is an experience of being itself, being as such, an experience in which being is revealed as a clearing, an open dimension of intelligibility for the appearing of beings in a time-space interplay of concealment and unconcealment in regard to the various modes and inflections of presence and absence that the grammar of temporalities articulates.

Although, as a student and young scholar, Heidegger vehemently rebelled against the scholastic theology in which he was educated, and moreover attempted to think about human existence in terms of a radically immanent, this-worldly transcendence, formulated in a distinctive philosophical terminology of his own free of theologically saturated concepts, I suggest that he never entirely purged his thinking of a theologically inflected metaphysics. Vestiges of a certain theological inspiration subtly persist, even in the secular Humanism to be found in the rhetoric of his post–World War II lectures and writings. These vestiges are particularly manifest in the rhetorical figure of destiny that is at the heart of his philosophy of history. And they continue to appear even *after* his forceful repudiation of an irremediably enigmatic interpretation of the "history of being" (GA 97: 382), referring to something that is neither a history in the familiar historiographical sense nor an interpretive metanarrative following the logic in an unfolding of a succession of ways of conceptually understanding and disclosing what it means for something to be. His "history of being," however, remained stubbornly obscure, an embarrassing problem—until it was eventually withdrawn into silence.

Basically, the meaning of *Geschick*, understood as signifying destiny, passed through three phases in Heidegger's thought. (1) In the 1920s, Heidegger's use of the word *Geschick*, meaning "destiny," carried a communitarian, nationalistic, culturally specific sense of destiny, a sense summoning the national culture of his native Germany to the achieving of its proper fulfillment, its so-called mission. In this use, he explicitly argued against the causality of fate; and he strongly repudiated all ontotheological, eschatological, and teleological interpretations, although it has sometimes seemed that, despite disclaimers, he remained to some extent under the influence of metaphysical, theological thinking during his early years as a scholar and academic. Something of an onto-theological sense occasionally seems to haunt his earliest use of the word. (2) But in the 1930s and the early 1940s, the word carried, and at least for a few years wholeheartedly encouraged, the sense of destiny belonging uniquely to National Socialism: an ontological nationalism and an ontological, cultural racism.

(3) In the late 1930s and the postwar years, Heidegger would still at times speak of destiny; but, as he began to twist free of the political ideology he once embraced, the question of destiny began to take on a diminished role in his thinking; and whenever it did appear, the word increasingly seemed to carry a sense of destiny that perhaps, finally, abandoned nationalism—even in its "merely" cultural version, and instead would bear witness to the human condition in its universality, representing his singular vision of a future transformed world in which we human beings would live together on this planet in a way worthy of our shared humanity—a way that would achieve and redeem what he regarded as the true "dignity" of our humanity. This universality, though, is never affirmed with the kind of reassurance we need to hear. Presumably it means to include *all* human beings in regard to their "humanity"—whatever that means. But, when he gives specific content to his vision, it is somewhat reminiscent of the utopian thinking in early German Romanticism, a poetic evocation of the communal life of a rural culture, and not a projection of an urban, cosmopolitan way of life. The images and rhetoric that he uses do not suggest a cosmopolitan, multicultural society and life. And yet, he will refer to characteristics constitutive of the supposed "essence" or "essential nature" of the human being. However, the building, dwelling, and thinking he conjures up in his utopian vision of the Fourfold (*Geviert*) do seem to be planetary, hence inclusive and universal, in its concern for the nature of our environment—our air, water, and earth. But, as I shall argue, it is not at all apparent that the *Geviert* is a gathering that takes place around each and every thing and welcomes, as into a democracy, all human beings, regardless of their differences.

So, I need to say here that I feel considerable dissatisfaction reading Heidegger's occasional invocations of "humanity" in the postwar years. All his thought ever provides seems to be nothing more than the celebration of an abstract humanity. For the word to be more than this, he would need to give it moral substance, arguing for human rights and civil rights, and for the importance of respecting and protecting identities and differences. There is virtually no guidance regarding what he actually means when he invokes "humanity." And, considering his early entanglement with National Socialism, we should be hesitant, if not reluctant, to think it carries forward the Enlightenment project. That connection to the Enlightenment will, however, always be what I have in mind when I appeal to our sense of humanity.

In his notebook (1947–1948), Heidegger confided—to his credit—serious misgivings about the "history of being" for which, in the decade after the publication of *Being and Time*, he had emphatically argued (GA 97: 382). But to the extent that his interpretation of "destiny" essentially depended on this notion of the "history of being," both the meaning and the usefulness of "destiny" would come into question. By the 1950s, however, invocations of *Geschick* were unquestionably disappearing (see GA 14: 50–51/OTB 41–42). Nevertheless, after Heidegger abandoned the culturally specific, nationalistic interpretation, it becomes difficult to determine how "destiny" could still fit into his project. His "Letter on Humanism" (1946) is frustratingly abstract; but, insofar as the question of our destiny is still at stake, we are somehow to understand it in the context of his version of Humanism.

In the post–World War II years, Heidegger refrained from giving "destiny" a significant role in his thinking about our inheritance of history and our responsibility for the future; but unfortunately, he also refrained from venturing to propose much substantive meaning for his vision of a "new Humanism": a transformed percipience, transformed humanity, and transformed world—unless we consider texts such as "Building Dwelling Thinking" and "The Thing" to indicate something of the substance: an ontologically grounded, ontologically oriented life. This is basically a vision that summons us to take responsibility for our disclosive relation to things: *what types* of entities can appear and be in our world and *how* they can appear and be in it. It is also a vision that, in projecting the Fourfold (*Geviert*), suggests a different relation to nature: a different way of dwelling on this earth and under its sky. Thus if, in the 1950s and after, his thought is still inspired by a vision of destiny—and this is not certain, then it seems to be making a claim to be a destiny for Humanism, a distinctive vision for humanity, for *all life* on this planet, and no longer only a vision for the German nation. One might wish, however, that if this interpretation is right, the inclusiveness of that vision had been more resolutely pronounced.

Nevertheless, even Heidegger's post–World War II invocations of *Geschick* justifiably cause suspicion, because, first of all, he never unequivocally repudiated the word's service during the terror of National Socialism and, second, because in the postwar years, he never clearly rendered with sufficient substance its *new* interpretation in the context of his new Humanism. What is his postwar vision with regard to the transformation of our *Mit-sein*, our being-with-others? There is, unfortunately, very little to inform our thinking. The word *Geschick* could of course still be used, free of destiny, simply to recognize the givenness of the historical situations we find ourselves in. So, in the postwar years (1947–1948), it seems that Heidegger increasingly recognized that he did not really need this word in order to conceptualize his project. The concept he recognized that his project required is *Ereignis*.

> In the *Ereignis*, nothing happens. Here there is no more happening [*Geschehen*]; no destiny [*auch kein Geschick*], either. In the *Ereignis*, the essence of history is abandoned [*verlassen*]. All talk of the history of beyng [*Seynsgeschichte*] is an embarrassment [*Verlegenheit*] and a euphemism. (GA 97: 382)

While insisting that the "history of being" is not a history in the normal historiographical sense of "history" and accordingly is not about the historical succession of conceptual interpretations of the meaning of being, that is, what it means for something—anything—to be, Heidegger left very much in the dark what exactly this history is about. Eventually, as I noted, the word *Geschick*, and, along with it, the enigmatic "history of being" in which it is supposed to figure, lost its usefulness and fell into the secrecy of a stubborn silence. In the seminar on "Time and Being," the philosopher says that, once thinking is working through the understanding of the *Ereignis*, thinking in terms of the *Seinsgeschick* is "at an end": Everything essential can be said without it (GA 14: 49–51/OTB 40–41). But if, on the one hand, the philosopher wanted finally to retract or deny the promise that we could ever attain a comprehensive, consoling meaning for history, on the other hand, with no more grandiose metaphysical or ontotheological temptations beckoning, the new focus on *Ereignis* enabled him to return his thought more wholeheartedly to an engagement with the plight of the world and correspondingly formulate, in the *Geviert*, his vision of a future for the destiny of which we are responsible. *Ereignis* is indeed the word and key that opens the final chapter in Heidegger's project of thought.

However, even after abandoning the *Seinsgeschick*, Heidegger, *sehr getrübt*, will continue to struggle with the idiom "Es gibt," unwilling to relinquish it in favor of the "poetic" "It is" (GA 14: 8–11/OTB 4–7). Thus, he continues to be haunted by, and to struggle with, the *Geschick* that seems to be implicit in the "Es gibt." I would like to try, if only as a polemical exercise, to rescue the idea of destiny by stripping it of all mythology, theology, teleology, and eschatology—and all poetizing celebration. There is no mysterious, hidden agent, no mysterious hidden agency, no numinous causality, no sending and giving, no dispensation from a source above the clouds. What is left? Simply the "given" historical situation we find ourselves "given" to engage—and the "Es gibt," the clearing, the openness of which gave us the very possibility of experiencing a world in the first place: the necessary, universal conditions of possibility letting the presencing of beings occur and take place. This "given," misleadingly glorified and called a "dispensation," refers simply to the inescapable factuality of the situations we are in. Nothing metaphysical needs to be invoked. Thus, the "grounding" of beings is not a metaphysical gesture, but rather a question of (1) recognizing the withdrawn, "hidden," and repressed or "forgotten" functioning of the ground—the context, clearing, world—in the figure-ground *Gestalt* and (2) *letting* that ground be what and as it essentially is.

However, these situations do have a history; and hidden in this history, almost buried, there are promising opportunities, possibilities, and potentials that have been ignored, neglected, blocked, or rejected. Historical memory (*Er-innerung*) can *retrieve* some of these promising opportunities, possibilities, and potentials from the inherited past of our heritage and realize their benefit for the making of our future. In the experience of the ontological *Ereignis*, we find ourselves appropriated, and in enowning our responsibilities, we are summoned to take up our "destiny," returning to the past we have inherited in order to begin retrieving and fulfilling its future promise as much as possible. This requires, as Heidegger would argue, (1) that we cease thinking of the past historiographically, that is, in terms of *Zeitlichkeit* as a linear, irreversible series in which the past is totally past, gone, and buried; and (2) that we begin thinking of historical time in keeping with the terms that Heidegger spells out in regard to the ontological dimension of "Temporalität." As I want to think of it, "destiny" is what, in the exercising of our freedom, we are able to make here and now of the conditions we are given to live with. Working with an *ontological* understanding and experience of historical time, those conditions are opened up to a past and a future.

Heidegger's word *Geschick*, and all its cognate, derivative, and related words, are very problematic, not only because of all the questions pertaining to a claim regarding destiny, but also because they are also doing the work that he characterizes by using words that refer to a sending, a giving or granting, a dispensation, a gift. In Heidegger's project of thought, *Geschick* does not mean only destiny. It also refers to a "giving" or "sending": what we are given by the world to live with. It seems to me that all these terms, these ways of thinking are caught up inescapably in metaphysics, in that it is difficult to rely on such idioms without projecting the agency of an agent, some mysterious source that sends or gives or dispenses and that "announces" in advance its coming. "Given" is ambiguous: We do use that word in everyday life to signify nothing more than the situations we confront; but "sent" (*geschickt*) really does seem to imply or suggest a sender. Heidegger let himself get entangled, unnecessarily, in the metaphysical and theological connotations that are not easily dismissed when he works with the two meanings of *Es gibt*: "It gives" and "there is." That flexible idiom can seem promising at first; but ultimately, it causes Heidegger stubbornly persistent problems. Eventually, though, he seems to clarify the matter in a way that escapes from metaphysics: What "gives" or "sends" or "grants" is always a clearing, a field of perception, or a universe of discourse, providing the conditions necessary for the presence and absence of beings to appear. In any case, it has certainly been challenging, even to the deeply religious, to think of the Shoah as a historical *gift* sent by God.

It is truly fascinating to read some of the passages in the text of Heidegger's 1962 Seminar on "Time and Being" where he is excruciatingly troubled and manifestly *struggling* to think the puzzling, enigmatic (*rätselhaften*) *Es* that figures in the locution *Es gibt*, at once separately from the meaning of the idiomatic way of asserting existence and yet also totally free of metaphysical echoes (GA 14: 21–23/OTB 16–18). Acknowledging his limitations, if not any ultimate defeat, he is finally compelled to say,

> We shall therefore abandon the attempt to determine "It" by itself, in isolation, so to speak. But this we must keep in mind: The It, at least in the interpretation available to us for the moment, names a presence of absence. (GA 14: 23/OTB 18)

I think Heidegger's attempt to work with the "Es gibt" is bound to remain exceedingly problematic, not only because of the difficulties that arise with the "Es," but also because of the problems that come with the "gibt," especially when it is glossed as a *sending*—a *Schicken*. Nevertheless, I think there is a way to retain the word *Geschick*, understanding it in a post-metaphysical way, as referring to destiny. Let us, to begin with, think of destiny as referring to *what we make* of the promising opportunities, potentialities, and possibilities that our time in the world, our situations, might make available to us in our exercise of freedom: opportunities, potentials, possibilities, some of them left behind in the past, forgotten, blocked, that we could retrieve from that past and take up for the sake of bringing us closer to the achievement of our shared historical sense of humanity.

However, it seems to me that the words related to *Geschick*, referring to a sending, a giving or granting, a dispensation, and a gift, are in effect holding us back, keeping us trapped in metaphysics. The German language creates here a metaphysical temptation that does not exist in the English language: *Geschick* is linguistically related to *schicken*, which means "to send." So, it is difficult to resist thinking of some mysterious metaphysical agency secretly at work in our destiny. To break out of metaphysics, we should not assume any agent or agency behind our world: no sending, no giving, nothing given, nothing sent. Heidegger's words are, I think, irremediably mischievous and misleading. Being is not a cause of things, but rather the necessary condition of their being and appearing. Being is the context of intelligibility and meaningfulness, the ground of appearance, the time-space clearing in which things can come into presence. And as such, being recedes; it withdraws, manifesting the dynamics of the figure-ground *Gestalt*. History is an intricate weave of contingent events and situations. There is nothing that we know of underneath or behind this weave. If that be so, then what is said to be sent or given, as by dispensation, is nothing other than, nothing more than, the events and situations we find ourselves having to live in and live with. The so-called dispensation is merely the factuality of our situation, our world—the world we find ourselves having to live in.

In our thrown-openness, we find ourselves confronting the givenness of the contingently given: our situations, conditions, circumstances. Confronting them, we have an opportunity to make of them something worthwhile, seeing if we can find, in the situations a confluence of contingent circumstances has given us, ways to retrieve and redeem historically missed opportunities, promising potentials, and overlooked possibilities: what was, what has been, and what still abides (*das Gewesene*), although it is as if it never was: Heidegger will call "das Un-geschehene," "the un-happened" (GA 94: 14; GA 34: 322). In these last two sentences, "given" is used in a way that does not draw us into ontotheology or metaphysics. It is used as a familiar and common way of acknowledging our circumstantial, situational, historical facticity.

What we find ourselves to have been "given"—including a past that still abides—does indeed make a claim on us. (On the difference between *das Vergangene*, the past as the bygone, and *das Gewesene*, the abiding of what has been, see GA 38: 103.) The "given" appropriates us. It is our responsibility to respond appropriately. We can give thanks for what has been disclosed only by treating what we have been given in the way that is most appropriate, most fitting.

What, then, is most fitting and most appropriate in responding to the *Seinsgeschick* (the dispensation of being) in the genocidal events of our world history? (1) Doing all we can possibly do to remember these historical events rightly, teaching the whole truth about them; (2) doing all we can possibly do to root out all forms of racism and intolerance; and (3) doing all we can possibly do to address the grievances, the resentments, the anxieties, and the rage that are major factors involved in the persistence of racism and intolerance.[20]

§10

My thinking has been formed in dialogue with many other philosophical minds. Here, I would like, even if only briefly, to situate my reading of Heidegger in relation to the thought of four interlocutors whose work has been especially important in my endeavor to formulate and propose for consideration an interpretation that is, I believe, comprehensive, coherent, and meaningful.

Richard Capobianco. I have read with pleasure his books *Engaging Heidegger* (2010) and *Heidegger's Way of Being* (2014).[21] There is much in Capobianco's interpretation and way of thinking that I like. In many ways, the paths on our adventures in thought nicely converge; and I enjoy our rich attunement. Above all, perhaps, we share a deep sympathy for the spirit of Romanticism that, in vestiges that bring a certain well-tempered joy, is retrieved and continued in Heidegger's project—although Capobianco's version, like that of Heidegger, is paradigmatically pastoral and bucolic, often seeming to evoke an idyllic world, whereas my Romanticism is a dream of *Sehnsucht* and melancholy troubled by the compelling reality of the commercialized, technologized, and painfully alienated life prevailing in the city and the brutal forms of intolerance manifest in the suffering of people living a rural life. Capobianco's second book concludes in a thought that I can wholeheartedly embrace, a thought that, indeed, lies behind much of my own work: the task to which Heidegger's thought summons us, he says, is "to revision ourselves, our relations, our *ethos* in accordance with the Being-way." But what does this mean? Arguing for this "Being-way," Capobianco speaks of "Being" as a gift for which the fitting response should be thankfulness. With pastoral scenes in mind, we can be moved to agree; but how does the "Being-way" respond to the Holocaust? Should we be grateful for the Shoah, the Holocaust? What we find ourselves to have been given by our historical situation does indeed make a claim on us. It appropriates us. It is our responsibility to respond appropriately. We can give thanks for what has been disclosed only by treating what we have been given in the way that is most appropriate, most fitting. I phrase my point this way because it must be recognized that not everything we have been given is obviously a blessing—not even a blessing in disguise, unless we are acrobats in linguistic obfuscation or charlatan magicians.

Capobianco emphasizes the importance, in the Being-way, of an attitude of "releasement"—*Gelassenheit*. But we need to distinguish between releasement as an ontological attitude and releasement as an ontic attitude. There is indeed wisdom in the ontological; but the ontic is not always wise or appropriate; it might even be morally reprehensible. For me, Capobianco's answer—an *ethos* of living in attunement with "Being"—needs much more specification. In this suggestion for living, what exactly does "Being" mean? I think it would be more helpful to think of that *ethos* in terms of the appropriation of attention: in question, then, would be our entering into a life of attentiveness, or mindfulness.[22] What is the relation between the "way of Being" and the conduct of an ethical life? What is the role of responsibility? Releasement and attunement must answer to the question of responsibility: responsibility for beings, responsibility for their being. How does *Sein* provide a model or guide for our comportment? It is unfortunate that many scholars have translated *Sein* using a capital letter that glorifies: "Being." And, after quoting four brief passages from Heidegger's published work, Capobianco writes, in this regard: "In my view, all recent scholarly efforts to maintain that Heidegger subordinated *Sein* to *Ereignis* (or any other term) simply founder."[23] All that I can say within the limits of this essay is that my disagreement with Capobianco in regard to being seems beyond reconciliation. He attributes to "Being" an independence that he claims is not theological and not metaphysical. But the way in which he characterizes this independence certainly makes it seem that "Being" plays the very same role of origin and agency that has always been attributed to God. This appearance is difficult to deny when, for instance, he quotes with manifest pleasure and approval[24] a passage from Heidegger's *Black Notebook* (GA 94: 304) in which, evoking a pastoral scene reminiscent of some of Thomas Cole's Hudson River paintings,[25] Heidegger says, "No matter how much the unrestrained distortion [*die losgelassene Verfälschung*] of everything rages [*sich austobe*], there remains for the wise [*dem Wissenden*] the mature calm of the mountain, the gathered illumination of the alpine meadows, the silent flight of the falcon, and the bright cloud in the expansive sky—that wherein the sublime stillness of the farthest nearness of beyng has already announced itself [*jenes, worin sich schon angesagt hat die grosse Stille der fernsten Nähe des Seyns*]." The passage begins with the Romantic evocation of a pastoral landscape: Although this invocation of *Seyn* can certainly tempt us to think of it as an independent, even world-transcendent source and agency, as I interpret the passage, it is attempting, albeit with unnecessary obscurity, to remind us of the *openness* of the clearing, as in the vision of Kalchas, the wise visionary who, rooted in the ecstatic dimension of temporality, can "fore-see" the future—not as prediction or prophecy, but simply by virtue of experiencing events from the standpoint of that ontological dimension of temporality where the three dimensions of time are gathered and intertwined.

It is true that there are textual passages in Heidegger's early period of thought wherein he says things suggesting a metaphysical transcendence, such as that "Being is abandoning us." Is that abandonment a mere figure of speech, an anthropomorphism not to be understood as seriously attributing that act, with its undeniable biblical resonance, to being? And if his thought-poem, "The Dawning of Being," the subject of my final chapter, is translated literally, it likewise attributes a certain metaphysical transcendence and agency to being. I cannot take this literally. It is perhaps most generously understood as a poetic expression of feeling despondent and helpless. As I read Heidegger, the claim for ontological independence cannot possibly be sustained in the light of his insisting on the belonging-togetherness of the human being and being. And "being itself" is, as he says very clearly and incontrovertibly in later texts, not other than the clearing that, by its very nature, arises and takes place as an openness that enables the being of beings to presence whenever and wherever a human being, understood as an embodied *Da-sein*, exists (GA 9: 337/PM 256: "so ist das Sein wesenhaft weiter als alles Seiende, weil es die Lichtung selbst ist"). What is "doing" the "sending" or "giving" is not other than *Seyn*, the clearing: that which essentially precedes (*wesenhaft weiter*) all beings and makes possible the appearing of beings in their presence and absence.[26] And the hoped-for continuing "generosity" of this dispensation can be "already announced" only because of the fact that the clearing is a temporally ecstatic openness. But, despite the uncanny wording that Heidegger surely knew would remind us of the Annunciation, nothing other than, or more than, the clearing is actually invoked, here, by Heidegger's words. The Romanticism that Capobianco and I share in melancholy nostalgia, longing, and hope must be tempered by an equally transcendental skepticism, reconciling in its own way the passion for the infinite and the recognition of limitation, our fate-imposed finitude. As Ralph Waldo Emerson's version of Transcendentalism expresses this point, acknowledging the unspeakable, a beyond always out of reach—but a beyond that is nevertheless finite.

> Thus is the unspeakable but intelligible and practicable meaning of the world conveyed to man, the immortal pupil, in every object of sense. To this one end of Discipline, all parts of nature conspire.[27]

In his implicit reconciliation of the sensible and the intelligible, Emerson encourages us to project, around every object of sense, a concealed, still unspeakable dimension of meaning: something like the representation of the gods in the gathering that takes place in Heidegger's *Geviert*. While Capobianco stresses the sublime dimension of concealment, the unspeakable, I want to stress the gathering that takes place around *every object of sense*—a transcendence of the ordinary within its ordinary time-space immanence.

Heidegger does seem to be suggesting that in the *Es gibt*, the *Es* names being as a source and agency behind the "gibt," as when he says, "The history of being means destiny of being in the sendings of which both the sendings and the *It* that sends forth hold back with their self-manifestation" (GA 14: 13/OTB 9). But despite some formulations like this one in which Heidegger seems to be suggesting that "being" in the relevant sense is a source independent of our presence as thrown-open *Da-sein*, I cannot agree with Capobianco's interpretation. Beings are independent of our existence, but being is not. The matter can be confusing, since Heidegger uses "being" in four different senses: (1) to express our recognition of the sheer fact that there are beings, speaking of the presencing, or *being*, of beings; (2) to refer to the "essence" we attribute to beings; and (3) to recognize that what it means for something to be can change, and has changed, in the course of history. What "gives" entities or "sends" them into their presencing within our world is being as the clearings (contexts of meaning, field of perception) that we in our bodily presence as *Da-sein* enter (GA 9: 337/PM 256). Being is neither the cause of beings nor their underlying essence, but rather that which arises and takes place as an openness within the shared world "reality," whenever and wherever a human being, understood as an embodied

Da-sein, exists; hence (4) there is the sense of "being" that construes it as a clearing that *enables* beings to emerge from concealment and appear for a while in a modality of presence in contexts of meaningfulness that are inherently always open.

I am not at all arguing here against religious and spiritual life. There is in this life a consciousness and sensibility, a practice of self-discipline and selflessness—call it religious or spiritual—that can encourage sympathy, kindness, generosity, hospitality, and other qualities of character that civilization has attempted to nurture. An authentic religious or spiritual life is not the problem. What I am arguing against is rather the role that Capobianco attributes to being, in effect identifying being as if it were really another way of thinking about God. To be sure, at various stages in the formulation and presentation of his project, Heidegger himself has encouraged such thinking, using words that we associate with the Christian religion and its theology in contexts that concern being. His personal struggles with a traditional religious background are reproduced in an ambivalence that appears in unresolved ambiguities troubling the interpretation of his philosophical thought. This means that we have to make consequential interpretive decisions.

François Raffoul. I like Raffoul's books on Heidegger, especially *The Origins of Responsibility*[28] and *Thinking the Event*.[29] In these two books, he concentrates on two of Heidegger's key words. For me, the origins of our responsibility for the fate of being, hence the fate of all beings, depends very much on our collective historical experience of being—the event of being (*Das Ereignis*). Our deepest, strongest, most steadfast sense of responsibility for being comes out of experiencing the event of being, being itself and as such, with recognition and understanding of the calling that the event bears. In regard to most of the fundamental matters, Raffoul's reading of Heidegger and mine happily converge. The one most outstanding difference, though, is his overwhelming emphasis on the unsettling expropriation that the experience of the event inevitably causes and on the finite limits of our ability to achieve the transformation of our world to which our responsibility is summoned. Recognition of our mortality, our weaknesses, and limitations—the *aporias* we encounter, resisting and blocking our way—is of course imperative. *Hubris* is a temptation that ultimately serves only to extend the reign of nihilism. However, there is, in Raffoul's texts, such an emphasis on negativity, on the deconstruction of any project, everything decisively interpreted as crucially, intrinsically eventuating, either in paradox or in aporia, such that it can become difficult for hope to overcome despair: so difficult, in fact, that the messianic redeeming of our sense of humanity and the world we have built that, after Derrida, Raffoul presumably wants to recognize, can seem virtually impossible. We need to balance ambition and humility, despair and hope, finitude and immanent transcendence. But how to move past the dead ends that the *aporias* seem to set before us remains an unresolved question. Perhaps Raffoul's most important contribution, like Derrida's, is to keep us honest and humble, recognizing the stumbling blocks that responsible thinking must not ignore. One more matter. I consider it crucial that the event of being not be appropriated by philosophical thought on the assumption that only such thought, with the weight of history behind it, can properly engage this event. Although it is an extraordinary event, it needs to be available outside that esoteric realm of thought if it is going to make a real difference in the character of life in the world. Our responsibility for being is outside the philosophical text. Raffoul wants to concentrate on the weakness of our cognitive and volitional powers with regard to the event of being: he deconstructs our approach to the event, challenging our metaphysical and epistemological assumptions and opening a way through the *aporias*. This outlines a noble and worthy scholarly pursuit with important implications for the continuation of Heidegger's project. But it is at this point that I want rather to leave the hermeneutics of being and the deconstructive logic of *aporias* and concentrate on the real *difference* that the experience of the ontological event actually makes in everyday life—in particular, in our ethical and political life.

Thomas Sheehan. I hugely admire Sheehan's reading of Heidegger, exemplified in his 2015 book, *Making Sense of Heidegger: A Paradigm Shift*.[30] I welcome that undertaking and am immensely indebted to his interpretive readings of Heidegger. They have inspired me with the courage to read Heidegger according to my own sense of what is at stake. It is a decisive relief to read an interpretation of Heidegger that endeavors to make good, sound sense of some exceedingly awkward, complicated, and abstract words and arguments. Moreover, in large measure, I happily agree with his interpretation. What I offer in relation to his work is, consequently, primarily in the nature of a supplement. The one, and perhaps only, point of divergence concerns his interpretation of *Ereignis*. For him, this key word is not to be interpreted as referring to an event (*Making Sense of Heidegger*, xvii, 234–35). He is certainly right in recognizing that, for Heidegger, the *Ereignis* is not, or not merely, not only, an event in world history in the *ordinary sense* of "event." And he is right in recognizing that Heidegger explicitly repudiates any attempt to think what it names in historiological terms. It is rather, for Heidegger, at least in the 1930s, a term essentially belonging to the "history" of being (*Seinsgeschichte*, *Geschick des Seins*). But I understand that to mean that it *is* nevertheless some kind of event, although an event of an *extraordinary* nature: an event, let us say, of *ontological* significance, an event concerning the experience of being as such, being itself, an event in which a fundamental ontological *difference* between being and beings is recognized as attention turns from beings to being as such. What the pre-Socratic philosophers Parmenides and Heraclitus experienced was a genuine event, a truly history-making event. For Heidegger, it was an inceptual event, not only inaugurating the discourse of metaphysics as a reflection on being but contributing in the realm of thought to the formation of the distinctive worldview and epoch that we identify with the ancient world of the West. Heidegger accordingly believed that a renewed attention, in our own time, to the ontological difference, and to being as such, could perhaps bring about another inception, another epoch in the meaning of being and the way in which we experience the being of beings. We need to appreciate the revolutionary importance of this event-oriented interpretation of the *Ereignis*. Of course, it is crucial to think of *Ereignis* as referring to an *ontological* event—not only an extra-ordinary *event* of singular ontological significance, but an event that is appropriating, appropriating *us*.

When Heidegger retrieves the pre-Socratics, it is to retrieve, as an event, their history-making inception, not only for the discourse of metaphysics, but, ultimately, for the ontological worldview that has unfolded its epochs in the Western world. And the intention behind this retrieving is to *make* history, *change* history: bring about another inception, a new understanding of being, of what it means to be. For Sheehan, however, it seems that the terms *Ereignis* and *Ereignung* refer first and foremost to propriation: the "structural *ap-propri-ation* of existence to its proper state as the thrown-open clearing" (Sheehan, *Making Sense of Heidegger*, 19). It is, he says, "the same phenomenon" as thrown-openness, the clearing, the essence of human being (Sheehan, *Making Sense of Heidegger*, xv). I agree with that interpretation; but if, as it seems, he gives more weight to propriation than he does to the event, then I would want to argue that he is giving less importance than is needed to the eventfulness of the *Ereignis*. In my judgment, propriation and event are *equally necessary* readings of "Ereignis." Propriation is not—or, in my reading, not only—an event; we must recognize, as Sheehan does, that it needs to be understood as a *process*—a process of self-examination and self-development that summons and calls us, appropriating us, to undertake it. It is, in part, Heidegger's way of thinking "authenticity" after *Being and Time*: answers, many possible, never more than transitory, to the existential questions "Who am I?" and "Who are we?" We also need to understand propriation in "structural" terms. Sheehan astutely recognizes the structural dimension; however, we need to explicate in more phenomenological detail how this structural dimension works its appropriation. And that requires recognizing, first of all, the fundamental and inseparable belonging-togetherness of *Mensch-Sein* and *Sein*. Second, it requires recognizing in the phenomenology of this relation the fact of our embodiment. Understanding the *Ereignis* as propriation requires what Nietzsche would call bodily incorporation: *Einverleibung*. Thus, third, the word requires recognizing the role or function of what Heidegger calls "our most fundamental disposition," the gentle law (*Ge-setz*) of our bodily nature, which lays out (*setzt*) our thrown-openness. This fundamental disposition, a pre-ontological attunement preceding the subject-object formation, can be bodily felt. However, although Heidegger describes the phenomenology of our relation to being in terms of an oscillation, a *Schweben* and *Schwingen* that Merleau-Ponty would describe as a reversibility and reciprocity, the felt body never figures in Heidegger's account. I surmise that that omission is the residue of a metaphysical construction of the body as substance that Heidegger failed to recognize and renounce. Fourth, it requires recognizing in this phenomenology our appropriation, our summons to assume responsibility for preserving and safeguarding being: our responsibility for sustaining the openness of the clearing, and for the very *being* of beings. Thus, after Sheehan's wonderfully illuminating reading of existential propriation in Heidegger's project, we need to flesh out the *Einverleibung* in order to understand concretely *how* the ontological event appropriates us. There is, then, more involved in the phenomenology of propriation as event, structure, and process than figures in the paradigm formulated in *Making Sense of Heidegger*. Nevertheless, this work makes the case for an interpretation that makes good sound sense by moving away from metaphysical temptations, reading "being" as the condition of intelligibility or meaning. It needs to be recognized, however, that "being" also refers to the space-time fields of perception, necessary condition for the possibility of concealments and unconcealments taking place in the space-time dimensions of perception. "Being" is not only what Sheehan, moving away from metaphysical projections, identifies as a matter of cognitive meaning, the meaning in and of the use of language. *Sinn* and *Bedeutung* are both also operative in sensory experience and perception.

Richard Polt. In his two informative and insightful books on Heidegger, *The Emergency of Being* (2006) and *Time and Trauma* (2019), Polt introduces, and stirs us to consider, important new approaches to Heidegger's project, bringing to our attention questions and contemporary problems in need of much more reflective engagement.[31] In what is perhaps his greatest difference from Sheehan, Polt's books emphasize how we should understand *Ereignis* as an *event* experienced in everyday life. Whereas Heidegger interprets it primarily in the context of the history of philosophical thought, although he recognizes its consequences and implications for the history and future of the Western world, Polt discerns the experience of being as such (the experience of what it means for anything to be), in our everyday life: it is not only the experience of a singularly extra-ordinary event, a history-founding, history-transforming event, designating both a genuinely originary turning-point in Western history and also the *possibility* of another such inceptual event, an origin of meaning setting in motion another very different epoch in the disclosure of being; it is also *any* event in which the experienced sense of being exceeds the understanding operative in present concepts and categories.

I like how, in his first book, Polt turns the danger and urgency of the crisis that Heidegger describes as nihilism, the abandonment of being, into an emergency in which promising possibilities for transformation might be emerging. In both works, it is being as *eventful*, as *exceeding* the sense of being as we have understood it, that motivates and informs Polt's thinking. For him, the key word *Ereignis* is an appropriating, and potentially unsettling, sometimes even traumatic event that "gives birth to our own being by calling it into question and urging us to decide who we are" (*Time and Trauma*, 109).

"We must each discover," he says, "the appropriating events of emergency in our own lives and communities." For it is not only a question of "the rare emergency that would found a world and an era," but also a question of "the smaller shocks and reversals that are frequent elements of our individual and collective lives (*Time and Trauma*, 7). The crises affecting our lives, especially ones involving questions of meaning and meaningfulness, are, according to Polt, times of emergency, times when, in the events that are taking place, our sense of how things are and what they are is disrupted, challenged, not only causing distress, suffering, and even, perhaps, great trauma; but they are also possible opportunities for the creative emergence of new possibilities for meaningful existence. Such is the essential message, a message of faith and hope, but one that does not neglect, distort, or deny the dangers, challenges, and trials that we, as human beings dwelling on this planet, are compelled to comprehend and responsibly, appropriately turn into opportunities for the transformative creation of new ways of living. Working with the concepts of emergency, emergence, sense, excess, and trauma, Polt provides a compelling reading of Heidegger, drawing on the key notion of *Ereignis* as event—an event that summons and challenges us, perhaps remaking the future that the past would otherwise impose. Working with his understanding of *Ereignis* as event, Polt is able to show—*eraügen*—how our appropriation in the experience of the ontological event—that is, how our experience and understanding of being—bears very concretely not only on the social, political, and moral crises of our time, but also on the way in which we inherit our history and attempt to appropriate its promising possibilities for the future.

What makes Polt's books so timely is that he extends Heidegger's strictly ontological interpretation of *Ereignis* so that it does not designate only an experience in which the meaning of being is contemplated, but can designate *any* event that profoundly unsettles our fundamental sense of things, even unto incomprehensibility, and challenges us to make of it an opportunity for greater self-examination and more creative living. And what makes the books so compelling is the care and insight with which such events are fleshed out and given experiential concreteness. Some of the events he considers, truly traumatic and estranging, exceeding the understanding in our present concepts and categories, can even challenge or disrupt our sense of who we really are. Polt's two books offer an extensive phenomenology capable of illuminating the historical and ontological character of significant events in our lives and our world, when a new sense of being emerges. Moreover, the books provide critical reflection on recognizable historical and contemporary *events* of ontological significance, crisis, and emergency. His books show just how illuminating it can be to interpret our world thinking with, in and from the perspective of the event. Such is the distinct virtue of Polt's two books, the latter of which concludes with an extremely timely, indeed urgent question: "Can a community be nourished and strengthened, not through a founding identity, but by sustaining and enhancing a public sphere in which responses to the question 'Who are we?' can be contested?" (*Time and Trauma*, 240). All around the world, nations have been thrown into struggles around this very question. But Polt's books confront and avert the danger to which Capobianco's reading of Heidegger is exposed, namely, that precisely in our time of crisis, we take refuge in Romantic fantasies and wishful thinking. Thus, when Polt writes that the appropriating event "is the inception that founds a world and lets being become an issue" (*Time and Trauma*, 109), he needs to acknowledge and name the crucial mediating medium that *joins* the event of being—the event as such—to the inception of philosophical discourse and the founding of a world, namely, the concrete *experience* of being as such, being itself as always *exceeding* the understanding we have. Strictly speaking, the event is not, first of all, the inception; rather, it is first of all the *experience* of being as such, revealing itself in an excess beyond our settled sense; and it is *that* intermediary experience which constitutes, and is represented in, the history-making event that is not only the inception of metaphysical thought but also the founding and emergence of a distinctive ontological epoch in the history of the world. Consequently, Polt argues that the *Ereignis* is an event that needs to be understood in terms of the phenomenology of propriation and authenticity as it bears on the question of who we are. Sheehan's books likewise emphasize this *experience* of being in our existential propriation as thrown-open, situated beings, leaving somewhat undeveloped the *Ereignis* as signifying the emerging of a new sense-making event in regard to our experience and understanding of being—that is to say, in regard to what has made sense to us.

In my work, I attempt to delve deeply into the phenomenology involved in the *Ereignis* (*Ereignung*) in order to propose a *reconciliation* of these two equally needed approaches, (1) *Ereignis* as event and (2) *Ereignis* as propriation, considering them to be not merely inseparable, but mutually requiring one another. In working out this phenomenology, I bring together and tie into a coherent, comprehensive interpretation the loose threads that Heidegger himself never clearly tied together: event and process, thrown-openness as the dis-positional structure of *Da-sein*, *Da-sein and Sein* in reversibility, interdependent belonging-together, and, finally, our responsibility for being. I also draw attention to how the fundamental thrown-openness of our bodily disposition figures in the *Ereignis* as an experience of being itself that stirs us to engage in a process of propriation.

None of the philosophers I have considered here take this bodily disposition into account, despite the fact that its incorporation of the ontological event is indispensable if we want to understand *why and how* the event of being as an ontological experience can bestir and appropriate us.[32] Even philosophers who have given attention to the human body have neglected to think about it in terms of its capacities and capabilities; and they have consequently ignored questions regarding their cultivation and development in the context of ethical life. I hope that, in this volume, I have elucidated and made sense of these matters, which Heidegger left to us in some very awkward and obscure formulations.

§11

There is, in Heidegger's project, what Walter Benjamin calls "a weak messianic ability" (*eine schwache messianische Kraft*), echoing in his own way Kant's phrase, "a weak ray of hope" (*eine schwache Strahl der Hoffnung*).[33] But the important point to bear in mind is that our destiny and its promise depend entirely on us! And, right now, I think we need to acknowledge that that promise seems to depend on a very weak power. Perhaps it begins when we enter into attentiveness—or say mindfulness. *Besinnung. Eingedenk-Sein.*

In imagining a future different from the past and better, above all, in regard to a different and better way of revealing being, Heidegger's project calls for retrieving missed possibilities and potentials from the past for the sake of appropriating and developing them to make a different future. The "Einkehr in das Ereignis" is thus also our appropriation as guardians of being: our appropriation for the future, the task of destiny.

Even in the 1936–1938 *Contributions*, while invoking "the last god" and saying that "the last god is not the end," Heidegger was urging us to direct our thinking toward another epochal beginning, understanding this as the beginning "of the measureless possibilities of our history" (GA 65: 411/ CP 326). "History," he says there, meaning "authentic" history, a history in the making of which we are engaged, should be understood in terms of "being as unfolding in events of appropriation [*Seyn als Ereignis*]" (GA 65: 494/CP 388). Hence, the *Ereignis* is not so much a mystery (*Geheimnis*) as it is a "home-coming" (*Heim-kehr*), a return to the sense and call of one's deepest nature, and the proper relation to being (see GA 65: 408/CP 323; GA 79: 70/BF 66). In question is our *ontological* responsibility, that is, our responsibility for being, a responsive openness, a "releasement" into openness, a responsibility that cannot be thought in terms of the opposition between active and passive. Nor can it be thought in terms of the opposition of the intelligible and the sensible.

But this process of retrieving historical possibilities requires confronting the fact that the conditions holding sway in the present epoch—the epoch of the *Gestell*, imposing a universal regime of total reification—obscure, distort, and even block our awareness, recognition, and understanding of these possibilities and potentials (see GA 7: 26–27/QCT 26). What *is* the *Geschick*? What have we been granted (*geschickt*) to work with? How can philosophical thought penetrate and overcome social, political, and cultural forms of distortion and blockage? These questions bring our thinking back to the *Ereignis*—back to being and its contemporary appropriation of our way of living. Thus, thinking about the destiny in our dispensation, we should not forget that, as the poet Wallace Stevens phrased it, "The final belief is to believe in a fiction, which you know to be a fiction, there being nothing else. The exquisite truth is to know that it is a fiction and that you believe in it willingly."[34] In concluding *Minima Moralia: Reflections from Damaged Life*, Theodor W. Adorno advises essentially the same process of appropriation or self-recognition in regard to the perspective of redemption.

> The only thing that can be responsibly practiced in the face of despair is to contemplate all things as they would present themselves from the standpoint of redemption [*vom Standpunkt der Erlösung*].

But he warns against failing to recognize the conditionality within which we project the fiction, or artifice, of the unconditional *Geschick*.

> The more passionately thought denies its conditionality for the sake of the unconditional, the more unconsciously, and so calamitously, it is delivered up to the world. Even its own impossibility it must at last comprehend for the sake of the possible. But beside the demand thus placed on thought, the question of the reality or unreality of redemption hardly matters.[35]

How does this bear on Heidegger's thought? In his first major work, *Being and Time*, Heidegger cannot emphasize enough the importance of giving thought to being—the question of being. But, although he briefly suggests it bears on ethical life, constituting "an orginary ethics," he leaves us quite in the dark, quite mystified, regarding the importance of this attention for our lives. Why does it matter whether we give thought to being—something that seems to be nothing but a useless abstraction? What we need to understand is that *it is for the sake of beings*—for the sake of *their* being, and *our* being as their guardians—that being matters. And so, what this means is that ontology—the particular ontology to which, in our time, we in the Western world, and increasingly in the Eastern, are committed, knowingly or not—makes an incalculable difference in regard to how we live, each one of us humans, with all other beings. And that means that our ontological commitments profoundly affect ethical life. There is no way to separate ethics from ontology. This is why being in all its four senses matters.

†

What our time requires is a critical confrontation, identifying, penetrating, and overcoming the social, political, and cultural factors currently blocking, obscuring, and distorting historical possibilities and potentials that, if retrieved and achieved in actuality, might turn our world of unnecessary suffering in a different direction, while also addressing the planetary emergency. But since there can be no guarantees, a good beginning would be, I suggest, Socratic work on ourselves, recognizing how we are woven into the text and texture of the world, connected to all living beings and dependent on all of nature. And we need to work up the courage to recognize and serve the truth, saying, of what is, that it is and of what is not, that it is not. After *Being and Time*, Heidegger called this Socratic work *ap-propriation*: *Er-eignung*. Socrates, who taught that the unexamined life is not worth living, thought of this critical reflexivity, or self-examination, as a way of "caring for one's soul" ("*epimeleia he'auto*").[36] For Heidegger, this process of propriation, becoming our potential, is inseparable from a dawning understanding of being. And that means not only understanding our inseparable belonging-togetherness with being, but understanding our responsibility for being—as it bears on all the different beings that figure in our ethical life.

A Spanish poet, José Ángel Valente, seems to be addressing that same experience of a merely dawning understanding in regard to the sense of being, writing, in "Memoria profética," a stanza of verse that warns us against forgetting the wisdom of the prophets, the seers, guardians of being, those who speak from the past and from the future to the needs of the present. At stake in the dawning sense of being [evoked in the metaphor of the Sun] is the awakening of *a deep sense of responsibility* for being as the promising gift of destiny (*Geschick*) in the hand of the human, those mortals wisely exercising their inherently limited freedom in such light as is given (*geschickt*) by, and in, the present conditions of the world. So, we turn now, as Heidegger always did, to one of the poets who speak to our time.

> Do not let the old prophets die,
> for they raise their voices against the greed that blinds our eyes
>   with dark oxides,
> voice that comes from the desert, naked animal that emerges
>   from the waters

> to found a reign of innocence,
> rage that unfolds the world in wings, the bird charred in the apocalypse,
> ancient words, lost cities,
> the awaited dawning of the sun as reassuring gift in the hands of the human.[37]

Like Heidegger and Adorno, I repudiate the delusion of a theologically inspired metaphysics that promises redemption only in the transcendence of mortal life and relieves us of our responsibility. At the heart of this responsibility for being is a redemption that affirms the promise hidden in our creaturely life and works for the salvation and glorification of this world, grounded with care on the earth and learning the limits of our measure from the infinite and immeasurable sky.

The time of our destiny (*Geschick*) depends on us—on how we make use of our freedom in receiving and appropriating wisely what the contingencies of nature and history have granted (*geschickt*) to us. Will we find what is promising in the situations we find ourselves given? Only time will tell.

Chapter 7

A Dawning Sense of Being

The mystery is not how things are in the world, but rather the fact that there is a world at all.

—Ludwig Wittgenstein, *Tractatus Logico-Philosophicus*

I am so happy, dear friend, so completely immersed in the sensation of sheer being.

—Johannes Wolfgang von Goethe, *The Sorrows of Young Werther*

Works of art may be defined as models of a nature that awaits no day, and thus no judgement day; they are models of a nature that is neither the theater of history nor the dwelling place of mankind. The redeemed night.

—Walter Benjamin, Letter to Florens Christian Rangs, 1923

In a collection of thought-poems, Heidegger attempted to condense his thinking, exercising the greatest possible restraint in order to let it come into expression wrought only through the richest, most telling, most compelling of words.

In what follows, I have interpreted and translated one of those thought-poems, offering not a "literal" translation—which, even if such a thing were possible, would, I believe, at the very least leave some of the meaning too dense and obscure, indeed virtually impenetrable, but rather instead a paraphrased interpretation, trying to be faithful both to the spirit of his thought and its sense. In undertaking this paraphrasing, I am indebted to Eoghan Walls, whose "more literal," but still inevitably interpretive translation has been useful, inspiring me to try rendering the thought-poem in a more accessible form without betraying or violating the tonality and dimensionality of its meaning.[1]

What makes the particular thought-poem that I have chosen to interpret and present here especially beautiful and worthy of attention is that it carries us back so vividly, as with such intense immediacy, to that extraordinary event, that moment in Western history, when, suddenly realizing their freedom to turn their attention away from the things of this world in order to reflect in wonder and awe on the very being of all these things, the earliest Greek philosophers first began to near, in their thinking, an understanding of being itself. We are carried back in time, as if to relive their experience, carried back to feel its existential meaning for them, while also contemplating their experience as an originating event in Western history, and in particular, as an event inaugurating the discourse of Western metaphysics—and consequently recognizing, in their philosophical reflections on that experience, their limitations, their unknowing: an appropriation and dis-position still concealed from them. What is dawning is a recognition of the ontological difference between beings and being, being as such, the necessary condition for the very possibility that beings can appear as present or absent in the fields of human experience. In a *schwebend*, pendulum-like rhythm, we are carried back in time to a certain historical dawn, and from there gently brought into the appropriation of a present from which we find ourselves envisioning the possibility of another dawn, dawn of what is still hidden, still to come, beckoning and summoning us to assume a necessary responsibility for being in the fitting exercise of our freedom. And, as Benjamin says, what art intimates is the promise of a redeemed night. And after that, the possibility of a new dawn.

Everything depends on our response (*Antwort*) to the claim by which, in the very nature of our inherent relation to being, we are summoned and our consequent assumption of responsibility (*Verantwortung*) for being: the "Verantwortung des Menschen für das Sein" (GA 11: 40n53/ID 32–33). Before we have become aware, we have always already been claimed by being, claimed in the disposition appropriating and attuning our embodiment, opening and exposing us to being. According to Heidegger, this means, given that we have today fallen into an epoch of nihilism affecting every aspect of our daily lives on earth, that we have a responsibility to take up and appropriate (*an-eignen*) the task (*Auf-gabe*) of preparing the way for a new epoch in the historical unfolding of the meaning of being—an experience and understanding of being more worthy of the promising possibilities in our guardianship (*Wächterschaft*) of the world and the earth on which we have built our civilization. It is in protecting being that we give appropriate recognition to the beings we encounter in our passage through the world—recognition to the truth of what they really are and how they figure, how they matter, and how they appear to be.

The first imperative of guardianship is attentiveness, not only as in *Aufmerksamkeit* (taking notice) but also as in *Besinnung* (mindfulness). Heidegger rarely, however, uses the somewhat quaint locution "*eingedenk sein*": being drawn into thought. In any event, it is a question of giving, or rather returning, from its forgotten beginning, the gift of thought to being.

Here, now, in a prose form that I think remains faithful to Heidegger's most deeply considered thinking, but departs from the misleading metaphysical deification of being in the original phrasing, as I suggest that it is not "Being" that is dawning, but rather *our sense of being* that is dawning, giving some hope, so to speak, for a new day in the emergence of our humanity and a new day for all life on this planet. Here, then, is what I will call Heidegger's song.

A Dawning Sense of Being

> While called to understand being, hidden from the very first,
> then retrieved into the hesitant, stammering beginning
> by an event of appropriation, a claim
> long unrecognized by themselves,
> and hidden from within their freedom,
> the ancient Greeks, even when finally almost able to think,
>   daringly,
> the clearing, with its concealed dispossession and estrangement
>   in appropriation,
> find themselves abandoned to their solitary destiny:
> freed in their ascent into the metaphysical, yet exceptionally
>   shy
> in the harvesting, the gathering, of all that comes to light
> in the invisible providence of dispensation,
> but still first to be enlightened by an appearance in the light.
> Viewed from there, gathering and listening

they were able to grow into looking
for the sake of truly seeing, whereby it became possible
to choose the clearest meaning for the eye;
and ever since, the world appears as it does,
a world framed from the viewpoint of visual presence: is.
So, the historical moment, when being comes into recognition
    and understanding, has been determined,
granting the appearance of beings
but itself only shining unnoticed among unreflective lights.
According to the measure of shining self-showing,
cognition itself becomes perception,
a looking that gives entitlement to appearance,
setting it forth in the keeping
of steadfast presence,
having forgotten its origins
in the thinking of the early poetry
hidden in the poesy of being;
so, the future itself in its own truth
has henceforth been veiled, a denial of itself,
close only in an estranged intimacy,
surprising distances in nameless futile beckonings,
in its own separation from awareness,
returning back to a once pure, deferred dispossession.
Perhaps this light, even though not
the illumination of the poetry
of appropriation,
will become the dawn
of what is still hidden from our understanding: what is to be
    cared for
in that freedom
that is not yet wholeheartedly sensed in the openness that is
    the truth
of being.
[See "The Enowning Claim" (*Eignis*).]

∽

In a footnote to this thought-poem, this song, drawing the relation between the ontological difference between beyng (being) and beings, that is, between the openness of the clearing and what presences *in* the clearing, Heidegger remarks, "Das Seyn ist die Wahrheit, ist die Heit der wahrenden Sparnis des Seins. Sein ist Seyn": "Beyng is truth, is the cheerful, or promising, glowing lighting of the nurturing protecting of the being of beings. Beyng is the clearing, openness for what presences" (my translation).

As Thomas Sheehan has argued with admirable scholarship, in Heidegger's way of thinking, there are four distinct senses of the word *Sein—Being*. This can cause considerable confusion and misunderstanding. In my brief recapitulation: (1) It is used to invoke that-which-is, expressing with wonder, awe, and a recognition of our limited powers of explanation and understanding the sheer fact that there is anything instead of nothing. (2) It is used to refer to the essence of something, but without assuming any metaphysical attribution of a final set end, purpose, or fully determinate, timeless meaning. For Heidegger, the essence of something is not eternal and immutable; instead it is exposed to the world, conceived in a dynamic process of interpretation that is open to the contingencies taking place in the world. The invocation of an essence is perhaps especially useful, however, as a way of challenging and resisting the reductionisms, reifications, and totalizations common in the *Gestell* of our time. In defending the being of a tree against its reduction to nothing but lumber, Heidegger will remind us to recognize its being. And in regard to the human being, the human *Dasein*, while defending our humanity against objectification, the invocation of being breaks with metaphysics, asserting that the meaning and purpose of our lives is not predetermined like the essence of a stone or tree, but entirely a question for our lives to answer. Although we enter the world with a certain bodily endowment, predispositions we are unable to escape, it is up to us to make of it what we will. So, "being" is that in terms of which beings as such are understood. (3) *Being* is used to refer to the *appearing* of beings, the *how* of their being, or presencing, in our world, whether in the mode of presence or in the mode of absence. As such, the term can become a way of urging ontological *Gelassenheit*, letting beings show themselves as they are. And (4) in its fourth sense, *being* refers to *that which makes possible* the phenomenology of presencing and appearing in our experience with beings. Accordingly, when Heidegger refers to that (*Es*) which "sends" (*schickt*), or "gives" (*gibt*) being, he is referring to the phenomenology of the clearing, the opening and exposing constitutive of our existence, as that which makes possible the presencing and appearing of beings. He is not attempting, as if still in metaphysics, to explain *why* there are beings instead of nothing by referring to being as the source, sender, and giver.

While the structure of these distinctions might remain over historical time and into the unknown future, what it means for something—anything—to *be* can undergo, and has in fact undergone, significant change in the course of Western history. The very being of beings as commonly experienced and understood in the past was very different from how that being of beings is commonly experienced and understood today. In his writings bearing on the history of philosophy, Heidegger succinctly but compellingly delineates the history of the Western relation to beings, noting that some of the transformations taking place as philosophical thought regarding the being of beings moved from ancient Greece to the Roman world, through the world of medieval Europe and the early modern world, eventuating in the way we of today experience and understand such being. Heidegger is unambiguous in his recognition of an epochal history of being, emphasizing how, in the Western world, *things* became *objects* and objects lost even their independent reality, becoming nothing but mere items of use. Thus, for instance, he notes how the subject-object relation that emerged in the time of Descartes is "only a historical variation of the relation we still recognize between the human being and the thing, insofar as things can be reduced [and have become nothing but objects"] (GA 77: 140/CPC 91).

If the logic of the historical unfolding of the conceptual transformations is quite clear, the confluence of factors contributing in various ways to these changes is of course beyond the competence of this logic to explain. But in any case, these factors are nothing mysterious: behind the historical changes, there is no metaphysical agency. That, however, does not relieve us of the formidable difficulties confronting any attempt, whether in concept formation, historiography, social theory or economic theory, to interpret the epochal changes that have occurred, and are still occurring, in our experience of being.

The uniquely ontological story that Heidegger tells is, like Hegel's, comprehensive; it also seems in many ways confirmed by our shared experience of "reality"—a "reality," however, that has emerged, in the course of time, from some deeply compelling illusions. Nevertheless, the ultimate test of the disclosive truth in his story lies, as Marx's *Eighteenth Brumaire* would argue, in its pragmatic power to suggest, motivate, and guide constructive changes in our attitudes and actions: "Humans make their own history," Marx wrote, "but they do not make it as they please; they do not make it under self-selected circumstances, but under circumstances existing already, given and transmitted from the past."

†

Passing, still early in the second decade of my life, many beguiling summer hours in my grandfather's vast encyclopedic library, I discovered, one day, a collection of George Santayana's books. Reading *The Last Puritan* to its end, I found a question for thought that has remained with me throughout my years in this world. It has served me well: "After life is over and the world has gone up in smoke, what realities might the spirit in us still call its own without illusion save the form of those very illusions which have made up our story?"

It is easy, reading Heidegger, to fall into metaphysical illusion. One might question from this viewpoint Heidegger's history of being (*Seinsgeschichte*). Heidegger himself expressed some strong reservations, perhaps recognizing that his interpretation of that history, committed to a problematic version of destiny, was irremediably metaphysical. Even so, he sought I think to remedy this problem, or at least counterbalance it, by turning our attention to *Dasein*'s appropriation and consequent ontological and ethical responsibility, set in motion by experiencing the event of being. But as he understood so profoundly, our sense of being is still only dawning.

Notes

Introduction

1. Benedict Spinoza, *Ethics*, Preceded by *On the Improvement of the Understanding*, ed. James Gutmann (New York: Hafner Publishing, 1960), 263–71.

2. Theodor Adorno, *Minima Moralia: Reflexionen aus dem beschädigten Leben* (Frankfurt am Main: Suhrkamp Verlag, 1951, 1969), 333; *Minima Moralia: Reflections from Damaged Life*, trans. E. F. N. Jephcott (London: Verso NLB, 1978), 247.

3. Spinoza, *Ethics*, 249. But see Dante, *The Inferno*. Trans. Robert Hollander and Jane Hollander (New York: Doubleday Random House, 2000), Canto VI: 107–8, 110: "quanto la cosa è più perfetta, / più senta il bene, / e così la doglienza": "the more perfect a being becomes, the more it is cognizant of the good, and for precisely that reason, it suffers all the more [in witnessing the misery and depravity of the world]" (my paraphrase).

4. Salman Rushdie, *Languages of Truth: Essays 2003–2020* (New York: Random House: 2021), 15.

5. Ontology, as that which concerns the being of beings, requires an ethics that calls for relating to beings in a way that is fittingly respectful of their nature, their being; and indeed, our ethics implies and requires a fittingly respectful engagement with regard to all beings. And see Jacques Derrida, "Violence and Metaphysics," in Alan Bass, trans., *Writing and Difference* (Chicago: University of Chicago Press, 1978), 121. "The phenomenon of respect requires the respect of phenomenality. And ethics requires phenomenology. In this sense, phenomenology is respect itself [. . .] Which is to say that ethics finds within phenomenology its own meaning, freedom, and radicality." I could not agree more wholeheartedly.

6. T. S. Eliot, *Collected Poems 1909–1962* (New York: Harcourt, Brace, and World, 1936), 133.

Chapter 1

1. Maurice Merleau-Ponty, *Phenomenology of Perception*, trans. Colin Smith (London: Routledge & Kegan Paul, 1962), 148.

210 | Notes to Chapter 2

2. Michel Foucault, "What Is Enlightenment?," in Paul Rabinow (ed.), *The Foucault Reader* (New York: Pantheon Books, 1984), 48.

3. Theodor W. Adorno, *Negative Dialectics*, trans. E. B. Ashton (London: Routledge & Kegan Paul, 1973), 365.

4. Jay M. Bernstein, "Intact and Fragmented Bodies: Versions of Ethics 'after Auschwitz,'" *New German Critique* 97, no. 1 (Winter 2006): 31.

5. Bernstein, "Intact and Fragmented Bodies, 32.

6. Adorno, *Negative Dialectic*s, 365.

7. Maurice Merleau-Ponty, "The Philosopher and His Shadow," *Signs*, trans. Richard C. McCleary (Evanston: Northwestern University Press, 1964), 167.

8. Foucault, *The Use of Pleasure*, trans. Robert Hurley (New York: Pantheon, 1995), 8.

9. Walter Brogan, "The Parting of Being: On Creation and Sharing in Nancy's Political Ontology," *Research in Phenomenology* 40 (2010): 300. Also see an exceptionally fine book by James R. Mensch, *Embodiments: From the Body to the Body Politic* (Evanston: Northwestern University Press, 2009) and the very useful review and summary of this book by Kathrin Morgenstern and Barbara Weber, "The Recovery of the Body," *Research in Phenomenology* 41 (2011): 441–49. For further reading, I cannot overestimate the significance of Eugene Gendlin's revised volume on *Experiencing and the Creation of Meaning: A Philosophical and Psychological Approach to the Subjective* (Studies in Phenomenology and Existential Philosophy), Evanston: Northwestern University Press, 1962, 1997. Also see the early trilogy by me, David Michael Levin: *The Body's Recollection of Being* (London: Routledge & Kegan Paul, 1985), *The Opening of Vision* (London: Routledge, 1987), and *The Listening Self* (London, Routledge, 1989). In addition, see my essay, "The Ontological Dimension of Embodiment: Heidegger's Thinking of Being," in Don Welton, ed., *The Body* (Malden, MA, Oxford, UK: Blackwell Publishers, 1999), 122–49. Since writing those works, however, I have significantly revised my way of thinking about being.

Chapter 2

1. Rainer Maria Rilke, *Poems 1912–1926*, An Unofficial Rilke, selected and translated by Michael Hamburger (Redding Ridge, CT: Black Swan Books, 1981), 72–73. The original German is included.

2. Maurice Merleau-Ponty, "Le monde sensible et le monde de l'expression": *Notes, 1953 Cours au Collège de France* (Geneva: Métis Presses, 2011), 100.

3. Merleau-Ponty, "Le monde sensible et le monde," 102.

4. David Morris, *Merleau-Ponty's Developmental Ontology* (Evanston: Northwestern University, 2018), 212. On motility, sense, and the field of being, see chapter 7, 199–246.

5. Rilke, *Duino Elegies*, bilingual edition, trans. J. B. Leishman and Stephen Spender (New York: W. W. Norton, 1939, 1963), bilingual edition, 33.

6. See Kathleen Freeman, ed. and trans., *Ancilla to the Pre-Socratic Philosophers* (Cambridge: Harvard University Press, 1978), 125. For Heidegger's discussion, see "The Age of the World Picture," GA 5: 103–10/QCT 143–51 and GA 90: 68–70.

7. On *Da-sein*, see GA 2: 56/BT 67; GA 5: 39–40/PLT 53; GA 9: 325, 372/PM 248, 283; GA 44: 26/N2: 26–27; GA 66: 328/M 291; GA 71: 140–41, 162, 247/E 120, 139, 213; GA 97: 175–76.

8. See Maurice Merleau-Ponty, *The Visible and the Invisible*, trans. Alphonso Lingis (Evanston: Northwestern University, 1968), 115 and 219.

9. See Merleau-Ponty's discussion of motility and gesture in *Phenomenology of Perception*, trans. Colin Smith (London: Routledge & Kegan Paul, 1962). And see *The Body's Recollection of Being* (London: Routledge & Kegan Paul, 1985), where I interpret gesture and motility in relation to Heidegger's reading of Heraclitus, arguing that they are bodily forms of the *logos* and its *legein*, gathering and laying out haptic, practical, gestural fields of intelligibility and meaning. Also see my chapter on "Usage and Dispensation: Heidegger's Meditation on the Hand," in *Gestures of Ethical Life: Reading Hölderlin's Question of Measure after Heidegger* (Stanford: Stanford University Press, 2005), 204–74. In addition, see my ruminations on writing in "Cinders, Traces of Darkness, Shadows on the Page: The Holocaust in Derrida's Writing," in Alan Milchman and Alan Rosenberg (eds.), *Postmodernism and the Holocaust* (Amsterdam and Atlanta: Rodopi, 1998), 265–86, reprinted in a revised version in *International Philosophical Quarterly* 43, no. 3, issue 171 (September 2003): 269–88.

10. Ann Umland, ed., *René Magritte: The Mystery of the Ordinary: 1926–1938* (New York: MoMA, 2013) and Lisa Lipinski, *René Magritte and the Art of Thinking* (London and New York: Routledge, 2019).

11. Jean-Luc Nancy, *Being Singular Plural*, trans. R. Richardson and A. O'Byrne (Stanford: Stanford University Press, 2000), 183.

Chapter 3

1. Heidegger, "Grundsätze des Denkens," in *Bremer und Freiburger Vorträge*, GA 79 (Frankfurt am Main: Vittorio Klostermann, 1994), Lecture I, 82–84; "Basic Principles of Thinking," in *Bremen and Freiburg Lectures*, trans. Andrew J. Mitchell (Bloomington: Indiana University Press, 2012), Lecture I, 78–80. I have altered the translation of "Zumutung," which conventionally means "imposition."

2. See Maurice Merleau-Ponty, *Phenomenology of Perception*, trans. Colin Smith (London and New York: Routledge & Kegan Paul, 1962), 219 ("Sense Experience"), 267 ("Space"), and 320 ("The Thing and the Natural World"). See also David Morris's truly outstanding book on *Merleau-Ponty's Developmental Ontology* (Evanston: Northwestern University Press, 2018).

3. Heidegger, *Die Geschichte des Seyns*, GA 69: 162; *The History of Beyng*, 139. And see "Der Spruch des Anaximander," *Holzwege*, GA 5: 346; "The Anaximander Fragment," *Early Greek Thinking*, 34.

4. Thomas Cole, "American Scenery," in *Proceedings of the American Lyceum*, in *The American Monthly Magazine* (January 1836), 7. And see Nicholas L. Guardiano, *Aesthetic Transcendentalism: Emerson, Pierce, and Nineteenth Century American Landscape Painting* (Lantham: Lexington Books, Rowman & Littlefield, 2017), 96–97. And see Cole's Lectures, vol. III (February 6, 1847), 107.

5. Thomas Cole, "Letter to Durand," in Louis Legrand Noble, ed., *The Life and Works of Thomas Cole* (New York: Sheldon, Blakeman, 1856), 248.

6. Heidegger, *Überlegungen II–VI*, GA 94: 304: "Aber wie auch die losgelassene Verfälschung von Allem sich austobe, noch bleibt dem Wissenden die gewachsene Ruhe des Gebirges, das gesammelte Leuchten der Matten, der schweigende Flug des Falken, die lichte Wolke am grossen Himmel—jenes, worin sich schon angesagt hat die grosse Stille der fernsten Nähe des Seyns." I thank Richard Capobianco for calling my attention to this textual passage. The translation and its interpretation are, however, my own; they both diverge from his because he attributes to what he calls "Being" an independence that seems to me to perpetuate an onto-theological, metaphysical interpretation that I believe Heidegger himself would dispute as being a speculative illusion.

7. Walter Homolka and Arnulf Heidegger, ed., *Ausgewählte Briefe von Martin und Fritz Heidegger* (Freiburg im Breisgau: Verlag Herder GmbH, 2016), §188, 87; my translation.

8. Walter Homolka and Arnulf Heidegger, *Ausgewählte Briefe von Martin und Fritz Heidegger*, §254, 123; my translation.

Chapter 4

1. Novalis (Georg Philipp Friedrich von Hardenburg), *Novalis: Philosophical Writings*, trans. Margaret Mahoney Stoljar (Albany: SUNY Press, 1997), Fragment no. 1, 21. For the German, see *Novalis Schriften, Historische-Kritische Ausgabe* (Stuttgart: W. Kohlhammer, 1960–2006), ed. Richard Samuel, Hans-Joachim Mähl, and Gerhard Schulz.

2. Heidegger, "Brief über den Humanismus," *Wegmarken*, 179; GA 9: 349; "Letter on Humanism," in *Pathmarks*, 265.

3. Novalis, *Novalis: Philosophical Writings*, Fragment no. 51, 31.

4. Mary Oliver, *Our World*, with photographs by Molly Malone Cook (Beacon Press, 2007), xii.

5. José Ortega y Gasset, *On Love: Aspects of a Single Theme* (New York: Meridian Books, 1957), 83. Heidegger would call this "field of attention" a clearing: a clearing that our presence as *Da-sein* makes.

6. "238. Die Rettung des Arzttums," *Reden und andere Zeugnisse eines Lebensweges*, GA 16: 586–87. Heidegger's wedding wishes for Peter Rees, the son of his deceased friend, Theophil Rees, is discussed by Andrew Mitchell in "Heidegger's Breakdown: Health and Healing Under the Care of Dr. V. E. von Gebsattel," *Research in Phenomenology* 46, no. 1 (2016): 94–95.

7. Stanley Cavell, *In Quest of the Ordinary: Lines of Skepticism and Romanticism* (Chicago: University of Chicago Press, 1988), 52–53.

8. Johann Gottfried von Herder, *Abhandlung über den Ursprung der Sprache, Ausgewählte Werke*, III (Leipzig: Bibliographisches Institut, 1900), 639–40; *Treatise on the Origin of Language*, in Michael N. Foster, ed., *Herder: Philosophical Writings* (Cambridge: Cambridge University Press, 2002), §3, 100.

9. For an interpretation differing from mine, I urge my readers to read Andrew J. Mitchell's book, *The Fourfold: Reading the Late Heidegger* (Evanston: Northwestern University Press, 2015).

10. In his interview with Dominique Janicaud, Jacques Derrida challenges Heidegger's emphasis on gathering (*Versammlung*), arguing that it perpetuates an oppressive, exclusionary system. Opposing this inherent regimentation, Derrida calls attention to the need for dissemination, dispersion, openness. Although I do not think Heidegger's "gatherings" are (intended to be) exclusionary, necessarily imposing oppressive, reifying identities, I fault Heidegger for not addressing this question and unequivocally repudiating the oppressive interpretation. See Dominique Janicaud, *Heidegger in France*, trans. François Raffoul and David Pettigrew (Bloomington: Indiana University Press, 2015), 356.

11. Theodor W. Adorno, "The Essay as Form," *Notes to Literature*, vol. I, trans. Shierry Weber Nicholsen (New York: Columbia University Press, 1991), 3; *Noten zur Literature, Gesammelte Schriften*, vol. 11 (Frankfurt am Main: Suhrkamp Verlag, 1974). The quote in Adorno's epigram comes from Goethe's unfinished drama, "Pandora."

12. Michel Seyeau, *Against the Event: The Everyday and the Evolution of Modernist Narrative*, trans. (Oxford: Oxford University Press, 2013), 12. And see Maurice Blanchot, "Everyday Speech," *The Infinite Conversation*, trans. Susan Hanson (Minneapolis: University of Minnesota Press, 1993), 238–45.

13. *Überlegungen II–VI (Schwarze Hefte)*, GA 94: 321; my translation.

14. Etymology supports Heidegger's attempt to imagine a redeeming return of the object to its original meaning as thing, reversing the course of material and cultural history. This is the redemptive functioning of memory at work in his project of thought. See *Wikipedia*.

15. Theodor Adorno, *Negative Dialektik, Gesammelte Schriften* (Frankfurt am Main: Suhrkamp Verlag, 1966), vol. 6, 62; *Negative Dialectics*, trans. E. B. Ashton (New York: Continuum, 1973), 52.

16. Rainer Maria Rilke, "Die Sonette an Orpheus," *Gesammelte Gedichte* (Insel Verlag, 1962), 510; *Sonnets to Orpheus*, part II, 5, 78–79.

17. See Rilke's 1918 letter to Marie von Bunsen, *Letters of Rainer Maria Rilke 1910–1926*, trans. and ed., Jane Bannard Greene and M. D. Herter Norton (New York: W. W. Norton, 1972), 176–77.

18. Rilke, letter to Marie von Bunsen.

19. See Rilke's letter to Witold von Hulewicz, November 13, 1925, in *Letters of Rainer Maria Rilke 1910–1926*, 374.

20. Rilke, letter to Witold von Hulewicz.
21. Rilke, letter to Witold von Hulewicz, 374–75.
22. Rilke, letter to Witold von Hulewicz, 375.
23. Walter Benjamin, "Kleine Geschichte der Photographie," *Gesammelte Schriften*, vol. II, part 1, 383; "Little History of Photography," trans. Edmund Jephcott and Kingsley Shorter, *Selected Writings 1927–1934* (Cambridge and London: Harvard University Press, 1999), 526. A provocative thought, considering the revolutionary cultural and art-historical influence of Andy Warhol's painting of Campbell's Soup cans.

24. In *Journey to the End of Night*, trans. Ralph Manheim (New York: New Directions, 1983, 108), the French writer Louis-Ferdinand Céline says: "To the eye, a small sardine tin lying upon the road at midday throws off so many reflections that it can take on the dimensions of an epiphany." How about thinking of it taking on the dimensions of a *Geviert*? In *The Equivocation of Reason: Kleist Reading Kant* (Stanford: Stanford University Press, 2007, 83), James Phillips quotes this passage and comments: "This car crash of a sardine can scintillates like a [Kantian] Idea." Indeed it does—and, set in a *Geviert*, it gathers mortals in relation to their ideals, recollecting their sublime vision—their Kantian Idea—of a morally perfected world. But I concur with Phillips's reluctance to presume even the possibility of completed perfection (*The Equivocation of Reason*, 40).

25. See Heidegger, *Die Frage nach dem Ding*, GA 41; *What Is a Thing?*, trans. W. B. Barton Jr. and Vera Deutsch (Chicago: Henry Regnery1967).

26. Heidegger, "Das Ding," *Vorträge und Aufsätze*, 163–81; GA 7: 167–87; "The Thing," in Albert Hofstadter, ed., *Poetry, Language, Thought*, 165–86. Since the near-final draft of this chapter was written, an excellent new translation by Andrew J. Mitchell of an *earlier* version of Heidegger's text on "The Thing" has been published in *Bremen and Freiburg Lectures* (Bloomington: Indiana University Press, 2012), 5–22. For the German, see "Das Ding," *Vorträge und Aufsätze*, GA 7: 167–87. I highly recommend Mitchell's translation, both for its content, different from the later version translated by Hofstadter, and for the quality of the translation; however, except for the textual quotes at the very beginning of this chapter, all my textual references to this text will be to the *earlier* translation of the *later* version rendered by Hofstadter, and using the 1950 lecture published in 1954 in *Vorträge und Aufsätze*. I have now added the pages in the *Gesamtausgabe*. For a historically oriented consideration of the topic, I recommend Wolfgang Rainer Mann, *The Discovery of Things* (Princeton: Princeton University Press, 2000).

27. Heidegger, *Die Frage nach dem Ding*, GA 41: 246; *What Is a Thing?*, 244. And see the superb "Analysis" by Eugene T. Gendlin that follows the translation of *What Is a Thing?*, 247–96.

28. Wallace Stevens, *Collected Poetry and Prose* (New York: The Library of America, 1997), 60–61.

29. Heidegger, *Die Frage nach den Ding*, GA 41: 44; *What Is a Thing?*, 46. And see a similar argument in, for example, Friedrich Nietzsche, *Beyond Good and Evil*, trans. Walter Kaufmann (New York: Vintage books, 1989), part I, §§20–21, 27–30.

30. Ute Guzzoni, "'Were speculation about the state of reconciliation permissible . . .': Reflections on the Relation Between Human Beings and Things in Adorno and Heidegger," in Iain Macdonald and Krzysztof Ziarek, ed., *Adorno and Heidegger: Philosophical Questions* (Stanford: Stanford University Press, 2008), 124–25.

31. See Theodor W. Adorno, *Gesammelte Schriften*, ed. Rolf Tiedemann (Frankfurt am Main: Suhrkamp Verlag, 1970ff), vol. 10, 742–46; vol. 6, 17. Hereafter, references to this edition will be abbreviated as GS, followed by volume and page numbers.

32. Adorno, *GS*, vol. 6, 192.

33. Adorno, *GS*, vol. 10, 602.

34. Adorno, *GS*, vol. 4, 47; vol. 6, 191, 345.

35. Adorno, *GS*, vol. 16, 92; vol. 18, 495.

36. Adorno, *GS*, vol. 4, 112.

37. Adorno, *GS*, vol. 6, 192.

38. See Martin Hägglund, *Dying for Time: Proust, Woolf, Nabokov* (Cambridge: Harvard University Press, 2012) and *This Life: Secular Faith and Spiritual Freedom* (New York: Anchor Books, 2020). How acknowledging our mortality makes us free.

39. Michel de Montaigne, "That to philosophize is to learn to die," *The Complete Essays*, trans. Donald Frame (Stanford: Stanford University Press, 1957), 62.

40. See Robert Reich, "Ukraine, climate change, and the common good," March 24, 2022 podcast (robertreich@substack.com).

41. To my mind, the greatest of all the poems in Walt Whitman's *Leaves of Grass* is perhaps his "Song of Myself." The title might suggest a narcissism. But in truth the poem is a song coming from the poet's sense of *Mit-sein*, a song celebrating the spirit of democracy in which the poet goes *out* of himself and names and receives and welcomes all beings to *come into* his sense of "self." See "Song of Myself," *Leaves of Grass* (New York: Doubleday, 1917), 33–109: "All truths wait in all things," he says there (stanza 30). And this thought is unfolded in the verses that follow, recognizing the hidden truth in a leaf of grass, the blackberry, a tree-toad, a mouse. "I find I incorporate gneiss, coal, long-threaded moss, fruits, grains, esculent roots [. . .] I ascend to the nest in the fissure of the cliff" (stanzas 31, 32). He is, in spirit, in vision, everywhere, going out of himself where "the mocking-bird sounds his delicious gurgles, cackles, screams, weeps" and where "the humming-bird shimmers," taking their lives into himself, moved by his caring, his sympathy (stanza 33). But his song does not gather only nature, only earth; it gathers all mortals as well. "I take part, I see and hear the whole" (stanza 33). The poem concludes (stanza 52) with his returning, in death, to the elements: "I depart as air [. . .], I bequeath myself to the dirt to grow from the grass I love."

The other great poem of his own *Geviert* bears the title "Salut au Monde!," Whitman, *Leaves of Grass*, 163–76. Here the poet finds himself asking himself: "What do you hear Walt Whitman?" And in answering this summons, the poet gathers into his hearing the voices of people all over the world, the sounds of people at work and at play, living their lives.

> I hear the workmen singing and the farmer's wife singing,
> I hear in the distance the sounds of children and of animals early in the day, [. . .]
> I hear fierce French liberty songs, [. . .]
> I hear the Coptic refrain toward sundown, pensively falling on the breast of the black venerable vast mother the Nile, [. . .]
> I hear the Arab muezzin calling from the top of the mosque,
> I hear the Christian priests at the altars of their churches, [. . .]
> I hear the Hebrew reading his records and psalms [. . .]

And after more of these invocations through hearing, the poet in Walt Whitman is summoned once again, asked this time what it is that he sees and hears. And once again he answers, gathering people into the fourfold of his sight, his vision, his hearkening. After naming and acknowledging the ordinary daily lives of people all over the world, their passions, hardships, struggles, achievements and joys, the poet confides in us.

> My spirit has pass'd in compassion and determination around the whole earth [. . .]
> I think some divine rapport has equalized me with them.

Whitman's songs are democratic gatherings, sincerely egalitarian, excluding no one. For even the thief and the murderer are still, after all, human beings, mortals whose violently tormented and destructive existence calls for an appropriate moral response. Such is Whitman's "Fourfold" as figure of democracy.

42. Regarding Derrida's criticism of Heidegger's "Versammlung," see footnote 9 above.

43. See the remarkable book by James R. Mensch, *Embodiments: From the Body to the Body Politic* (Evanston: Northwestern University Press, 2009) and the very useful review and summary of this book by Kathrin Morgenstern and Barbara Weber, "The Recovery of the Body," *Research in Phenomenology* 41 (2011): 441–49. Also, regarding democracy and its public space, see John Dewey, *The Public and Its Problems* (New York: Henry Holt, 1927; Athens: Ohio University Press, 1980) and *Democracy and Education* (New York: Macmillan, 1916; The Free Press, 1944); Hannah Arendt, *The Human Condition* (1958; Chicago: University of Chicago, 1998) and an anthology, *The Promise of Politics* (New York: Schocken, 2005); Jürgen

Habermas, *The Structural Transformation of the Public Sphere*, trans. Thomas Burger (Cambridge: MIT Press, 1989) and *The Theory of Communicative Action*, 2 vols., trans. Thomas McCarthy (Boston: Beacon Press, 1981).

44. Heidegger, *Rede und andere Zeugnisse eines Lebensweges, 1910–1976*, GA 16: 671.

45. See Heidegger, "Nur noch ein Gott kann uns retten," "The Spiegel Interview," trans. William J. Richardson, in Thomas Sheehan, ed., *Heidegger: The Man and the Thinker* (Chicago: Precedent, 1981), 57.

46. Salman Rushdie, *Languages of Truth: Essays 2003–2020* (New York: Random House, 2020), 24–25.

47. Walt Whitman, "Song of Myself," *Leaves of Grass*, stanza 30, page 70.

Chapter 5

1. Walter Benjamin, "Das Kunstwerk im Zeitalter seiner technischen Reproduzierbarkeit," *Gesammelte Schriften* (Frankfurt am Main: Taschenbuch, Suhrkamp Verlag, 1939), I.2, 471–508; "The Work of Art in the Age of Mechanical Reproduction," *Illuminations*, trans. Harry Zohn (New York: Schocken Books, 1969), 217–42. Also see Walter, Benjamin, "Eduard Fuchs, der Sammler und der Historiker," *Gesammelte Schriften* (Frankfurt am Main: Taschenbuch, Suhrkamp Verlag, 1977), II.2, 503–4; "Edward Fuchs: Collector and Historian," in Howard Eiland and Michael W. Jennings, ed., *Walter Benjamin: Selected Writings, 1935–1938* (Cambridge: Harvard University Press, 2002), vol. III, 283.

2. Howard Caygill, *Walter Benjamin: The Colour of Experience* (London: Routledge, 1998), 92. And see Walter, Benjamin, "Eduard Fuchs, der Sammler und der Historiker," *Gesammelte Schriften*, II.2, 468; "Edward Fuchs: Collector and Historian," in *Walter Benjamin: Selected Writings, 1935–1938*, 262: For dialectical historical materialism, "It is an irretrievable image of the past which threatens to disappear in any present that does not recognize itself as intimated in that image. [. . .] To put to work an experience with history—a history that is originary for every present—is the task of historical materialism. The latter is directed toward a consciousness of the present which explodes the continuum of history." Also see Benjamin's discussion of what he means by calling a work of art "original" in his "Epistemo-Critical Prologue," *The Origin of German Tragic Drama*, trans. John Osborne (London and New York: Verso, 1998), 45; "Ursprung des deutschen Trauerspiels," *Gesammelte Schriften, Taschenbuch*, I.1, 226–27.

3. Felix Klee, ed., The *Diaries of Paul Klee 1898–1918* (Los Angeles: University of California, 1968), 313. I think Vermeer, Chardin, and Constable are painters whose works immediately suggest those "happier" times. Abstraction in the Western world began in earnest, I think, when there was a widespread sense that the historically inherited way of life—social mores, political and economic

systems, the international order—was in its entirety rapidly fragmenting, collapsing and changing, while new technologies emerged, altering old habits and relations. Abstraction mirrors the breakdown, the confusion, the anxiety of our time, but also boldly exhibits the assertiveness of a new freedom, a new energy, a new confidence, using new materials, new techniques, and new forms of presentation.

4. John Berger, *Ways of Seeing* (London: Penguin, 1990), 37.

5. See Alison McDonald's conversation with Hirst, reported in "In the Studio: Damien Hirst's Veil Paintings," *Gagosian Quarterly*, Fall 2021.

6. See Vincent Pécoil, "Steven Parrino: Natures Mortes Vivantes" (New York: Gagosian exhibition catalog, 2007), reprinted in *Gagosian Quarterly* (New York: April 2019) and see *Steven Parrino*, exhibition catalog (Basil: Gagosian Basil, 2022).

7. Mark Fisher, *Ghosts of My Life: Writings on Depression, Hauntology and Lost Futures* (Winchester, UK and Washington, DC: Zero Books, 2014). This thought, that we have lost the future because we have lost the promise hidden in the past, is an elaboration of Walter Benjamin's writings on the philosophy of history.

8. Maurice Merleau-Ponty, *Phenomenology of Perception*, trans. Colin Smith (London: Routledge & Kegan Paul, 1962), 29–30 and 53.

9. Merleau-Ponty, *Sense and Non-Sense*, trans. Hubert Dreyfus and Patricia Allen Dreyfus (Evanston: Northwestern University, 1964), 72.

10. The key to my terminology briefly interpreting the history of art, primarily in painting and sculpture:

- Ancient art

- Byzantine art

- Medieval art

- Early Modern art: eighteenth- and nineteenth-century art

- Latest Modern art: nineteenth-century art and early-twentieth-century art (Impressionism, Expressionism, Cubism, Surrealism, Dada)

- Post-Modern art: Modernist self-reflection (art questioning reflection on its own historical essence), Abstract Expressionism, Minimalism, Pop Art, Neo-Realism, Neo-Modern art (satirical, ironic, deconstructive return to Latest Modern art), Installation and Performative art.

11. See Vincent Scully, *The Earth, the Temple and the Gods: Greek Sacred Architecture* (New York and London: Frederick A. Praeger, 1969). I attempted to find out whether Scully was acquainted with Heidegger's essay, but was unable to get an answer. Be that as it may, Scully's extensively researched book splendidly fills out Heidegger's argument with an abundance of photographs, historical documentation, references to mythology, and architectural fieldwork. I am sure that, if Heidegger

had been able to read Scully's work, he would have enjoyed it. It implicitly supports Heidegger's argument. But if there is any one argumentative theme that stands out in Scully's book, it is surely that the archaic origin of the Greek temples and their placement in the landscape is an emphatically matriarchal religion.

12. But see Maurice Merleau-Ponty, "Cézanne's Doubt," in *Sense and Non-Sense*, trans. J. Wild (Evanston: Northwestern University Press, 1964), 16. And see Merleau-Ponty, "Eye and Mind," in *The Primacy of Perception*, trans. James Edie (Evanston: Northwestern University Press, 1964), 12–42.

13. See Günther Seubold, "Heideggers nach-gelassene Klee-Notizen," *Heidegger Studies*, 9 (1993), 5–12. And see Heidegger's 1959 words to his friend, Heinrich Wiegand Petzet, *Auf einen Stern zu gehen: Begegnungen mit Martin Heidegger 1926–1976* (Frankfurt: Societäts Verlag, 1993.

14. See Paul Klee, *Kunst-Lehre: Aufsätze, Vorträge, Rezensionen und Beiträge zur bildnerischen Formlehre* (Leipzig: Reclam, 1991). And see Dennis J. Schmidt, *Between Word and Image: Heidegger, Klee and Gadamer on Gesture and Genesis* (Bloomington: Indiana University Press, 2013) and Stephen Watson, *Crescent Moon over the Rational* (Stanford: Stanford University Press, 2009).

15. Paul Klee, *Das Bildnerische Denken*, ed. Jurg Spiller (Basel: Schwabe, 1964), 92.

16. Heidegger, "Die Kunst und der Raum," GA 13: 210.

17. GA 12: 204. And see Andrew Benjamin, "Matter and Movement's Presence: Notes on Heidegger, Francesco Mosca, and Bernini," *Research in Phenomenology*. 42 (2012): 343–73.

18. See Heinrich Wiegand Petzet, *Encounters and Dialogues with Heidegger, 1929–1976*, trans. Parvis Emad and Kenneth Maly (Chicago: University of Chicago Press, 1993), 143.

19. Merleau-Ponty, "Cézanne's Doubt," *Sense and Non-sense*, 13–14.

20. Merleau-Ponty, *Phenomenology of Perception*, 241–42, 298.

21. Merleau-Ponty, *Phenomenology of Perception*, vii.

22. Merleau-Ponty, *Phenomenology of Perception*, xiv.

23. Andrew J. Mitchell, *Heidegger Among the Sculptors: Body, Space and the Art of Dwelling* (Stanford: Stanford University Press, 2010). And see David Farrell Krell's review of Mitchell's book, "Heidegger and the Art of Sculpture," *Research in Phenomenology* 42 (2012): 117–29. Also see Julian Young, *Heidegger's Philosophy of Art* (Cambridge: Cambridge University Press, 2001) and Iain D. Thomson, *Heidegger, Art, and Postmodernity* (Cambridge University Press, 2011).

24. Thomas Houseago, quoted in the Gagosian Gallery catalog for September 2021 exhibit in London.

25. For Clement Greenberg, see *The Collected Essays and Criticism*, 4 vols., John O'Brian, ed., Chicago: University of Chicago Press, 1993, and *Art and Culture: Critical Essays* (Boston: Beacon Press, 1961). For Michael Fried, see *Art and Objecthood* (Chicago: University of Chicago Press, 1998).

26. See Wieland Schmied, *Francis Bacon: Commitment and Conflict* (New York: Prestel, 2006).

27. Alex Ross, "Music Fills the Rothko Chapel," *The New Yorker* (March 14, 2022).

28. In this regard, see Walter Benjamin's discussion of an experience with color that defies the subject-object metaphysics, in "Der Regenbogen: Gespräch über die Phantasie," *Gesammelte Schriften*, VII.1, 19–26.

29. Walter Benjamin, "Goethe's Wahlverwandtschaft," in *Gesammelte Schriften*, ed. Rolf Tiedemann and Hermann Schweppenhauser (Frankfurt am Main: Suhrkamp, 1991), vol. I, 125.

30. Regarding Alberto Burri, see Emily Barun, ed., *Alberto Burri: The Trauma of Painting* (New York: The Guggenheim Museum, 2015) and Germano Celant, ed., *Alberto Burri* (New York: Mitchell-Innes & Nash, 2008). And see Rainer Maria Rilke, "Duineser Elegien," *Gesammelte Gedichte* (Frankfurt am Main: Insel-Verlag, 1962), First Elegy, 441.

31. Walter Benjamin, "Die Farbe von Kinde aus betrachtet," *Gesammelte Schriften* (Frankfurt am Main: Suhrkamp Verlag, 1985), VI, 110–12.

32. Howard Caygill, *Walter Benjamin: The Colour of Experience* (London: Routledge, 1998), 84–85.

33. See Heidegger's *Introduction to Phenomenological Research*, trans. Daniel Dahlstrom (Bloomington: Indiana University Press, 2005), 7.

34. On Jackson Pollock, see Michael Fried, *Art and Objecthood* and see the excellent study by Michael Schreyach, "Pre-objective Depth in Merleau-Ponty and Jackson Pollock," *Research in Phenomenology* 43 (2013): 49–70.

35. See Merleau-Ponty, *The Phenomenology of Perception*, trans. Colin Smith (London: Routledge, 1962) and *The Primacy of Perception*, trans. James Edie (Evanston: Northwestern University Press, 1964), 12–42.

36. See Merleau-Ponty, *Phenomenology of Perception*, 214.

Chapter 6

1. A much briefer, earlier version of this chapter was published in the Heidegger Circle annual journal *Gatherings* 2022.

2. Henry Miller, *Big Sur and the Oranges of Hieronymus Bosch* (New York: New Directions, 1957).

3. Hannah Arendt, *Between Past and Future* (New York: Enlarged Penguin Edition, 1977), 227.

4. Gregory Corso, excerpt from "The Golden Dot," in *The Golden Dot: Last Poems of Gregory Corso*, ed. Raymond Foye (New York: New Directions, 2021).

5. Heidegger's word *Lichtung* does not mean an illuminating *light* but refers rather to the *clearing* that opens a region to the light. The word must be inter-

preted in a topology working with four pairs of distinctions: (1) light/lighting in the sense of the clearing for light to enter; (2) ontic/ontological; (3) figure/ground; and (4) unconcealment/concealment. In his *Phenomenology of Perception*, Maurice Merleau-Ponty makes pairs of distinctions that implicitly correspond to Heidegger's: "The lighting is not on the side of the object; it is what we assume, what we take as the norm, whereas the object lighted stands out before us and confronts us. The lighting is neither color nor, in itself, even light; it is anterior to the distinction between colors and luminosities" (311). Also consider this: "Lighting and reflection [. . .] play their part only if they remain in the background as discreet intermediaries, and lead our gaze instead of arresting it" (310). It is satisfying to find such affinities and correspondences between two such different philosophical projects. What may surprise Heidegger scholars is that, in effect, Heidegger's phenomenology of perception is really not different from Merleau-Ponty's late phenomenology, as in, for instance, his "Working Notes" in *The Visible and the Invisible*. Unfortunately, Heidegger has an affinity for thinking in terms of abstract singulars, essences: the poet, the word, the hand, the thing, . . . the clearing, although manifestly we need to be able to think in the plural. Heidegger also leaves somewhat vague and elusive how exactly the openness of the clearing relates to *Da-sein*'s thrown-openness and to the world. But see GA 15: 345/FS 547: He wants, he says, to emphasize "the openness of being itself, rather than the openness of *Dasein* in relation to the openness of being." But what is that relation? How does it function? In his *Zollikon Seminars* (Z 223 /ZS 178), he says: "The human being is the guardian of the clearing, of the appropriating event [*des Ereignisses*]. He is not the clearing himself, nor the entire clearing, nor is he identical with the whole of the clearing as such. But, as the one ecstatically 'standing out' into the clearing [. . .], he is related to, belongs, and is appropriated by the clearing." This still leaves some ambiguity, because wherever *Da-sein* is in its thrown-openness, there is—or say, there occurs—a clearing.

6. Henry David Thoreau, ed. Carl Bode, *Walden* (New York: Viking, 1947), 366.

7. Ralph Waldo Emerson, "Nature," in Carl Bode, ed., *Essays and Lectures* (New York: Library of America, 1983), 9. But today, as Heidegger pointed out, our city lights compete with, and ultimately conceal, the starry sky of the night. And the selfish, self-interested, ruthlessly competitive form of "individualism" that dominates our contemporary American society could not be more at odds with the "individualism" that Emerson praised in his essay on "Self-Reliance."

8. On "Ereignis" as an event regarding the meaning of meaning, see Richard Polt, *The Emergency of Being* (Ithaca: Cornell University Press, 2006) and *Time and Trauma: Thinking Through Heidegger in the Thirties* (London and Lanham: Rowman & Littlefield, 2019) and François Raffoul, *Thinking the Event* (Bloomington: Indiana University Press, 2020).

9. Ludwig Wittgenstein, *Tractatus Logico-Philosophicus*, trans. David F. Pears and B. F. McGuinness (London and New York: 1961), Proposition 6.44. And see

his *Tagebücher 1914–1916, Werkausgabe*, vol. I (Suhrkamp Verlag, 1984), 181: "The aesthetic wonder is that the world exists."

 10. Regarding the fundamental connection between the ethical and the ontological, see David Wood's very insightful essay, "Some Questions for my Levinasian Friends," in Eric Sean Nelson, Antje Kapust, and Kent Still, eds., *Addressing Levinas* (Evanston: Northwestern University Press, 2005), 155–57.

 11. Heidegger, GA 29–30: 11/FCM 8. The aphorism can be found in *Novalis: Philosophical Writings*, trans. and ed., Margaret Mahoney Stoljar (Albany: SUNY Press, 1997), 135.

 12. William Wordsworth, *The Prelude* (Baltimore: Penguin, 1971), Book II, 86.

 13. Merleau-Ponty, *Phenomenology of Perception*, 264–65.

 14. Heidegger, "Der Satz der Identität," GA 11: 37–48; "The Principle of Identity," in *Identity and Difference*, trans. Joan Stambaugh (Chicago: University of Chicago, 1969), 29–39. And see Merleau-Ponty's articulation of that same phenomenology of belonging-togetherness in *Phenomenology of Perception*, trans. Colin Smith (New York: Routledge & Kegan Paul, 1962), 216, where he observes that, "to say that I have a visual field is to say that by reason of my position I have access to and an opening upon a system of beings, visible beings, that these are at the discretion of my gaze in virtue of a kind of *primordial contract* and through a gift of nature [. . .]." Italics added.

 15. Thomas Sheehan, *Making Sense of Heidegger: A Paradigm Shift* (London: Rowman & Littlefield, 2015), 255n24.

 16. In *Phenomenology of Perception*, 100, Merleau-Ponty describes how the word *here* applies to one's body, in effect nicely defining it as *Da-sein* and *legein*.

 17. Merleau-Ponty, *Phenomenology of Perception*, 347; see also, 215, 254.

 18. On the importance of "disposition" in Heidegger's project, see GA 20: 375–76/HCT 272 and GA 65: 217–24/CP 187–92. On "the gentlest law," see GA 12: 248/OWL 128.

 19. And see Merleau-Ponty, *The Visible and the Invisible*, trans. Alphonso Lingis (Evanston: Northwestern University Press, 1968), 123, 142. What Heidegger calls an oscillation (*Gegenschwung*) and vibration (*Schweben*), Merleau-Ponty describes as a reciprocity and reversibility.

 20. Albert Camus: "We have not overcome our condition, and yet we know it better. We know that we live in contradiction, but we also know that we must refuse this contradiction and do what is needed to reduce it. Our task as [humans] is to find the few principles that will calm the infinite anguish of free souls. We must mend what has been torn apart, make justice imaginable again in a world so obviously unjust, give happiness a meaning once more to peoples poisoned by the misery of the century. Naturally, it is a superhuman task. But superhuman is the term for tasks [we] take a long time to accomplish, that's all." Albert Camus, *Lyrical and Critical Essays*, trans. Ellen Conroy Kennedy (New York: Alfred A. Knopf, 1968, Vintage Books, 1970).

21. Richard Capobianco, *Engaging Heidegger* (Toronto: University of Toronto, 2010) and *Heidegger's Way of Being* (Toronto: University of Toronto, 2014).

22. In an apothegm reminiscent of Malebranche's thought that "attention is the natural prayer of the soul," Simone Weill wrote: "Attention is the rarest and purest form of generosity." *First and Last Notebooks*, republished in *Gravity and Grace*, trans. Arthur Wills (New York: G. P. Putnam's Sons, 1952; Lincoln: University of Nebraska Press, 1997), 169.

23. Richard Capobianco, *Heidegger's Way of Being*, 95–96.

24. Capobianco, *Engaging Heidegger*, 204.

25. Although many of Thomas Cole's paintings—idyllic pastoral scenes—give expression to a deeply felt Romanticism, he was nevertheless an unblinking observer of nature, very committed to calling attention to the ways in which our rush into industrialization is increasingly threatening the environment. See his series of five paintings, "The Course of Empire" (1833–1836), currently owned and exhibited by the New York Historical Society. He could not share in the spirit of faith and optimism that Heidegger expressed here in the *Black Notebook*, GA 94.

26. To be sure, Heidegger sometimes speaks in a way that can be misleading, suggesting being as an independent source, or agency, as when he says: "The history of being means destiny of being in the sendings of which both the sendings and the It that sends forth hold back with their self-manifestation" (GA 14: 13/OTB 9). But, contrary to Capobianco's reading of Heidegger, the "It" that sends (namely, the "Es gibt") and the sending are not separate; and the "It" is not any kind of being. The being that "sends" or "gives" is the clearing that our bodily presence as thrown-open *Da-sein* opens. On this and many other key matters, I highly recommend François Raffoul, *Thinking the Event* (Bloomington: Indiana University Press, 2020).

27. Ralph Waldo Emerson, "Nature," in *Emerson: Essays and Lectures*, ed. Joel Porte (New York: Library of America, 1983), 32.

28. François Raffoul, *The Origins of Responsibility* (Bloomington: Indiana University Press, 2010).

29. Raffoul, *Thinking the Event* (Bloomington: Indiana University Press, 2020).

30. Thomas Sheehan, *Making Sense of Heidegger: A Paradigm Shift* (London: Rowman & Littlefield, 2015).

31. Richard Polt, *The Emergency of Being* (Ithaca: Cornell University Press, 2006) and *Time and Trauma: Thinking Through Heidegger in the Thirties* (London and Lanham: Rowman & Littlefield, 2019). For a different approach to the eventfulness of the event of being, giving us different insights into the importance of the event, see François Raffoul, *Thinking the Event* (Bloomington: Indiana University Press, 2020).

32. In this regard, see, for example, Kevin Aho, *Heidegger's Neglect of the Body* (Albany: SUNY Press, 2009); David Farrell Krell, *Daimon Life: Heidegger and Life-Philosophy* (Bloomington: Indiana University Press, 1992); David Michael Levin, *The Body's Recollection of Being* (London: Routledge & Kegan Paul, 1985)

and the Opening of Vision (London: Routledge & Kegan Paul, 1987); Daniela Vallega-Neu, *The Bodily Dimension in Thinking* (Albany: SUNY Press, 2005); and Daniela Vallega-Neu, *Heidegger's Poietic Writings from* Contributions to Philosophy *to* The Event (Bloomington: Indiana University Press, 2018).

33. See Immanuel Kant, *Kritik der Urteilskraft* (Hamburg: Felix Meiner Verlag,1959), §80, 285; *Critique of Judgment*, trans. Werner S. Pluhar (Indianapolis: Hackett, 1987), 304; and Walter Benjamin, "Über den Begriff der Geschichte," *Gesammelte Schriften* (Frankfurt am Main: Suhrkamp Verlag, 1974), vol. I, pt. 2, 697–98; "Theses on the Philosophy of History," trans. Harry Zohn, in Hannah Arendt (ed.), *Illuminations* (New York: Schocken, 1969), 257–58.

34. Wallace Stevens, "Adagia," in *Collected Poetry and Prose* (New York: The Library of America: 1997), 903. He was perhaps recalling what George Santayana said at the end of *The Last Puritan*: "After life is over and the world has gone up in smoke, what realities might the spirit in us still call its own without illusion save the form of those very illusions which have made up our story."

35. Theodor W. Adorno, *Minima Moralia: Reflexionen aus dem beschädigten Leben* (Suhrkamp Verlag, 1951), 333–34; *Minima Moralia: Reflections from Damaged Life*, trans. E. F. N. Jephcott (London: New Left Books, 1974), 247.

36. Plato, *Apology* 382, in *Platonis Opera*, ed. John Burnet (Oxford: Oxford University Press, 1958).

37. José Ángel Valente, *Material memoria 1977–1992*, Obra poética 2. Trans. David Kleinberg-Levin.

Chapter 7

1. See "Die Frühe des Seyns," in *Gedachtes*, GA 81: 68–69. Despite the challenge, an admirable English translation—by Eoghan Walls—of a selection of the *Gedachtes* is now available: *Thought Poems: A Translation of Heidegger's Verse* (Rowman & Littlefield, 2021). I have seen the translation and have drawn rich understanding from it, but my paraphrase suggests an interpretation that diverges from his translation in a number of ways, notably in saying, in order to explicitly avoid the metaphysical hypostatization of being, that what is dawning is the *sense* of being, not being itself. Being is not some entity that could be dawning; only beings dawn: the sun, the morning; and metaphorically, a thought. But in a sense, being itself *is* dawning: dawning *in our awareness and recognition*, as reflection finally turns from beings to being. And in this awareness and recognition lies the dawning possibility of another epoch in the history of being, another interpretation of what it means to be. Heidegger's wording, however, is precisely what lends support to Richard Capobianco's interpretation of being as something that itself can dawn, as if it were an entity. Being itself can dawn only in a metaphorical locution. But that concession will never satisfy metaphysics. Here is the German original.

Weil ins Sein gerufen, doch verhehlt erst
eingefreyt dem noch verhaltnen Anfang
aus Ereignis,
unvertraut dem selbst noch lang
fortan gehehlten Freyn,
doch einstig zugetraut der kaum gewagten
Lichtung noch verborgener Enteignung
aus Ereignis
sind die Griechen in ihr
einziges Geschick entlassen:
frei dem Aufgang, auserlesen scheu
der Lese, der Versammlung alles Lichten
in die unscheinbare Fügung,
also erst gelichtet einem Schein von Licht.
Aus ihm erblickt, gedeihen
Sammeln und Vernehmen als der Blick
zum Sehen, das allein vermag
zu wählen sich den augenhaften Sinn,
dem darum Welt seither im Aussehn
weltet, als die Aussicht sichtsam anwest: ist.
Dass künftig Sein entschieden bleibt,
verschenkend dem Erscheinen sich
ins mitscheinend aber ungedachte Lichte.
Nach dem Mass des scheinenden Sich-Zeigens
wird Erkennen selber das Ersehen,
Schauen, Zustehn auf das Aussehn,
her es stellend in die Ständigkeit
anwesenden Bestehens
und vergisst zuvor die Herkunft
aus dem Denken früh verhehlter
Dichtung am Gedicht des Seyns, das
Zukunft selber in der eignen Wahrheit
sich seitdem verhüllt, Versagnis ihrer selbst,
als diese nahe nur in ungenahter Nähe,
jäher Ferne namenloser Wink
ins eigene Scheiden
weg zu rein versparter einstiger
Enteignung.
Wohl das Licht,
doch nicht
die Lichtung aus der Dichtung
des Ereignens

wird zur Frühe
die verhüllte noch, die Freye
jener Freyheit,
die nicht selber Wahrheit ist
des Seyns.
[siehe: Eignis]

Bibliography

Abbreviations for works by Heidegger cited or quoted
Abbreviations for translations of Heidegger works cited or quoted
All works in the *Gesamtausgabe* have been published in Frankfurt am Main, Germany by Verlag Vittorio Klostermann.

Gesamtausgabe (Frankfurt am Main, Germany)

GA 1   *Gesamtausgabe*, vol. 1. *Frühe Schriften* (1912–1916). Ed. Friedrich-Wilhelm von Herrmann, 1978.

GA 2   *Gesamtausgabe*, vol. 2. *Sein und Zeit* (1927). Ed. Friedrich-Wilhelm von Herrmann, 1977. Also published separately by Max Niemeyer, Verlag, Tübingen, Germany (1st ed.), 1927. The 7th edition (1953) was used for the English translations.

GA 3   *Gesamtausgabe*, vol. 3. *Kant und das Problem der Metaphysik* (1929). Ed. Friedrich-Wilhelm von Herrmann, 1991 (2nd ed., 2010).

GA 4   *Gesamtausgabe*, vol. 4. *Erläuterungen zu Hölderlins Dichtung* (1936–1968). Ed. Friedrich-Wilhelm von Herrmann, 1981, 2012 (rev. ed.).

GA 5   *Gesamtausgabe*, vol. 5. *Holzwege* (1935–1946). Ed. Friedrich-Wilhelm von Hermann, 1977.

GA 6.1 *Gesamtausgabe*, vol. 6, part 1. *Nietzsche* I (1936–1939). Ed. Brigitte Schillbach, 1996.

GA 6.2 *Gesamtausgabe*, vol. 6, part 2. *Nietzsche* II (1939–1946). Ed. Brigitte Schillbach, 1997.

GA 7   *Gesamtausgabe*, vol. 7. *Vorträge und Aufsätze* (1936–1953). Ed. Friedrich-Wilhelm von Herrmann, 2000.

GA 8   *Gesamtausgabe*, vol. 8. *Was heißt Denken?* (1951–1952). Ed. Paola-Ludovika Coriando, 2002.

GA 9   *Gesamtausgabe*, vol. 9. *Wegmarken* (1919–1961). Ed. Friedrich-Wilhelm von Herrmann, 1976, 1996 (rev. ed.).

GA 10   *Gesamtausgabe*, vol. 10. *Der Satz vom Grund* (1955–1956). Ed. Petra Jaeger, 1997.

GA 11   *Gesamtausgabe*, vol. 11. *Identität und Differenz* (1955–1963). Ed. Friedrich-Wilhelm von Herrmann, 2006.

GA 12   *Gesamtausgabe*, vol. 12. *Unterwegs zur Sprache* (1950–1959). Ed. Friedrich-Wilhelm von Herrmann, 1985.

GA 13   *Gesamtausgabe*, vol. 13. *Aus der Erfahrung des Denkens* (1910–1976). Ed. Hermann Heidegger, 1983, 2002 (rev. ed.).

GA 14   *Gesamtausgabe*, vol. 14. *Zur Sache des Denkens* (1927–1968). Ed. Friedrich-Wilhelm von Herrmann, 2007.

GA 15   *Gesamtausgabe*, vol. 15. *Seminare* (1951–1973). Ed. Curd Ochwadt, 1986, 2005 (2nd rev. ed.).

GA 16   *Gesamtausgabe*, vol. 16. *Reden und andere Zeugnisse eines Lebensweges* (1910–1976). Ed. Hermann Heidegger, 2000.

GA 17   *Gesamtausgabe*, vol. 17. *Einführung in die phänomenologische Forschung* (1923–1924). Ed. Friedrich-Wilhelm von Herrmann, 1994.

GA 19   *Gesamtausgabe*, vol. 19. *Platon: Sophistes* (1924–1925). Ed. Ingeborg Schüßler, 1992.

GA 20   *Gesamtausgabe*, vol. 20. *Prolegomena zur Geschichte des Zeitbegriffs* (1925). Ed. Petra Jaeger, 1979, 1988 (2nd rev. ed.), 1994 (3d rev. ed.).

GA 21   *Gesamtausgabe*, vol. 21. *Logik. Die Frage nach der Wahrheit* (1925–1926). Ed. Walter Biemel, 1976, 1995 (rev. ed.).

GA 22   *Gesamtausgabe*, vol. 22. *Die Grundbegriffe der antiken Philosophie* (1926). Ed. Franz-Karl Blust, 1993.

GA 24   *Gesamtausgabe*, vol. 22. *Die Grundprobleme der Phänomenologie* (1927). Ed. Friedrich-Wilhelm von Herrmann, 1975.

GA 26   *Gesamtausgabe*, vol. 26. *Metaphysische Anfangsgründe der Logik im Ausgang von Leibniz* (1928). Ed. Klaus Held, 1978, 1990 (2nd rev. ed.), 2007 (3d rev. ed.).

GA 27   *Gesamtausgabe*, vol. 27. *Einleitung in die Philosophie* (1928–1929). Ed. Otto Saame and Ina Saame-Speidel, 1996, 2001 (rev. ed.).

GA 28   *Gesamtausgabe*, vol. 28. *Der deutsche Idealismus (Fichte, Schelling, Hegel) und die philosophische Problemlage der Gegenwart* (1929). Appendix: "Einführung in das akademische Studium" (1929). Ed. Claudius Strube, 1997.

GA 29–30   *Gesamtausgabe*, vols. 29–30. *Die Grundbegriffe der Metaphysik. Welt—Endlichkeit—Einsamkeit* (1929–1930). Ed. Friedrich-Wilhelm von Herrmann, 1983.

GA 31   *Gesamtausgabe*, vol. 31. *Vom Wesen der menschlichen Freiheit. Einleitung in die Philosophie* (1930). Ed. Hartmut Tietjen, 1982, 1994 (rev. ed.).

GA 33   *Gesamtausgabe*, vol. 33. *Aristoteles, Metaphysik Θ 1–3. Von Wesen und Wirklichkeit der Kraft* (1931). Ed. Heinrich Hüni, 1981, 1990 (2nd rev. ed.), 2006 (3d rev. ed.).

GA 34   *Gesamtausgabe*, vol. 34. *Vom Wesen der Wahrheit. Zu Platons Höhlengleichnis und Theätet* (1931–32). Ed. Hermann Mörchen, 1988, 1997 (rev. ed.).

GA 35   *Gesamtausgabe*, vol. 35. *Der Anfang der abendländischen Philosophie: Auslegung des Anaximander und Parmenides* (1932). Ed. Peter Trawny, 2011.

GA 36–37   *Gesamtausgabe*, vols. 36–37. *Sein und Wahrheit* (1933–34). Ed. Hartmut Tietjen, 2001.

GA 39   *Gesamtausgabe*, vol. 39. *Hölderlins Hymnen "Germanien" und "Der Rhein"* (1934–1935). Ed. Susanne Ziegler, 1980, 1989 (rev. ed.).

GA 40   *Gesamtausgabe*, vol. 40. *Einführung in die Metaphysik* (1935). Ed. Petra Jaeger, 1983.

GA 41   *Gesamtausgabe*, vol. 41. *Die Frage nach dem Ding. Zu Kants Lehre von den transzendentalen Grundsätzen* (1935–1936). Ed. Petra Jaeger, 1984.

GA 42   *Gesamtausgabe*, vol. 42. *Schelling: Vom Wesen der menschlichen Freiheit* (1809) (1936). Redacted version, Ed. Ingrid Schüßler (Tübingen, Germany: Max Niemeyer, 1988).

GA 43   Gesamtausgabe, vol. 43. *Nietzsche: Der Wille zur Macht als Kunst* (1936–1937). Ed. Bernd Heimbüchel, 1985.

GA 44   *Gesamtausgabe*, vol. 44. *Nietzsches metaphysische Grundstellung im abendländischen Denken: Die ewige Wiederkehr des Gleichen* (1937). Ed. Marion Heinz, 1986.

GA 45   *Gesamtausgabe*, vol. 45. *Grundfragen der Philosophie. Ausgewählte "Probleme" der "Logik"* (1937–1938). Ed. Friedrich-Wilhelm von Herrmann, 1984.

GA 46   *Gesamtausgabe*, vol. 46. *Zur Auslegung von Nietzsches II. Unzeitgemäßer Betrachtung "Vom Nutzen und Nachteil der Historie für das Leben"* (1938–1939). Ed. Hans-Joachim Friedrich, 2003.

GA 47   *Gesamtausgabe*, vol. 47. *Nietzsches Lehre vom Willen zur Macht als Erkenntnis* (1939). Ed. Eberhard Hanser, 1989.

GA 48   *Gesamtausgabe*, vol. 48. *Nietzsche: Der europäische Nihilismus* (1940). Ed. Petra Jaeger, 1986.

GA 51   *Gesamtausgabe*, vol. 51. *Grundbegriffe* (1941). Ed. Petra Jaeger, 1981, 1991 (rev. ed.).

GA 52.   *Gesamtausgabe*, vol. 52. *Hölderlins Hymne "Andenken"* (1941–1942). Ed. Curd Ochwadt, 1982.

GA 53   *Gesamtausgabe*, vol. 53. *Hölderlins Hymne "Der Ister"* (1942). Ed. Walter Biemel, 1984.

GA 54   *Gesamtausgabe*, vol. 54. *Parmenides* (1942–1943). Ed. Manfred S. Frings, 1982.

GA 55   *Gesamtausgabe*, vol. 55. *Heraklit* (1943, 1944). Ed. Manfred S. Frings, 1979, 1987 (rev. ed.).

GA 58.   *Gesamtausgabe*, vol. 58. *Grundprobleme der Phänomenologie* (1919–20). Ed. Hans-Helmuth Gander, 1992.

GA 60   *Gesamtausgabe*, vol. 60. *Phänomenologie des religiösen Lebens* (1918–1921). Ed. Matthias Jung, Thomas Regehly, and Claudius Strube, 1995, 2011 (rev. ed.).

GA 61   *Gesamtausgabe*, vol. 61. *Phänomenologische Interpretationen zu Aristoteles. Einführung in die phänomenologische Forschung* (1921–22). Ed. Walter Bröcker und Käte Bröcker-Oltmanns, 1985, 1994 (rev. ed.).

GA 63   *Gesamtausgabe*, vol. 63. *Ontologie. Hermeneutik der Faktizität* (1923). Ed. Käte Bröcker-Oltmanns, 1988.

GA 64   *Gesamtausgabe*, vol. 64. *Der Begriff der Zeit* (Vortrag, 1924). Ed. Friedrich-Wilhelm von Herrmann, 2004.

GA 65   *Gesamtausgabe*, vol. 65. *Beiträge zur Philosophie (Vom Ereignis)* (1936–1938). Ed. Friedrich-Wilhelm von Herrmann, 1989, 1994 (rev. ed.).

GA 66   *Gesamtausgabe*, vol. 66. *Besinnung* (1938–1939). Ed. Friedrich-Wilhelm von Herrmann, 1997.

Bibliography | 231

GA 67   *Gesamtausgabe*, vol. 67. *Metaphysik und Nihilismus* (1938–1939, 1946–1948). Ed. Hans-Joachim Friedrich, 1999.

GA 69   *Gesamtausgabe*, vol. 69. *Die Geschichte des Seyns* (1938–1940). Ed. Peter Trawny, 1998, 2012 (rev. ed.).

GA 70   *Gesamtausgabe*, vol. 70. *Über den Anfang* (1941). Ed. Paola-Ludovika Coriando, 2005.

GA 71   *Gesamtausgabe*, vol. 71. *Das Ereignis* (1941–1942). Ed. Friedrich-Wilhelm von Herrmann, 2009.

GA 72   *Gesamtausgabe*, vol. 72. *Die Stege des Anfangs* (1944). Ed. Friedrich-Wilhelm von Herrmann.

GA 73.1   *Gesamtausgabe*, vol. 73.1. *Zum Ereignis-Denken* (1932–1970s). Ed. Peter Trawny, 2013.

GA 73.2   *Gesamtausgabe*, vol. 73.2. *Zum Ereignis-Denken* (1932–1970s). Ed. Peter Trawny, 2013.

GA 77   *Gesamtausgabe*, vol. 77. *Feldweg-Gespräche* (1944–1945). Ed. Ingrid Schüßler, 1995, 2007 (2nd rev. ed.).

GA 79   *Gesamtausgabe*, vol. 79. *Bremer und Freiburger Vorträge. 1. Einblick in das was ist: Bremer Vorträge 1949. Das Ding—Das Ge-stell—Die Gefahr—Die Kehre, 2. Grundsätze des Denkens: Freiburger Vorträge 1957.* Ed. Petra Jaeger, 1994.

GA 81   *Gesamtausgabe*, vol. 81. *Gedachtes* (1910–1970). Ed. Paola-Ludovika Coriando, 2007.

GA 82   *Gesamtausgabe*, vol. 82. *Zu eigenen Veröffentlichungen.* Ed. Friedrich-Wilhelm von Herrmann, 2018.

GA 89   *Gesamtausgabe*, vol. 89. *Zollikoner Seminare* (1959–1969). Ed. Peter Trawny, 2017.

GA 94   *Gesamtausgabe*, vol. 94. *Überlegungen II–VI* (*Schwarze Hefte*, 1931–1938). Ed. Peter Trawny, 2014.

GA 95   *Gesamtausgabe*, vol. 95. *Überlegungen VII–XI* (*Schwarze Hefte*, 1938–1939). Ed. Peter Trawny, 2014.

GA 96   *Gesamtausgabe*, vol. 96. *Überlegungen XII–XV* (*Schwarze Hefte*, 1939–1941). Ed. Peter Trawny, 2014.

GA 97   *Gesamtausgabe*, vol. 97. *Anmerkungen I–V* (*Schwarze Hefte*, 1942–1948). Ed. Peter Trawny, 2015.

Gesamtausgabe Volumes with the English Translations Consulted, and with Abbreviations

Author's Comments

1. Not all the volumes of the *Gesamtausgabe* have been translated into English.

2. In the translation of some GA volumes, texts appearing together there have been separated, so their translation will only be found scattered in more than one English publication.

3. Most of the published translations I have used have been modified after I consulted the original German texts. In presenting these altered translations, in some cases altered in major ways, I have not hesitated to exercise a freedom that some scholars will no doubt challenge. Communicating and sharing the meaning is more important than dogmatic devotion to all the words. Judgment is required. But I have attempted, as much as possible, to make the thought that the texts convey more easily accessible and more comprehensible, giving words to the philosopher's thought that might faithfully and adequately express it in more idiomatic English. At this moment in time, I consider that attempt to be more important than producing translations that reproduce with obsessive exactitude the awkward grammar and style that expresses and reflects Heidegger's struggles to say something profoundly new and difficult.

4. The German text will be referenced first, and the English translation will follow.

Abbreviations

AM   *Aristotle's "Metaphysics" Θ 1–3: On the Essence and Actuality of Force.* Trans. Walter Brogan and Peter Warnek. Bloomington: Indiana University Press, 1995.

BaT   *Being and Truth.* Trans. Gregory Fried and Richard Polt. Bloomington: Indiana University Press, 2010.

BC   *Basic Concepts.* Trans. Gary E. Aylesworth. Bloomington: Indiana University Press, 1993.

BCAP   *Basic Concepts of Ancient Philosophy.* Trans. Richard Rojcewicz. Bloomington: Indiana University Press, 1997.

BF   *Bremen and Freiburg Lectures: Insight into That Which Is and Basic Principles of Thinking.* Trans. Andrew Mitchell. Bloomington: Indiana University Press, 2012.

BPP   *The Basic Problems of Phenomenology.* Trans. Albert Hofstadter. Bloomington: Indiana University Press, 1982.

| BPPh | *Basic Problems of Phenomenology: Winter Semester 1919/1920.* Trans. Scott M. Campbell. London: Continuum, 2013. |

| BQP | *Basic Questions of Philosophy: Selected "Problems" of "Logic."* Trans. Richard Rojcewicz and André Schuwer. Bloomington: Indiana University Press, 1994. |

| BT | *Being and Time.* Trans. John Macquarrie and Edward Robinson. New York: Harper & Row, 1962. |

| BTS | *Being and Time.* Trans. Joan Stambaugh. Revised and with a Foreword by Dennis J. Schmidt. Albany: State University of New York Press, 2010. |

| BWP | *The Beginning of Western Philosophy: Interpretation of Anaximander and Parmenides.* Trans. Richard Rojcewicz. Bloomington: Indiana University Press, 2015. |

| CP | *Contributions to Philosophy (Of the Event).* Trans. Richard Rojcewicz and Daniela Vallega-Neu. Bloomington: Indiana University Press, 2012. |

| CPC | *Country Path Conversations.* Trans. Bret Davis. Bloomington: Indiana University Press, 2010. |

| CPE | *Contributions to Philosophy (From Enowning).* Trans. Parvis Emad and Kenneth Maly. Bloomington: Indiana University Press, 1999. |

| CT | *The Concept of Time. The First Draft of "Being and Time."* Trans. Ingo Farin. London: Continuum, 2011. Also see *The Concept of Time* (bilingual edition), trans. William McNeill (Oxford, UK: Blackwell, 1992) and "The Concept of Time" in *Becoming Heidegger: On the Trail of His Early Occasional Writings, 1910–1927*, ed. Theodore Kisiel and Thomas Sheehan (1st ed.) (Evanston, IL: Northwestern University Press, 2007). |

| DT | *Discourse on Thinking.* Trans. John M. Anderson and E. Hans Freund. New York: Harper & Row, 1966. |

| E | *The Event.* Trans. Richard Rojcewicz. Bloomington: Indiana University Press, 2013. |

| EF | *Schelling's Treatise on the Essence of Human Freedom.* Translation of the Niemeyer edition. Trans. Joan Stambaugh. Athens: Ohio University Press, 1985. |

| EGT | *Early Greek Thinking.* Trans. David F. Krell and Frank A. Capuzzi. New York: Harper & Row, 1975. |

| EHF | *The Essence of Human Freedom: An Introduction to Philosophy.* Trans. Ted Sadler. London: Continuum, 2002. |

EP *The End of Philosophy.* Trans. Joan Stambaugh. New York: Harper & Row, 1973.

ET *The Essence of Truth: On Plato's Cave Allegory and "Theaetetus."* Trans. Ted Sadler. London: Continuum, 2002.

FCM *The Fundamental Concepts of Metaphysics: World, Finitude, Solitude.* Trans. William McNeill and Nicholas Walker. Bloomington: Indiana University Press, 1995.

FS *Four Seminars.* Trans. Andrew Mitchell and François Raffoul. Bloomington: Indiana University Press, 2003.

GI *German Idealism.* Trans. Peter Warnek. Bloomington: Indiana University Press.

H *Heraclitus: The Inception of Occidental Thinking and Logic: Heraclitus' Doctrine of the Logos.* Trans. Julia Goesser Assaiante and Shane Ewegen. London: Bloomsbury, 2018.

HB *The History of Beyng.* Trans. William McNeill and Jeffrey Powell. Bloomington: Indiana University Press, 2015.

HCT *History of the Concept of Time: Prolegomena.* Trans. Theodore Kisiel. Bloomington: Indiana University Press, 1992.

HGR *Hölderlin's Hymns "Germania" and "The Rhine."* Trans. William McNeill and Julia Ireland. Bloomington: Indiana University Press, 2014.

HI *Hölderlin's Hymn "The Ister."* Trans. William McNeill and Julia Davis. Bloomington: Indiana University Press, 1996.

HP *Elucidations of Hölderlin's Poetry.* Trans. Keith Hoeller. Amherst, NY: Humanity Books, 2000.

HR *Hölderlin's Hymn "Remembrance."* Trans. William McNeill and Julia Ireland. Bloomington: Indiana University Press, 2018.

HS *Martin Heidegger and Eugen Fink. Heraclitus Seminar 1966/67.* Trans. Charles Seibert. University, AL: University of Alabama Press, 1979. Reprint: Evanston, IL: Northwestern University Press, 1993.

ID *Identity and Difference.* Trans. Joan Stambaugh. New York: Harper & Row, 1969.

IM *Introduction to Metaphysics.* Trans. Gregory Fried and Richard Polt. New Haven, CT: Yale University Press, 2000.

IMM *An Introduction to Metaphysics.* Trans. Ralph Manheim. New Haven, CT: Yale University Press, 1959.

IP	*Introduction to Philosophy*. Trans. William McNeill. Bloomington: Indiana University Press.
IPR	*Introduction to Phenomenological Research*. Trans. Daniel O. Dahlstrom. Bloomington: Indiana University Press, 2005.
KPM	*Kant and the Problem of Metaphysics*. Trans. Richard Taft (5th, enlarged ed.). Bloomington: Indiana University Press, 1997.
LQT	*Logic: The Question of Truth*. Trans. Thomas Sheehan. Bloomington: Indiana University Press, 2010.
M	*Mindfulness*. Trans. Parvis Emad and Thomas Kalary. London: Continuum, 2006.
MFL	*The Metaphysical Foundations of Logic*. Trans. Michael Heim. Bloomington: Indiana University Press, 1984.
N	*Nietzsche*. Ed. and trans. David Farrell Krell. 4 vols. New York: Harper & Row, 1979–1987. Translation includes revised versions of GA vols. 43, 44, 47, and 48.
N1	*Nietzsche*, vol. I: *The Will to Power as Art (1936–1937)*. See GA 6.1 and GA 43.
N2	*Nietzsche*, vol. II: *The Eternal Recurrence of the Same and the Will to Power (1937)*. See GA 6.2 and GA 44.
N3	*Nietzsche*, vol. III: *The Will to Power as Knowledge and as Metaphysics (1940)*. See GA 6.1 and GA 47.
N4	Nietzsche, *Nihilism (1939)*. See GA 6.1 and GA 48.
NUM	*Interpretation of Nietzsche's Second Untimely Meditation*. Trans. Ullrich Haase and Mark Sinclair. Bloomington: Indiana University Press, 2016.
OBT	*Off the Beaten Track*. Trans. Julian Young and Kenneth Haynes. Cambridge, UK: Cambridge University Press, 2002.
OHF	*Ontology—The Hermeneutics of Facticity*. Trans. John Van Buren. Bloomington: Indiana University Press, 1999.
OTB	*On Time and Being*. Trans. Joan Stambaugh. New York: Harper & Row, 1972.
OWL	*On the Way to Language*. Trans. Peter D. Hertz and Joan Stambaugh. New York: Harper & Row, 1971.
P	*Parmenides*. Trans. André Schuwer and Richard Rojcewicz. Bloomington: Indiana University Press, 1992.

PIA	*Phenomenological Interpretations of Aristotle: Initiation into Phenomenological Research.* Trans. Richard Rojcewicz. Bloomington: Indiana University Press, 2008.
PLT	*Poetry, Language, Thought,* trans. Albert Hofstadter. New York: Harper & Row, 1971.
PM	*Pathmarks.* Ed. William McNeill. Cambridge, UK: Cambridge University Press, 1998.
PR	*The Principle of Reason.* Trans. Reginald Lilly. Bloomington: Indiana University Press, 1991.
PRL	*The Phenomenology of Religious Life.* Trans. Matthias Fritsch and Jennifer Anna Gosetti-Ferencei. Bloomington: Indiana University Press, 2004.
PS	*Plato's "Sophist."* Trans. Richard Rojcewicz and André Schuwer. Bloomington: Indiana University Press, 1997.
P2	*Ponderings II–VI: Black Notebooks 1931–1938.* Trans. Richard Rojcewicz. Indiana University Press, 2016.
P7	*Ponderings VII–XI: Black Notebooks 1938–1939.* Trans. Richard Rojcewicz. Indiana University Press, 2017.
P12	*Ponderings XII–XV: Black Notebooks 1939–1941.* Trans. Richard Rojcewicz. Indiana University Press, 2017.
QCT	*The Question Concerning Technology and Other Essays.* Trans. William Lovitt. New York: Harper & Row, 1977.
QT	*The Question Concerning the Thing.* Trans. James Reid and Benjamin Crowe. London: Rowman & Littlefield International.
RZL	*Reden und andere Zeugnisse eines Lebensweges* (1910–1976). Ed. Hermann Heidegger (Frankfurt am Main, Germany: Vittorio Klostermann, 2000).
WIP	*What Is Philosophy?* Trans. Jean T. Wilde and William Kluback. New Haven, CT: College & University Press, 1958.
WCT	*What Is Called Thinking?* Trans. J. Glenn Gray. New York: Harper & Row, 1968.
WT	*What Is a Thing?* Trans. W. B. Barton and Vera Deutsch. Chicago, IL: Henry Regnery, 1967.
ZSE	*Translation: Zollikon Seminars: Protocols—Conversations—Letters.* Trans. Franz Mayr and Richard Askay. Evanston: Northwestern University Press, 2001.

This is a translation only of *Zollikoner Seminare: Protokolle, Gespräche, Briefe*. Ed. Medard Boss. Frankfurt am Main, Germany: Klostermann, 1987.

ZSG Not in the *Gesamtausgabe*: *Zollikoner Seminare: Protokolle, Gespräche, Briefe*. Ed. Medard Boss. Frankfurt am Main, Germany: Klostermann, 1987.

Index

Adorno, Theodor W., 3, 20, 79, 85, 96–98, 159, 198, 200
Anaximander, 49, 54, 57, 66
Appropriation, 3 meanings of, 169–70
Arendt, Hannah, 148
Aristotle, 1, 5, 6, 12, 19, 41, 93, 94, 99, 123
Authenticity, 54, 58, 81, 83, 105, 111, 162, 164, 168–73, 190, 192, 196–97
Auschwitz, 20

Bacon, Francis, 129
Barlach, Ernst, 124
Basquiat, Jean-Michel, 129
Beckett, Samuel, 109
Befindlichket (situatedness), as a clearing in the world, 157; as *Geworfenheit*, 32, 55, 157
Being (*Sein*), four senses of, 149–51, 205–06; in relationship to us human beings (*Mensch*), 21–22, 29, 37, 77, 88, 97, 119, 141, 151–52, 167, 178, 193; responsibility of human beings for, 169, 202
Benjamin, Walter, 91, 113–14, 132, 138, 197, 201, 202
Benn, Ben, 129
Berg, Alban, 98
Bernstein, Jay, 20
Blanchot, Maurice, 83

Blaue Reiter, 143
Bluemner, Oscar Florianus, 129
Boss, Medard, 151
Botticelli, Sandro, 133
Bourgeois, Louise, 140
Braque, Georges, 128
Brogan, Walter, 23
Burri, Alberto, 132, 143

Calasso, Robert, 111
Capobianco, Richard, 155, 177, 186, 187–90
Cavell, Stanley, 76
Caygill, Howard, 113, 138
Cézanne, Paul, 122, 125, 142
Chamberlain, John, 125
Chillida, Eduardo, 124, 126
Cole, Thomas, 68, 69, 187
Corso, Gregory, 148
Cranach, Lukas the Elder, 143

Dante, Alighieri, 209n3
Da-sein, 1, 5, 24–25, 32–34, 46, 51, 56, 63–64, 69–70, 84, 93–94, 110–11, 116, 140, 146–47, 151–52; as our *Geworfenheit* and *Befindlichkeit*, 155–57; as power to be disclosive, 171–72; as situated in its being in the world, 178; in its belonging to being, 140, 166–67

De Kooning, Willem, 131
Democracy, 19, 105–08, 112
Derrida, Jacques, 191, 209n5, 213n10
Descartes, René, 1, 5, 9, 34, 60, 93, 94, 117, 118, 135, 163, 177, 206
Dispositions, 1, 7, 12; as our most fundamental, 5, 148, 168, 172, 176–77, 193, 196, 202, 205, 222n18; as the gentlest of laws, 11, 176–77, 196
Dubuffet, Jean, 129

Einkehr (return), as entering into the event of being, 73; as *Heim-kehr*, 165–67
Eliot, T. S., 1, 14
Emerson, Ralph Waldo, 153, 189
Ereignis, 158, 164–66, 168–70, 192; and authenticity, 172–73; and the *Es gibt*, 155, 157; and destiny (the *Geschick*), 156–57, 160, 178, 182–83; and the *Geheimnis* as *Heim-kehr*, 165, 197; as an event of being, 13, 21, 37, 111, 145–49, 154, 156; as calling for a process of appropriation and propriation, 25, 88, 162–63, 166, 169–70, 176, 192–93, 196; as calling for our responsibility and guardianship, 151, 183, 190; as a singular event of history-making significance in the history of philosophy and world, 191–92; as an event that could happen to anyone at any time, 171, 193–96

Feldman, Morton, 131
Fisher, Mark, 114
Flavin, Dan, 141
Fried, Michael, 127
Friedrich, Caspar David, 143
Foucault, Michel, 19, 23
Furtenagel, Lukas, 134

Geheimnis, 164–68
Gelassenheit, 29, 40–41, 83–84, 98, 187
Gendlin, Eugene, 210n9, 214n27
Geschick (destiny), 4, 36, 41, 67–68, 71, 77, 155; depends on our use of freedom; 200; *two senses of,* 156–57
Gestalt, 10, 68, 77–79, 84, 88–91, 100, 139; *and the Gestell*, 10, 78, 109; and the *Geviert*, 77–78
Gestell, 79–81, 97, 100, 108–09, 139, 142, 197; and the *Geviert*, 84–85
Geviert (Fourfold), 75–84, 86, 88, 100, 180–82; and democracy, 91–92, 107–08, 112
Geworfenheit (thrownness into the world), 25, 32–34, 37, 51–55, 64, 84, 116, 146, 157, 164
Giacometti, Alberto, 124, 126
Goethe, Johannes Wolfgang, 79, 132, 201
Gossaert, Jan, 134, 135
Greenberg, Clement, 127
Grünewald, Mattias, 143
Guzzoni, Ute, 96–98

Hals, Frans, 133
Hearkening, 82, 90, 98
Hegel, Georg Wilhelm Friedrich, 70, 93, 115, 123, 138, 206
Heiliger, Bernard, 124
Heraclitus, 30–32, 37, 49, 80, 90–93, 111, 170, 192
Herder, Johann Gottfried, 76
Herodotus, 148
Hölderlin, Friedrich, 30, 31, 39, 70, 71, 109, 111, 119, 145, 166
Homer, 49–51, 57
Humanism, 4, 75, 78, 106, 112, 136, 154, 170, 179–82
Husserl, Edmund, 2, 8, 9, 55, 63, 163, 177, 178

Johns, Jasper, 130
Judd, Donald, 100, 120, 136, 137

Kabakov, Emilia, 140
Kabakov, Ilya, 140
Kafka, Franz, 78, 109
Kalkas, 49–73
Kandinsky, Wassily, 124, 142
Kant, Immanuel, 21, 93, 94, 99, 116–19, 123, 127, 128, 135, 174, 197
Kelly, Ellsworth, 137
Kiefer, Anselm, 132, 143

Leibniz, Gottfried Wilhelm, 93
LeWitt, Sol, 137
Lichtung (clearing): 24, 28–29, 33, 37–38, 46, 50–58, 60–73, 84, 93, 103, 108, 139, 141, 145–53, 157–58, 165–66, 173–79, 183–85, 188–90; is being, 145–46; ontological lighting vs. ontic lights, 220–21n5

Magritte, René, 39, 113, 129
Malbranche, Nicholas, 5
Malevich, Kazimir, 137
Manet, Éduard, 135
Marx, Karl, 1, 206
Matisse, Paul, 130, 142
Mehretu, Julie, 132
Merleau-Ponty, Maurice, 2, 17–18; exposes the pre-objective dimension prior to subject-object formation, 8–11, 60, 116–19, 125, 142, 167, 176–79; interprets *Sein-Mensch-sein* connection, 29, 166–67, 177–79; on "essence," 33; on reversibility and reciprocity, 9–10, 22, 29, 63, 119, 139–40, 193; on the emergence of the *Gestalt*, 139; on "universal flesh," 127; on what Heidegger called the pre-ontological, 10, 139, 167; worked out the "ontological rehabilitation of the sensible," 22, 24.
Metaphor, 10–11, 17–18, 78, 91–92, 165; interpreting the "gods," 77. 108–11
Michelangelo, 27
Miller, Henry, 23
Moira, 65, 67, 69, 80, 152
Mondrian, Piet, 128
Montaigne, Michel de, 104–105
Morris, David, 29

Nancy, Jean-Luc, 23, 46
Nietzsche, Friedrich, 35, 40, 86, 96, 110, 119, 123, 143, 193
Novalis (Friedrich von Hardenberg), 70, 75, 166

Oliver, Mary, 75
Ontological, as a question about what something is, 127–28; 127; as an event concerning being, 17, 21, 168–69; and another epoch in the history of being, 40, 163–64; and its relation to the ethical, 161, 198, 207; and *Mitsein*, 24; and nihilism, 28, 39; and *Temporalität*, 52, 183; and the *Da-sein*-being structure, 93–94; and the promise of a future *Geschick*, 71, 177–79; and van Gogh's shoes, 122; as responsibility for being, 173, 207; as the difference between being and beings, the lighting and the light, 79–80, 159, 192, 202–04; as the dimension of the clearing, 70; as pointing to the relationship with being that precedes and underlies the subject-object structure, 117; as revelatory events, 154; in nationalism and

Ontological *(continued)*
racism, 180; in the developing stages of hearing, 82–83; in the inception of metaphysical though in Greece, 155; involves responsibility for the being of beings, hence for being itself, 45, 171, 197; in the two reigning modalities of being, *Zuhandensein* (being ready to hand) and *Vorhandensein* (being present in and for contemplation and reflection, 115–16; vs. ontic, 1–2, 40–41, 117, 187–88; vs. pre-ontological, 1–2, 10, 14, 20, 24, 119, 139–40, 149–51, 165–67, 183; what being "announces," 71
Ortega y Gasset, José, 75

Parmenides, 38–41, 44, 49, 65–68, 80, 94, 171, 173, 192
Parrino, Steven, 114
Periander, 53
Picasso, Pablo, 123, 130
Plato, 5, 10, 50, 61, 62, 71, 72, 90, 123, 162
Pollock, Jackson, 128–129, 139, 142
Polt, Richard, 158, 177, 193–96
Promise of happiness, 2, 14, 60, 65, 71, 77, 88, 112, 136, 143–44, 159, 173, 200; depends on us, 197, 200; in the thing, 90, 103, 105–06; of transformation, 109, 112
Protagoras, 31

Raffoul, François, 177, 180, 191
Rauschenberg, Robert, 132
Reich, Robert, 107
Responsibility for being, 5, 10–11, 17, 20–22, 24, 39, 45–46, 72, 91, 94, 101, 104, 108, 111, 146–49, 153, 158, 161–62, 164–66, 168–74, 176, 181, 187, 190–91, 193, 196–97,
199–200, 202, 207
Richter, Gerhard, 128, 129, 132, 143
Rilke, Rainer Maria, 27–30, 76, 84, 86–89, 132, 148, 160
Rodin, Auguste, 124, 126
Rorty, Richard, 159
Ross, Alex, 131
Rothko, Mark, 131, 137
Rushdie, Salman, 10
Ryman, Robert, 137

Salgado, Doris, 140
Santayana, George, 207
Schelling, Friedrich Wilhelm Joseph, 3, 70, 119
Schiller, Friedrich, 116, 119
Seeing, stages of development, 83
Serra, Richard, 140
Seyeau, Michel, 83
Sheehan, Thomas, 147, 174, 177, 191–93
Sittow, Michel, 133
Socrates, 13, 21, 30, 104, 172, 199
Spinoza, Baruch, 2–8, 12
Stella, Frank, 128
Stevens, Wallace, 95, 198
Subject-object structure, 9–11, 18, 21–22, 58, 60, 81, 94, 96–98, 117–19, 167, 177, 193; is only a historical variation, 206

Temporalität, 56, 62–63, 183; vs. *Zeitlichkeit*, 52
Thoreau, Henry David, 151
Turrell, James, 141
Twombly, Cy, 45, 129, 132

Valente, José Angel, 199–200
Van der Weyden, Roger, 134
Van Gogh, Vincent, 122, 127, 129, 137, 142
Velázquez, Diego, 133, 134
Vienna Secession, 143

Wächterschaft (guardianship), 23, 45.
　171, 203
Wahrnehmung (perception), 53–54,
　61–63, 98
Warhol, Andy, 91, 137, 214
Weill, Simone, 5
Whiteread, Rachel, 140

Whitman, Walt, 91–92, 107–08, 112,
　215–216n41
Wittgenstein, Ludwig, 158, 201
Wood, David, on the inseparability of
　ontology and ethics, 161
Wordsworth, William, 89, 167
World, 150

www.ingramcontent.com/pod-product-compliance
Lightning Source LLC
Chambersburg PA
CBHW030539230426
43665CB00010B/951